Chopard

"Passione"

Mille Miglia Gran Turismo XL Chrono. Mechanical passion, technology, power and flowing curves: there is a wealth of striking similarities between the automobile and watchmaking worlds.

Chopard presents the new "Mille Miglia GT XL Chrono", a chronograph equipped with integrated pushers. This powerful and distinctive model features a blend of cutting-edge technology and sophisticated design. Its original split-level counters and the tachometric scale engraved on the bezel make this a highly contemporary and particularly legible timing instrument. Measuring 44 mm in diameter, the steel case is water-resistant to 100 metres and houses a self-winding movement chronometer-certified by the COSC.

Mille Miglia Gran Turismo XL Chrono: available in steel with a 1960s Dunlop Racing rubber strap (ref. 168459-3001)

›› Contents

14
AC COBRA
THE ULTIMATE SPORTS CARS?

{ FEATURES }

100

132

110

176

212

220

» Welcome

TREAT YOURSELF TO A SPORTS CAR

'There are so many good cars out there, and most are easier than ever to own'

If there's anything that can help you forget the bad things in life it's owning and driving a classic sports car. Stress at work? Go for a drive with the top down. Meant to be decorating the lounge? Sneak out to the garage instead and revel in real man's DIY.

There are so many good cars out there, and most are easier than ever to own. Parts are better made, decent tools are cheaper, specialists are more switched on to our needs. And consequently the quality of restored cars is much higher.

Some classics have shot up in value over the past five years, such as six-cylinder Jaguar E-types. But there are others that are still true bargains, from Triumph Spitfires to 1980s Porsche 911s. Buy one now and you could find that your little automotive indulgence also proves to be a rising finanical asset. What a bonus!

This publication is packed with buying guides on a massive variety of classic sports cars, as old as the wonderful MG T-types or as new as the exciting Lotus Elise and Exige. Read them, enjoy them – but most important of all, use them to help you buy the car you've always promised yourself.

David Lillywhite

IN ASSOCIATION WITH

CLASSIC SPORTS CAR
BUYING GUIDE

Editorial office
Octane, 1 Tower Court, Irchester Road,
Wollaston, Northants NN29 7PJ, UK
Tel: +44 (0)207 907 6585. Fax: +44 (0)1933 663367
Email: info@octane-magazine.com
Website: www.octane-magazine.com

Advertising office
Octane Media Advertising Dept, 19 Highfield Lane,
Maidenhead, Berkshire SL6 3AN, UK
Tel: +44 (0)1628 510080. Fax: +44 (0)1628 510090
Email: ads@octane-magazine.com

Managing editor:	David Lillywhite
Art editor:	Rob Gould
Designer:	Dean Lettice
Staff writer:	Jack Carfrae
Editorial manager:	Janet Mills
Production:	Sarah Bradley
	Paul Hardiman
Contributors	Richard Dredge
	Malcolm McKay
	Simon Goldsworthy
Advertising director:	Sanjay Seetanah
Advertising sales:	Samantha Snow
	Sue Farrow
	Madeleine Lillywhite
Advertising production:	Anisha Mogra
	Kerem Kolcak
Publisher	Geoff Love
Newstrade director	Martin Belson
Marketing manager	Alex Seeberg
Managing director	Ian Westwood
Group finance director	Ian Leggett
COO	Brett Reynolds
CEO	James Tye
Chairman	Felix Dennis

Classic Sports Car Buying Guide is published under licence fro
Octane Media Ltd, a subsidiary company of Dennis Publishing
Limited, United Kingdom. All rights in the licensed material bel
to Felix Dennis, Octane Media or Dennis Publishing and may ne
reproduced, whether in whole or in part, without their prior w
consent. Octane is a registered trademark.

Repro by Octane Repro, AT Graphics
Printed by SouthernPrint

Distribution Seymour, 2 East Poultry Avenue,
London EC1A 9PT. Tel: +44 (0)207 429 400

Periodicals Postage paid @ Emigsville, PA.
Postmaster: send address corrections to Octane Media c/o 33
Pacific Ave, Suite 404, Virginia Beach, VA 23451

Octane ISSN 1740-0023 is published monthly by Octane Media
USPS 024-187

The text paper used within this magaz
is produced from sustainable forestatic
from a chain of custody manufacturer

CONTRIBUTORS

PAUL HARDIMAN
HE'S CLASSIC through and through and brings his considerable knowledge to every project he works on.

SARAH BRADLEY
WITH CLASSIC motorcycles and hot rods as her everyday transport, Sarah lives and breathes old vehicles.

RICHARD DREDGE
HAS ONE MAN ever produced so many fully-researched, accurate and entertaining buying guides? We think not – a hero!

ROB GOULD
DESIGN GURU and classic fan Rob is usually responsible for the look of *Octane* magazine – this was his labour of love...

DEAN LETTICE
DEAN'S WORK on the design of the Classic Sports Car Buying Guide may yet earn him enough to add to his Mini buying fund.

BUYING A CLASSIC

A good classic sports car is something you'll love for years. A bad one will drive you mad, so read this and choose carefully

Words: Richard Dredge Photography: www.magiccarpics.co.uk

What to buy

» Your budget will dictate what classic you can buy, but in any price band there will be all sorts of car types available. You need to work out whether you want something fun or practical, mainstream or off-beat.

» Continue to narrow down your field by working out what sort of age your classic should be. Many classics are surprisingly usable on an everyday basis; if the car is more than a toy you'll need something reasonably practical and frugal.

» If you want something that's really off-beat such as a low-volume sportscar or an American import, bear in mind that specialists will be few and far between. Also parts could be harder to get and may be more costly.

» You can't beat the buzz of driving a convertible on a sunny day, but most cheap open-topped classics leak like sieves. A leaky classic that's stored outside is a recipe for disaster, so be wary unless you've got a garage.

» Any classic built (but not necessarily registered) before January 1, 1973 is entitled to free road tax. Other running costs to think about include insurance (get a quote before buying), fuel bills and both parts and servicing costs.

►► What to look for

Bodywork and trim

Overhauling engines and gearboxes is usually the cheapest and easiest part of any restoration; it's the bodywork that will get you...

Fixing bodywork properly takes time and skill; it may be worth getting a professional to do some of the trickier bits as it'll take them a lot less time than it'll take you. Also bear in mind that a complete restoration project is often easier (but more costly and time-consuming) than a quick patch up, because it's easier to get to everything once a car is stripped down.

1 If a car has been badly pranged it can be difficult to attain proper alignment of everything, so make sure all panels line up properly. Check for rippled inner wings and  shutlines that are all over the place – sorting these can be very costly, if not impossible. Unless you've got specialist bodywork skills, you're best avoiding any car that's been in a major shunt because you'll never get everything to line up.

2 Reshelling is common, as it's often more economical to source a decent used bodyshell than to patch up a badly damaged one. Although the legality of this is sometimes questionable, it's usually safe – unlike the cut 'n' shut. This is likely to affect only recent classics – but still ensure the car doesn't consist of two cars welded together across the middle. Don't even consider a cut 'n' shut, but a properly reshelled classic makes a great buy.

3 If you're considering an especially demanding restoration, check panel availability first. Panels are often extinct, and  where repro parts are offered, the quality is variable. Often you'll need to create your own panels; for hidden items such as inner wings that may be fine, but outer panels can be very demanding because of their subtle contours. Unless you're a whizz on the wheeling machine, you might need an easier project.

4 Rust is the most common issue, so check every nook and cranny for paint damage, microblistering or bubbling. Common rust traps include the sills  and wheelarches, so run a magnet over them to check for filler. Seams and brightwork also frequently harbour rot, as do rain gutters. Cosmetic rust needn't be a problem, but structural rot could be, depending on your metal-bashing skills. Structural areas include the sills, bulkheads and any floorpan crossmembers.

5 Other areas to check include the door bottoms plus the front and rear valances, which often rot from the inside out. Also look at the leading edge of the bonnet and trailing edge of the bootlid; these start to corrode, get left, then dissolve. These areas aren't structural, but can be tricky to repair without specialist skills. Also ensure the rubber seals are intact; they perish then let water into the cabin.

6 If the car has a sunroof, make sure it's not leaking and that its surround hasn't corroded. Lift the bonnet and see what state the inner wings and battery are in, and look  closely at the bulkhead. If this has corroded it'll mean an engine bay strip down (and possibly dashboard removal) to effect proper repairs – extremely time-consuming, but not usually that difficult. If the car has MacPherson strut front suspension, look at the strut tops for corrosion.

7 Check the floorpans from underneath (including the spare wheel well) and lift any trim for a view from inside. Repairs to these areas can be time-consuming, as  you may have to remove fuel and brake pipes and mechanical parts such as brake or suspension systems – but once stripped, repairs are usually straightforward. Finish by checking the doors aren't dropping because of rotten A-posts or worn hinges; the former is often very difficult because of poor accessibility.

8 Any car with a separate chassis needs careful inspection, as effecting proper repairs can mean removing the bodyshell – and you can't skimp, because a chassis gives a car most of its strength. Check the entire chassis for corrosion, along with stress cracks where sections meet – especially around suspension mountings. Repairs are usually easy, but it's common to have to remove fuel and brake lines or mechanical parts such as the suspension, before work can begin.

9 Exterior trim can cause headaches, with some model ranges having many different trim specifications. Light units get broken while chrome trim gets  pitted, and replating mazak isn't usually possible so you need to find new parts. A lot of repro stuff is badly made and original bits are often unavailable or overpriced – so check all the exterior trim parts are present and in good nick or get costs for replacements.

10 Ensure door panels, carpets and seat covers are in good nick. Also make sure the wood trim, headlining and hood (if it's a convertible) are sound as these  often need professional help to revive. Newton Commercial remanufactures trim for some classics; otherwise it's a case of scouring autojumbles or buying from fellow club members.

How to buy

» Having looked at the considerations overleaf, create a shortlist of the classics you think would suit your circumstances. Get along to a few classic car shows and talk to people who already own the cars, getting a feel for them.

» Establish what the running costs will be for your chosen classic; look at how much the insurance will be as well as what specialists charge for parts and labour. Be realistic about maintenance requirements, which will be greater than for a modern.

» Look at a range of examples of your chosen car before you buy; even if you think the first car you see is an absolute minter, looking further may show it to be not as good as you think, or overpriced for what it is.

» Give any potential purchase a thorough inspection; it's worth putting it through an MoT if you're in doubt. This is effectively a cheap inspection, although you can get a full professional inspection done as an alternative; it'll be costly though.

» In terms of where to buy, classic car rallies, classifieds and specialist magazines are worth a look, along with www.octane-magazine.com. For the greatest peace of mind it's best to buy from a specialist classic car dealer.

How to run

» Joining an owners' club will enable you to home in on the best specialists for your car. Also, you should find it easier to track down parts as well as solve problems if they crop up.

» As a general rule, the older the car the greater its servicing requirements. However, most classics were simply engineered, so DIY maintenance isn't as daunting as you might think. Buy a

manual and you could save a fortune in maintenance costs.

» Make sure you insure the car on a specialist classic policy. Doing this will ensure that you get what the car is worth in the event of a total loss, as its value is agreed when you take out the cover.

» Even if you don't do many miles each year, give the car a service before you put it away for the winter, including an oil change. Refreshing the lubricant and filter annually is the best thing you can do to preserve the engine.

» When winter comes round, make sure the car is stored properly if you're not going to use it. Fit a battery conditioner and get the engine up to temperature once a month to make sure you don't have problems with bits seizing up.

›› What to look for

Mechanical parts

Most classics are like big Meccano kits; if you treat items such as the engine, gearbox and back axle as sealed units, you can just swap bits over with relatively little hassle. The cost of rebuilding these items can be very high, so get an idea of replacement costs before you inspect your potential purchase. At least brakes, steering and suspension are usually cheap and easy to sort – but not always!

1 Don't start the engine until you've inspected the bodywork and interior, giving it time to cool down if the owner has run it up to temperature before your arrival. Look for bad oil leaks and suspect  out-of-balance carburettors if the engine runs unevenly. A worn engine will usually smoke badly, but even the most knackered powerplant can be rebuilt – although costs can be very high if it's something exotic or rare.

2 Knocking sounds on start up indicate bearing wear, caused by oil starvation, high mileage or hard use. Continuous rumbling signals worn main bearings while  clattering from the top of the engine means the valve clearances need adjusting or something (probably the camshaft) has worn. Only the latter means a top-end rebuild; the others mean the bottom half needs reviving – and that's usually costly unless you just fit a used powerplant.

3 Make sure no water has collected at the bottom of the radiator, signalling leaks; a recore is usually £100+. Get the engine hot (to ensure the thermostat  hasn't been removed) and if there's an electric fan, make sure it cuts in at the required temperature. Then switch off the engine and try to restart it a few seconds later; hot starting problems can be hard to sort out.

4 On the test drive, if the car has a manual gearbox, change up and down through the gears quickly, to reveal any synchromesh weaknesses. While doing this  listen out for any whining from the gearbox and diff; rebuilding these is usually £250+ apiece, although first gear whine is normal on many classics. Check the overdrive works, if fitted; most (but not all) problems are electrical and easy to fix.

5 Clonks as you release the clutch signal that the universal joints on the propshaft and/or the driveshafts have worn out. Replacement is usually cheap and easy, but if there's a vibration at a certain speed it's because the propshaft is out of balance; a replacement is normally £100-£150. Also ensure the clutch isn't slipping; replacement parts are usually cheap but labour charges can increase the cost considerably.

6 Sourcing replacement steering boxes is often tricky, but originals tend to be durable with the possibility of adjusting out wear in most cases – if this has already been done, there might be stiff spots as a result. Steering racks are usually easier to source; they wear through use or because the rubber gaiters on each end have split, allowing dirt in, accelerating wear. Rebuilt racks are £40+; power assistance quadruples this cost.

7 The dampers are shot if you press down sharply at each corner and the car doesn't settle quickly. Leaf and coil springs wear out or break; the latter should be obvious from underneath, but wear isn't so easy to detect. Look at the ride height; if the car is sitting low at one end or the other it's time for new springs. Replacement dampers and springs are normally cheap, and they're easy to renew.

8 Uneven tyre tread wear may show that the tracking is out or it could show more serious problems such as misaligned suspension – especially if the car  has been rebuilt. It could also be that the suspension bushes are worn. If the latter is the case, a visual inspection should suffice, but vague steering can also be the result. Also listen for worn wheelbearings; they rumble as you corner.

9 Pressed steel wheels rust, while wires suffer from worn splines and damaged spokes – replacements are around £60-  £100 each. Alloy wheels can suffer clearance problems if they're oversized. Braking systems are usually simple, but servos pack in (so you have to push the pedal harder to stop), wheel cylinders leak and brake pipes corrode. They're individually cheap to fix, but if it all needs doing the bill could be extra-large.

10 Most classics have simple electrics, but problems can arise from poor earths, dodgy connections and brittle looms.  Looms are cheap but fitting is tricky, while sourcing components such as switchgear and instrumentation can be impossible. If any upgrades have been carried out (such as an alternator conversion or extra spotlights etc), make sure the work has been done properly. Also check there's no chafing anywhere; electrical shorts could lead to a conflagration.

HOW TO INSURE YOUR CLASSIC

Make sure you get the best (and most appropriate)
deal possible on your classic insurance policy

So, you've got your hands on the classic of your dreams, or perhaps your restoration project is finally finished. Your beloved car is sitting, waiting to be driven, but first, you've got to insure it.

Yes, it's widely known that choosing insurance is one of the least glamorous parts of owning a classic, but having the correct cover is absolutely essential to make sure your pride and joy is fully protected.

With an ever-increasing range of different policy options coming on to the market, the choice for enthusiasts can seem complicated.

That's why Paul Matthews, of specialist insurer Footman James, is on hand to explain some of the key policy choices, to make the choice for you that bit easier.

'It sounds simple, but I would recommend more than anything that owners of classic vehicles don't just chose the cheapest policy when it comes to insurance,' he explains.

'Coping with a stolen vehicle or accident is distressing enough already, especially when it is your treasured classic, so the last

thing you need on top of that is the added stress of a difficult insurance claim.

'That's why it really is worth taking the time to talk to specialist insurers, like Footman James, who can offer you the best possible protection for your classic.'

Standard policy cover

What can you expect from a standard policy? European and UK breakdown cover, legal expenses cover, road rage personal accident cover and emergency travel cover are included in all Footman James classic policies.

However, Paul explains: 'Most other companies don't include these as standard, so if you are shopping round for insurance, you must remember to take this into account when comparing prices.

'Different insurers include different services as standard, so it's essential that you find out

exactly what you are getting for your money. That is the only way to truly compare policies.'

Agreed value

It's every classic owner's nightmare but if, heaven forbid, your pride and joy should come to grief, 'agreed value' can be a life-saver.

Agreed value means the vehicle's true value is confirmed when you first take out your insurance policy.

Paul Matthews continues: 'With this option, because the value of the vehicle has already been confirmed, it doesn't have to be negotiated or proven after an incident, taking that extra stress away.

'Where the car is declared a write-off – i.e. it is beyond repair within the true value (however, repairable within DVLA guidelines) most enthusiasts are keen to rebuild their pride and joy, so in some cases we offer a cash settlement and retention of salvage.

'The customer is then free to source the parts and restore their vehicle to its former glory, if they choose to.

'However, if your classic has only suffered minor damage, then taking it to the first bodyshop that springs to mind just isn't on, so make sure that your insurer, has an established network of specialist clubs, dealers and repairers which can be trusted to do a good job.'

More than one classic?

For those lucky people out there who are the proud owners of more than one classic, multi-vehicle cover, which allows several classics to be insured on one policy, is ideal.

This results in a lower premium, and means motorists only have to remember the one renewal date instead of several.

Multi-vehicle cover makes life a whole lot easier for classics collectors and provides better value for money than seemingly cheap one-off quotes for individual vehicles.

'Many classics owners might not want to risk taking their much-loved vehicle on everyday

errands such as the weekly supermarket run, and instead have a modern vehicle as their daily run-around,' explained Mr Matthews.

'Footman James allows for modern vehicles to be included on our multi-vehicle policies, as long as the majority of the vehicles on the policy are classified as "classic". Multi-vehicle is rapidly becoming one of our most popular policy choices, with a 20 per cent increase in people signing up to it in the past two years.'

Limited mileage

With our wonderful British weather, it is no wonder that many enthusiasts only take their classics out for a spin on the odd occasion when the sun shines, so if this applies to you, limited mileage is the perfect option.

Through limited mileage policies, enthusiasts who don't notch up a large number of miles in their classic each year, can benefit from a cheaper premium. It is usually offered in various bands, such as 1500, 3000 and 4500 miles per year.

It works on the principle that the fewer miles you drive, the less your risk of an accident, therefore, the cheaper your insurance. Cars that are more than 30 years old automatically qualify for unlimited mileage, which is usually charged at the same premium as the 3000-mile option.

Laid-up cover

As show season has come to an end, and the colder weather sets in, classics across the country are stowed away in the sheds and garages to ride out the winter. However, many classics owners forget to insure their vehicle properly when laying it up for the winter. Even though the vehicle is not on the road, it is still vital to ensure the paperwork and insurance is right.

Just because your car is resting, or even in pieces, does not mean laying-up is risk-free. Fire, theft and even animals knawing away at the upholstery are still, unfortunately, commonplace so it's essential to safeguard the vehicle.

Laid-up cover suits the many devoted enthusiasts who have bought their vehicle as a restoration project or purchased a classic that needs a fair bit of general maintenance work.

It also covers the vehicle whilst it is on static display at an exhibition in the UK, including whilst it is being transported by trailer to and from an event.

Paul Matthews adds: 'As well as the correct insurance, it is also essential to submit a Statutory Off Road Notice (SORN) to the DVLA. This replaces road tax and ensures your classic is legally off the road. It's worth remembering that the Government has now launched a clampdown on uninsured and untaxed vehicles, and has set up a motor insurance database – a nationwide bureau to cross-reference car registrations with insurance details, which the police have immediate access to. So a classic

without SORN or a valid tax disc might seem hidden away to you, but it is still detectable to the authorities.'

Modifications

It might be extremely tempting it is to give your Jaguar XK that extra oomph under the bonnet, but before you set about it, make sure your insurer is told about any modifications to your vehicle. In brief, if you don't declare any changes made, your insurance could be invalid.

Very small alterations are unlikely to send your insurer into a panic, but any major changes, especially if they are performance or safety related, must be declared.

Car club membership

As well being part of a group of enthusiasts who are as passionate about their cars as you are, being a car club member can have significant insurance benefits.

'Footman James is in partnership with a number of vehicle clubs around the country, and our club insurance schemes offer members exclusive club rates. Each policy taken out also earns money for the club on a commission basis, so there are perks all round,' added Mr Matthews.

'We also have a dedicated club contact, Emma Merwood, who is a familiar face at club events across the country and keeps us in touch with exactly what enthusiasts are looking for from their insurance provider.'

'It works on the principle that the fewer miles you drive, the less your risk of an accident, therefore, the cheaper your insurance'

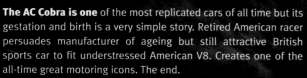

The AC Cobra is one of the most replicated cars of all time but its gestation and birth is a very simple story. Retired American racer persuades manufacturer of ageing but still attractive British sports car to fit understressed American V8. Creates one of the all-time great motoring icons. The end.

Simple indeed, but an almost identical treatment didn't work so well for Rootes and Sunbeam. The same racer inserted a similar 260in Ford and Borg-Warner gearbox into the Alpine – another elegant Brit – and although numerically it outnumbers the Cobra (7000 Tigers were made between 1964 and 1967, against just over 1000 Cobras), it hasn't acquired the same kind of status. So what was it that made the Cobra so special?

The question is timely, because it is now 50 years since the Ace – the car that started it all – first saw the light of day. Designed for AC Cars by John Tojeiro, it bore an uncanny resemblance to the Ferrari Barchettas of the day but otherwise didn't seem particularly special when it went on the market in 1953 wearing a price tag of £1439. Power came from AC's own single overhead cam 2-litre six, a design dating from 1919, producing about 80bhp at 4500rpm with the rest about as simple as it gets. A ladder frame chassis made of 3in diameter steel tubes, with independent wishbone suspension and telescopic dampers at both ends, each sprung by a transverse leaf across the top, pinned in the middle so that each »

ACE IN THE PACK

The AC Ace is best known simply as the father of the Cobra. We drive Ace, Cobra 289 and Cobra 427 to see which is really the best of the line

Words: Mark Hales   Photography: Michael Bailie

Above right
AC Ace, a veteran of Le Mans and 300,000 miles, may look a little faded in places but it's still a bundle of fun on twisty roads.

half does one side. It was typical of a breed and wasn't, as the modern designers would put it, a very stiff platform. The undeniably attractive hand-crafted aluminium body, which was mounted on flimsy hoops, could do little to tighten it.

John Deveson's fading metallic green Bristol-BMW engined example you see in the pictures still looks exquisitely well proportioned, slim and elegant, perfectly poised on a set of unfeasibly skinny Michelin X tyres. It is certainly no garage queen, restored with the sheen of modern paint, but looks well-used and nicely worn in all the right places.

I then learnt it had been in the Deveson family since 1960, during which time it had recorded an unbelievable 300,000 miles. In the three years before that, after it emerged from the Thames Ditton factory in November 1956, it had raced at Mallory Park, Silverstone and Brands in the hands of its first owner and survived a rollover before passing to a Mrs Jane Waugh, who in 1959 loaned the car to Ken Rudd of Ruddspeed fame (the same man who boosted the Zephyr engines to 170bhp as an option in the last 36 Aces). He entered it for that year's Le Mans where it finished seventh overall and won the 2-litre class. Mrs Waugh drove it there, then drove it back again. Via Paris, of course...

I learnt that the disc brakes which glinted through the painted wheel spokes were an extra at £17.50 while the Bristol engine option added a more substantial £360. AC had soon realised that its home-grown example was convenient but not exactly lively, but Bristol's neat little pushrod six gave around 125bhp at 5750rpm and in 1956 enabled the Ace to reach 60mph from rest in under ten seconds with a top speed of 125mph; figures almost identical to those of a modern Ford Focus 1.8, but more than respectable at the time. Even after all those years and all those miles, the buff leather of the Ace's

upholstery whiffed like leather should and the flimsy doors still shut with that signature thwack.

Most people know by now that the Cobra that followed in 1963 was a marriage of expediency involving this elegantly English Ace and the 260 cubic inch iron boat anchor destined for a Canadian Ford pick-up truck. Ford as a company had realised that racing success appealed to the younger market it had begun to covet and marketing guru Lee Iacocca was looking for a tool to defeat Chevy's Corvette in domestic events. Ford did what it knew how to do and set out to buy Ferrari but Ferrari strung out the negotiations then refused to sell even at an inflated figure – a technique to which the mighty Blue Oval was not accustomed...

Enter Carroll Shelby, a rare American who had raced outside his native land. He was perfectly placed to take advantage of the Ford-Ferrari rebound although his motivation was rather more personal. It was the same Enzo Ferrari who had refused to pay Shelby – the 1959 Le Mans winner – his worth as a driver and the American wanted a big stick with which to settle the score. Meanwhile, back in Blighty, the supply of Bristol engines for the Ace had dried up. AC had started fitting the bigger and heavier 2.5-litre straight six from the Ford Zephyr, in various stages of tune. The timing was spot on. AC could see the new lease of life that might come from a larger and lazier eight-cylinder engine, which didn't need modifying and which Ford was keen to supply. Shelby helped with the installation and the result was the Cobra – powered by Ford.

The first versions differed little in layout to the last Ford-engined Aces of 1963 and the chassis looked almost identical, even down to the worm and peg steering with its central bellcrank (Deveson has an argument about permissible play at the MoT station once a year), but a large amount of detail work

'The Bristol engine is crisp and willing and wails like a saxophone on drugs, and the swift response says the Ace is light and quick – 100mph comes up in no time'

AC Ace (Bristol Engine)

SPECIFICATIONS

Engine
1971cc, in-line six cylinder, overhead valve, three downdraught carburettors

Power
125bhp @ 5750rpm

Torque
122lb-ft @ 4500rpm

Transmission
Four-speed plus optional overdrive

Suspension
Front and rear: independent, lower wishbones, transverse leaf spring, telescopic dampers

Brakes
Discs front, drums rear

Performance
0-60mph 9 secs, top speed 117mph

Weight
1845lb (837kg)

Value
£40,000
(price at launch £2011)

Left
Tall Bristol-BMW pushrod six just clears the Ace bonnet..

'The AC 289 featured a real chassis improvement
in the shape of rack and pinion steering –
an off-the-shelf MGB item'

Cobra 289
SPECIFICATIONS

Engine
4727cc, Ford V8,
overhead valve. Four-
choke carburettor (four
twin-chokes on test car)

Power
300bhp @ 5750rpm
(360bhp on test car)

Torque
285lb-ft @ 4500rpm

Transmission
Four-speed with optional
close-ratio gearset

Suspension
Front and rear:
independent, lower
wishbones, transverse
leaf spring, telescopic
dampers

Brakes
Discs all round

Performance
0-60mph 5.5secs, top
speed 138mph

Weight
1210lb (953kg)

Value
£100,000
(price at launch £2454)

Left
Engine modifications,
including these four
downdraught
Webers plus a hot
cam and high-
compression pistons
give 360bhp..

had been carried out at Shelby's insistence. There was a lot of gusseting to beef up the chassis ladder and the attachments for differential and suspension while the body was attached more firmly with bigger hoops to support it in the hope of adding some more stiffness to the whole structure. Springs and shock absorbers were toughened to cope with extra weight and the potential of extra performance and disc brakes replaced the rear drums, but the aluminium body that covered it all was little changed. The longer nose was already a feature of the Zephyr Aces but the arches were widened to accommodate the Cobra's wider wheels and bigger tyres. The engine for the first production versions was a single carburettor 260 cubic inch (4.2-litre) V8, which gave out about 160bhp (less than the best Ruddspeed Zephyr) but a mountain of torque. I remember a party piece with a similarly motivated Tiger that involved driving all the way from rest to 100mph in top gear only.

The yellow car you see in the pictures belongs to powder coatings magnate John Andon and started life as a roadgoing Mk2, which first featured the 289 cubic inch (4.7-litre) 300bhp engine from the High Performance Mustang and a real chassis improvement in the shape of rack and pinion steering (an off the shelf MGB item). Otherwise there were few other changes at the factory. This one has since been turned into a racer by Cobra experts Uniclip Automotive of Byfleet, which has wrought more engine modifications (four downdraught Webers, cams and pistons) to give a fairly conservative 360bhp, or about the amount a racer would have had in the day. Stiffer suspension, tougher brake pads and a set of period-spec Dunlop L-section race tyres complement the extra but in reality these are still only detail differences from the original and very similar to the upgrades you could have ordered at the factory should you

have wished. The rather more visible modern additions are the rollover hoop, the modern seat and belts and smaller steering wheel, of which more later.

Which brings us to Joe Eagle's Mk3, or the Big Red One. This is number 183 of 260 cars made in kit form at Thames Ditton and sent out to the US for assembly (hence the left-hand drive) and it embodies the first real differences in layout. The ladder chassis remains but the tubes are an inch bigger in diameter and there are subframes front and rear to carry top wishbones and coil spring/damper units in place of the leaf springs – a change which the chassis engineers from Ford USA helped to design.

Every possible opportunity was taken to add more rigidity to the frame and suspension components, while the engine was a massive, all-iron big-block 427 (or 428) cubic inch (7-litre) Ford, which pushed out about 400bhp and, according to Eagle, does ten miles to the gallon 'if you're lucky'... And this with a tank of 15 gallons. Something says this was made for parading along Californian beaches rather than grand touring. The body boasted even fatter wheelarches to accommodate massively wide 15in wheels and tall profile tyres (the 7.5in front and 9.5in wide rear 'Sunburst' pattern magnesium alloys fitted to Eagle's car are the 'narrow' option). All of which makes it look a much bigger car until you see the trio together in profile.

It was time to drive and, as the progenitor, the Ace would be first. Lever my legs beneath the wheel and, instead of thwacking the door, add pressure from the outside until the chrome lever clicks shut. Press the starter and hear the whirr followed by a wonderful crackle from the two tiny looking pipes jutting beneath the offside rear wing. Poke a heavy clutch, ease forward a long lever, which has a surprisingly short and snicky

Above right
Cobra 427 is easily
identifiable thanks to
the wider arches but
underneath it's coil
springs and 427
engine that make
the difference.

throw, and off we go. The Bristol engine – rebuilt in 1997 – is crisp and willing and wails like a saxophone on drugs. The swift response says the Ace is light and quick – 100mph comes up in no time and, as always with light cars, there seems to be more when you push the accelerator. But then you try the brakes. My right knee is firmly wedged against the wheelrim and I can only reach the edge of the brake pedal. Heeling and toeing is impossible and I couldn't contemplate racing the car.

Forget that for a moment and turn the wheel. The nose points, then points that bit more than you asked for, so you unravel a little lock. Then you add a touch to get back on course. Then you unravel a little. It's a process that goes on through the corner. Meanwhile the steering seems to tighten depending on how much you ask of it. Hard to decide what message it wants to send, but meanwhile the chassis is actually quite composed, gently undulating between push at the nose and loose at the tail as the corner unfolds. Or maybe not even that. More like a walk each side of a line which constantly prompts you to react.

And it was a theme which would play throughout, with minor variations. John Andon's Mk2 was so much easier to sit in that it makes you wonder why a wheel smaller by an inch and a seat thinner by much the same amount could make such a difference. I well remember driving a proper original Mk2 most of the way to Le Mans for a Ford demo and it was just like the Ace only faster and with a heavier clutch and hotter cockpit.

It can't be just me who found the original uncomfortable, so as always, I don't know why they didn't do something about it. But by comparison, Andon's car was more precise in its responses. Part of this could be the tightening up of chassis and suspension that went on back in 1964, and part could be the bigger Dunlop crossplies, which are always sharper than an

equivalent radial, especially when the suspension was designed for similar tyres. But the rack and pinion steering was much better too, despite wider rubber. It didn't tighten or stick and you got messages back from the road, some in the form of kick back over the bumps, but messages nonetheless. But then when you upped the effort a bit, the same fidget crept in. I remember a stint at Goodwood in Nigel Hulme's Cobra, the official AC entry for the 1963 Le Mans which finished seventh and was much as it would have been then. You added a squeeze of lock, then waited for the car to respond, unwound it, then added again. Or maybe, depending on the corner, you added a similar squeeze and waited for the response, which turned out to be a massive slide you hadn't asked for, or deserved.

Uniclip's Bill Shepherd is one of the fastest men in these cars and says it shouldn't do that, not on a dry road at least, but he also admits that the Cobra's flimsy chassis will always make itself felt, and is something 'you have to factor into the set-up'. That would be nice to experience because I have done a fair few laps in all sorts of Cobras and all have done exactly the same: fidgeted then fought back at some inopportune moment. You can never seem to get a nice drift going where the car stays more or less composed, holding a yaw which is neither understeer push or tail loose in the way you can in an E-type or Ferrari 250, both of which were contemporaries of the Cobra.

On the other hand, the Cobra does have some unique strengths; the homologated weight was a mere 880kg (the original Ace road car weighed 765 dry), which Shepherd says is realistic without cheating (compare with the lightweight E-type which we are assured cannot legally meet its 922kg target) so, even if the Ford V8's 400bhp was a bit optimistic at the time, it came from an engine which displaced a litre more than the

'Even if the Ford V8's 400BHP was a bit optimistic at the time, it came from an engine which displaced a litre more than the Jaguar's and had the torque and low down pulling power to deal with the gaps between four gears'

Cobra 427
SPECIFICATIONS

Engine
6984cc, Ford V8, overhead valve. Four-choke carburettor

Power
390bhp @ 5200rpm (competition spec 480bhp)

Torque
475lb-ft @ 3700rpm (comp spec 460lb-ft)

Transmission
Four-speed with optional close-ratio gearset

Suspension
Front and rear: independent, upper and lower wishbones, coil springs, telescopic dampers

Brakes
Discs all round

Performance
0-60mph 4.2secs, top speed 138mph

Weight
1936lb (880kg)

Value
£200,000 (price at launch $7000)

Left
The 427 is fitted with iron big-block 427 (or 428) cubic inch Ford motor with almost 400bhp in standard spec.

'Touch the accelerator and, simple pushrod and iron though it may be, the engine's instant energy rocks the car in response... connect that to the wheels and the car moves in a similar way'

Jaguar's and had the torque and low down pulling power to deal with the gaps between four gears. On the track, this meant dealing with traffic was so much easier because you would see a gap, plant and go. Lose your momentum in an E-type, or even more relevant, the GTO with its 'little' 3-litre engine, and you'd lost your main advantage. The other point about light weight is that, even if the chassis can't offer an elegant handling balance, the driver doesn't have to battle with extra mass when it gets out of shape. There are plenty of cars where you have to wait for everything to settle before you can get on with it.

The Mk3 then, should have been an attempt to wring some final improvements from a 1950s design in order to compete with the emerging semi-monocoque GTs. There's no doubt that it rides better, feeling taut but absorbing the shocks rather than chopping and jittering over them and it's much more comfortable; the seat doesn't even need to be right back for me and there's plenty of room between thighs and wheel rim. Just as well, because the clutch necessary to deal with 400 iron horses needs muscles of Garth to depress.

The gearshift too is similarly proportioned with a long throw, wide gate and tough syncros. That said, it's irrelevant with 7 litres because you can leave it in top gear most of the time, but it's a strange contrast with the Mk2's shift, which is short and changes as quick as you can move the lever. The engine, though, is rather less inspiring. The exciting thing about even lightly modified small-block American V8s – like the one in Andon's Mk2 – is the way they spin up when you touch the accelerator. Simple and pushrod and iron they may be, but the instant energy rocks the car in response and when you connect that to the wheels, the car moves in a similar way. The 7-litre, though, seems to take longer, as if the mass within takes more stirring.

There is no question about the performance, mind you. On a damp road, wheelspin is never more than a toe's-worth away and having started it, you'd better be careful about how you back off. The drag from that huge engine is akin to yanking on the handbrake. Drive it smoothly and it feels more composed and classier than the other two. Press on, though, and it reverts to type. There's that little fidget, the push, then the yaw, and it takes longer to recover from each. Whether the huge Cooper Cobra radials (235/70R15) don't actually suit the car despite their name, is hard to say but it would be interesting to try the car on some big crossplies.

You get the impression that the Mk3 was inspired by the notion that bigger has to be better. Shelby, Ford and AC did what they could to cope with the bigger engine and the wheels and tyres, but you get the feeling that any dynamic advantage has simply been used up by the extra weight (about 1200kg), leaving you back where you started. The Mk3 makes a great statement about bodybuilding and the power that surely lies within, and in a straight fight it would have an advantage over the Mk2. Where the road turns, though, as roads in Europe do, it probably couldn't outrun the leaner, more athletic model.

As a racer, the Cobra embodies the oldest recipe for success known to engineers. More power in less weight than most means you can endure some compromises elsewhere. As a road car the Cobra is about statement as much as anything. It looks and sounds raw and muscular and, as you drive past, people cannot help but know that. And there is still the way it looks. As long as the huge wheels and tyres and side exhausts and bull bars stay on the shelves at the go-faster shop, there is the obvious purpose which can't really be hidden, but just enough of the elegance that defined the Ace to keep it handsome. That I think, is the real answer to our question...

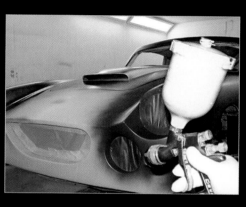

ALFA ROMEO SPIDER (1966-1993)

The once-controversial Spider is now viewed as the classic Italian
ragtop – but what should you look out for when buying?
Words: Richard Dredge Photography: www.magiccarpics.co.uk

It's hard to believe that one of today's
most revered classics was greeted
mainly with cries of dismay when it was
first unveiled at the 1966 Geneva salon.
Slated for being gimmicky and
unattractive, the ugly duckling has
matured over the past 42 years to
become a much sought-after swan.

When the Spider was initially shown,
many disliked the look of those early
cars. Then, as the model evolved
its design became increasingly
controversial; the final variants are
plasticky and something of an acquired
taste. However, the response has always
become far more enthusiastic once
the car has been driven – a slick
gearchange, lusty twin-cam engine
and superbly responsive chassis add
up to a dynamic delight.

The lifespan of the Spider was long

and complex, with four different engines
offered and an equal number of
incarnations – all of which shared the
same superstructure. But it doesn't
matter which derivative you choose, it's
always going to be a great drive thanks
to wonderfully sonorous powerplants
and a chassis that is so communicative
you truly feel you're at one with the car.

As with many cars of the 1960s and
'70s, the eighth owner some 40 years
down the line wasn't really at the
forefront of the designers' minds
when the models were conceived.
Consequently there are many traps for
the unwary. Rust protection was pretty
much non-existent and repairs are often
complex and expensive. Buy a good one
and it'll take years off you; jump in
without looking and you could end
up ageing very quickly!

If you don't want to get caught out,
you will need to spend at least £5500 on
a car that's usable and shouldn't require
any significant work. Even better if you
can stretch to £8000 for a Series 3 or
£10,000 for an earlier model; these kind
of figures will secure you something
that's really good.

Looking for a quality Duetto? You'll
need more in the region of £15,000 – but
for that you'll be able to get one of the
best cars out there. If you'd prefer a
challenge, you could buy a restoration
project for £1500 upwards, but be
warned: putting one of these cars back
together is not the same as with your
typical Meccano-like Triumph or MG.

Engine
The all-alloy twin-cam fours fitted
to the Spider are renowned for their

'Originally slated for being gimmicky and unattractive, the ugly duckling has matured into a much sought-after swan'

sweetness, the basic design having first been used in 1954. However, they don't take neglect very well, and a common malady is for the head gasket to blow, giving the usual tell-tale signs of white emulsion in the oil.

One of the rules which is often broken by owners is to let the engine warm up thoroughly before exercising it – being an all-alloy unit this is especially important. As long as the motor has been serviced properly (preferably with 3000-mile oil-change intervals and the correct anti-freeze) it should last for 120,000 miles before needing a rebuild.

One of the things that doesn't help the potential buyer is the fact that Spider engines can still appear healthy long after a rebuild is due. The nature of the unit means it'll always sound a bit thrashy with noise emanating from the

timing chains and valvegear, but it shouldn't be unduly unpleasant.

Oil pressure should not fall below half way on the clock (4kg/sq cm) once above tickover, and make sure you check the air cleaner: if the engine is on its way out, this will have traces of oil from the breather pipe.

Other weak spots are the O-rings below the camshaft bearings. If these have failed there will be a trio of oil trails down the side of the engine block (from the head) or traces of oil in the cooling system's header bottle.

Because of its cast alloy construction, the engine block is easily damaged by frost. Modern sealing compounds can hide this quite effectively, so check the thermostat housing for evidence of them. Also, engine mountings have a habit of failing (especially on the

exhaust side), so you should make sure you rock the motor via its cam covers to check these.

Transmission

Apart from some US-spec Series 4 models, all Spiders were fitted with a five-speed gearbox. This should be quiet and easy to use – the first problem you'll encounter is likely to be worn syncromesh on second ratio. It's probable that the gearchange won't be too sweet until the box has fully warmed through, but once up to temperature it shouldn't be at all baulky.

The clutches originally specified were prone to wearing out quickly, but by now most have been replaced with much stronger units. Meanwhile, the back axle rarely gives any trouble as it's the same as is fitted to the heavier saloons and

»

'The all-alloy twin-cam fours fitted to the Spider are renowned for their sweetness, but do not take neglect very well'

coupés. Any whines coming from it could indicate that there is trouble ahead. The most likely cure is a replacement axle, and the most cost-effective solution is buying a secondhand unit for around £100.

Rear hub bearings can be a problem as they're not very easy to replace. There's a shrink-ring used to retain the bearing, but if you're not too handy with the toolkit a specialist will ask around £50 to fix each side.

Suspension, steering and brakes

Right-hand-drive cars were fitted with recirculating-ball steering, but some Spiders were reputedly equipped with a worm and roller set-up. Neither system normally gives problems, but the bottom steering joints do wear to cause MoT failure.

If you need to buy lower ball joints, don't go for the cheapest available as some aren't really up to scratch – generous tolerances give enough play to produce an immediate MoT failure. The bushes within both the steering and suspension systems are also wear-prone, as are those in the rear suspension's trailing arms. Another area that gets neglected is the central reaction trunnion locating the rear axle. These are cone-shaped rubber bushes which quickly wear out, allowing the back wheels to feel unstable. When replacing this it is worthwhile fitting a bush made of harder rubber or nylon, available from specialists.

As if that's not enough, there's another fault which often afflicts the Spider's suspension: the Metalastik bushes in the wishbones. There are four bushes, all of which can be affected by seizure as a result of water getting into the trunnion. If left, the wishbones can be damaged by the undue strain.

Replacing these is a big job, and again you should be wary of cheap bushes. At the same time check the lower spring pans for rust. Furthermore, inside the pan is an aluminium shim that tends to dissolve with the passing of time. These are selectively fitted in order to control the height of the suspension. This isn't easy on older cars, but EB has shims ranging in thickness up to 10mm.

Another job that's well worth doing every 20,000 miles or so is to ensure the tracking, caster and camber are set correctly. To get the best handling out of the car the suspension must be set up very accurately, but it's not easy to find somebody who can do it properly. A good bet is BenAlfa in Westbury, Wiltshire, which charges £140.

Check the anti-roll bar mountings, which will probably have corroded and may need to be welded up. Front anti-roll bars often pull out of their retaining links as the bushes tend to be of poor quality, but new links complete with bonded bushes are available for £20.

As well as brake servos leaking, the master cylinders are particularly prone to bore wear. A regularly used car may

From above left
Parts for the cabin are easy to find, making renovation of Italian classic easier than ever.

need a new cylinder within four years of replacement. If you're looking at a right-hand-drive model that was built between 1970 and 1978, it's fitted with a dual cylinder which costs £195.

Brake calipers can corrode and seize up, and after years of having to settle for rebuilt units which were sometimes not that great, it's now possible to purchase new ones again. They're the same price whether you're buying for the front or the rear: £130 apiece.

Bodywork, electrics and trim
The Spider's biggest problem is rust, and it is not an easy model to restore properly or inexpensively. The Spider's lack of any corrosion protection from new means signs of rot on the car will have come from the inside out. By the time it's visible it'll be much worse underneath, so it's normal for three-quarters of the cost of a Spider restoration to be on the bodywork.

Because the cars were so badly protected from the elements, it's likely that every machine you inspect will have had some restoration – and probably major work at that. One of the first areas to rot is the crossmember under the radiator – on Kamm-tail cars there are two plates which are fitted on either side of the radiator. They meet the lower panel where water gets trapped, eventually rotting through.

Also badly affected are the rear of the sills,

the wheelarches (especially the back ones, which are double-skinned) and floorpans. The seams where the front valance meets the wings also harbour rust.

The lower half of each rear wing will have seen better days, due to a blocked drainage pipe which runs from the hood scuttle to an outlet in the chassis. Although the area may look presentable, there's a good chance it's been patched and is not as solid as it appears.

While you're checking the back of the car, pay attention to the trailing edge of the bootlid as well as the spare wheel well – leaks will cause the latter to fill with water, with predictable results. The fuel tank mounts are also vulnerable to rot.

From inside the car it's possible to inspect the base of the footwell for rotting floorpans, along with the inner sill wall and the seat runners. Also check the condition of the A-posts, which will cause the doors to sag once they start to rot significantly.

Other weak spots include the front jacking points and the peak of the wheelarches. Any sign of bodged repairs in these areas means major expense to put right. Also inspect the front and rear valances, both of which rot from the inside out thanks to mud getting trapped behind and retaining moisture.

The front wings need to be examined very carefully, as they rust along the edges, seams and even the indicator repeaters. At »

Alfa Romeo 2000 Spider Veloce (1971-1977)
SPECIFICATIONS

Engine
All-alloy, DOHC
1962cc, two Weber
DCOE carbs

Power
130bhp @ 6000rpm

Torque
137lb ft @ 3500rpm

Transmission
Five-speed manual
rear-wheel drive

Brakes
Front: Discs
Rear: Discs
Servo-assisted

Suspension
Front: Coil-over damper
with double wishbones,
anti-roll bar
Rear: Live-axle, coil
springs, trailing arms,
anti-roll bar

Weight
2245lb (1020kg)

Performance
Top speed: 118mph
0-62mph: 8.8sec
Fuel consumption:
24.8mpg

Value
Cost new: £3848,
Value now:
£6000-£11,000

TIMELINE
» **1966:** Alfa Romeo unveils its all-new Spider, unofficially tagged the Duetto. The first Spiders (badged 1600) have a 1570cc engine and two twin-choke Webers to give 109bhp, 103lb ft and 111mph.

» **1968:** The 1750 Spider debuts at the 1968 Brussels motor show, still with a boat-tail; its 1779cc engine is reckoned to be the finest incarnation of Alfa's twin-cam powerplant, with 118bhp and 127lb ft giving 116mph. Changes include an alternator instead of a dynamo, a brake servo as standard and suspension tweaks. Harsh Italian tax laws also lead to the introduction of a 1290cc Spider Junior, aimed at the home market – RHD cars are rare. 89bhp equates to a 110mph top speed, but three-quarters of the cost of a 1.8-litre car ensures strong sales.

» **1970:** The Duetto bodystyle is superseded by the Kamm-tailed version, still with the 1779cc engine. It is six inches shorter than its predecessor, and its revised dashboard has cowled instruments in place of the original ones set in a flat dash.

» **1971:** The engine size is increased to 1962cc and the car becomes the 2000 Spider Veloce. A limited-slip diff is standard, and styling changes include a broader front grille, recessed door handles and modified sidelights.

» **1977:** Official UK imports of the Spider stop, but some cars aren't actually sold until 1978. However, Spiders continue to be imported (including 1983-1989 Series 3 models) by companies such as Bell & Colvill.

» **1990:** Official imports resume, with LHD only. These Series 4 machines are structurally the same as 1970s models but with a heavily-restyled nose and tail. The interior is also spruced up and electronic fuel injection is installed along with variable valve timing. An official right-hand-drive conversion is £2200, taking the overall price to £18,550.

» **1993:** Production ceases, a year before the introduction of the all-new GTV-based front-wheel-drive Spider.

the front of the wheelarch there's a ledge which traps mud and rots through, and at the rear there's a removable panel which protects the structure behind. If the vendor has nothing to hide, they should hopefully allow you to remove the plate and see what condition the panelwork behind is in.

As well as the rust problems, there's a good chance that the bodyshell has been subjected to parking nudges. This is thanks to the difficulty of seeing the corners, and also because the bumpers fitted offer little protection. Check the bootlid to see if it aligns properly all round, and ensure there are no crumples in the front wings which have been filled to disguise the extent of the damage. The complexity of the boat-tailed car's construction means restoration is an even more involved process than that for the later models.

The Spider's electrical system is very simple, so the worst malady is likely to be rusty connections. If you're looking at a car with air-conditioning make sure the system is working properly – the same models are likely to have electric windows, which will probably be suffering from sticky motors.

As well as the seat trim falling apart quite readily, door trim panels can warp. Also, the rubber mats fitted to early cars are not easy to replace. Thankfully pretty much everything is available to spruce up the interior. The seat covers in the Series 4 Spider (1990-94) wear the quickest. They're a combination of vinyl or leather with Alcantara, and replacements start at £160. The hood has always been noted for its ease of use, but replacement is not for the amateur. It has a tendency to get damaged easily in operation and

is prone to leaking even when working correctly. Factory-fitted tops have always tended to leak at the upper windscreen point, but some aftermarket hoods have been redesigned to obviate the problem.

Conclusion
Buying a Spider isn't to be taken lightly, and if you're thinking of purchasing a car imported from America you could be setting yourself up for huge amounts of grief thanks to the specification differences between US-market cars (which featured Spica fuel injection from 1969) and European models. However, the parts supply situation is better now than it's been for years. Because of the car's complex structure it's worth looking into who has done any work and, if possible, getting hold of supporting pictures to show it being done. It's easy to buy an example which has been badly restored and will end up costing you even more to put right than an honest car needing a complete rebuild. But find a good Spider and you'll wonder why everybody doesn't have one!

» **Thanks to Kevin at EB Spares for all his help.**

£150.60

FOOTMAN JAMES
Insurance specialists. At your service.

1968 Alfa Romeo Spider
Value: £10,000
Quote: **£150.60** (£50x/s unlimited mpa)

AUSTIN-HEALEY 100

Often overlooked in favour of the 3000, the lovely 100/4 is the unsung Healey hero

Words: Richard Dredge Photography: www.magiccarpics.co.uk

THE AUSTIN-HEALEY 100

> 'With less weight in the nose, the 100/4 has the best balance of all the Big Healeys'

There's an old adage that original is best. In the case of the Austin-Healey that's hard to argue against. With its torquey 'four', ultra-clean lines and almost vintage handling, the 100 appears to offer less on paper than its pokier and more highly specified newer siblings. However, slide behind the wheel and you'll soon see why everyone is clamouring for a 100. With less weight in the nose, the 100/4 has the best balance of all the Big Healeys, while the four-cylinder car was actually faster than the six-cylinder model that replaced it.

The Healey Hundred first saw the light of day at the London Motor Show in October 1952. The brainchild of Donald Healey, the 100 was built to slot between cheap sports cars such as the MG T-series and costly ones like the XK120. Designed by Gerry Coker, the 100 was so named because it could crack the magic 100mph barrier – but it would prove too costly for Healey to build by themselves. The potential demand for such a desirable sports car would also have been a problem for Healey; the solution was a deal with Austin which led to lower prices and a final production figure of over 70,000 units.

Austin-Healey Club official Phil Gardner owns a late example (BN2) of the model and is currently restoring a 1954 BN1; he's convinced the 100 is the pick of the Big Healey crop.

'Many enthusiasts opt for the late 3000 convertibles, only to realise after a while that the 100 is nicer to drive, even if it's less practical. While the six-cylinder cars make great tourers, the four-cylinder models are genuine sports cars.

'Values have held steady in recent years, with supply and demand being fairly well matched – although really good cars don't come up that often. You can still buy a running car for £12,000, but you need to fork out half as much again for a nice one. The best examples will go for over £25,000, if sold by a dealer.'

Engine

The 100's engine is an unstressed truck unit, which should give 200,000 miles before serious attention is needed. A full rebuild costs £3000, and that's if you do the work yourself. Four-cylinder cars

THE *Austin Healey* 100

often leak oil, but this can be minimised; if the engine has been rebuilt ask if the crankshaft's scroll-type rear main oil seal has been replaced with a modern lipped version.

These engines also weep water between the head and block; Denis Welch can modify the waterways to eliminate it, but as long as you keep an eye on things there's no cause for concern. Just check the compression if you think there's something awry and monitor the oil to ensure there's no build up of emulsion where the oil and water have mixed. Oil consumption can hit 250 miles per pint, while oil pressure should be 45-50psi, dropping to 20-25psi at idle. Some engine components are getting hard to find.

'Values have held steady in recent years: you can still buy a running car for £12,000 but the best examples will go for £25,000'

Transmission

The 100 had an A90 saloon-sourced four-speed gearbox, with first gear blanked off to give just three speeds – but overdrive on second and third effectively raised this to five ratios. In August 1955 the A90 unit was superseded by the Westminster's 'box, this time with four speeds and overdrive. These gearboxes are tough, but a lack of first gear syncromesh can lead to damaged teeth, and spare parts for the early three-speed gearboxes are now extremely scarce.

If the overdrive isn't working, the chances are the fault is electrical: the most likely culprits will be either the solenoid or the dash switch.

Rear axles often leak oil, which then seeps from the end of the axle casing onto the rear brake linings. Replacing the seal is a half-hour job; running the axle low on oil is not recommended.

Suspension, steering and brakes

Front damper mountings work loose and lever-arm dampers leak. The rear springs also sag and, as ground clearance

Above
Headscarf, cloth cap, gently rolling English countryside – the 100/4 lets you buy into the dream.

»

'If you're looking for an original right-hand-drive 100, remember that nearly 90 percent of Big Healeys were built for export to America'

Austin-Healey 100

SPECIFICATIONS

Engine
2660cc in-line four, overhead valves, cast-iron head and block, two SU carburettors

Power
90bhp @ 4000rpm

Torque
114lb ft @ 2500rpm

Transmission
Three-speed manual, overdrive, rear-wheel drive

Suspension
Front: independent by coil-and-wishbone, lever-arm dampers, anti-roll bar. Rear: live axle with semi-elliptic leaf springs, Panhard rod, lever-arm dampers

Brakes
Drums all round, no servo

Weight
925kg (2035lb)

Performance
Top speed 106mph
0-60mph 8.5sec

Value
Cost £1063 new
Value now £15,000-25,000

was always tight, exhaust systems get damaged through grounding.

The cam-and-peg steering boxes often leak, but as long as they're oiled regularly they don't need rebuilding. If the steering feels loose it's probably because of worn bushes and kingpins.

All 100s had drum brakes all round and, while there was no servo, if maintained properly the brakes will happily pull the car up. The standard 48-spoke wire wheels are fragile, which is why 72-spoke versions are often fitted instead. Splines can wear and cost £50-70 a corner to fix – check for wear by reversing the car and listening for clonks. As long as the splines are greased and the spinners kept tight, the splines shouldn't wear particularly quickly.

Some Indian-sourced wheels bought in the 1980s can give problems. Poorly made, they're often not quite round, which leads to vibration. Another problem with wire wheels is that they're frequently not balanced properly, and sometimes the knock-off spinners are not tightened correctly because owners don't like to risk damaging the chrome.

Bodywork, electrics and trim

The Big Healey's weak spots are its chassis and bodywork. Rustproofing wasn't carried out on the production line, so unless the car has been fettled and/or pampered it's likely there'll be corrosion.

The ladder-frame chassis is simple, but it can be damaged with the slightest knock – even a minor nudge on the front corner will lead to kinks. Check to see if the main rails are straight – any distortion will indicate accident damage – and check whether the car pulls to one side of its own accord. If the car has been in a shunt it's possible to straighten out the chassis, but this is very expensive.

Chassis corrosion is also a problem, with the main rails and outriggers all suffering from tinworm. Beware of bodged chassis and floorpan repairs. Because the floorpans and bulkhead are welded to the chassis, many people won't effect a proper repair. The whole of the bottom nine inches of the car is susceptible to rot, which means floorpans, sills, wings and wheelarches need careful inspection. Inner sills are

structural and difficult to repair. These need to be checked from inside the car, but carpeting can make inspection tricky.

The front shroud is particularly difficult to restore properly, as it consists of several alloy sections welded together and there are compound curves galore. Although it's not able to rust, parking knocks can wreak havoc with the soft metal. The metal is so soft that it's possible to collect dents in alloy panels just by leaning against them while working on the car.

The rear section can be the same, and it's equally susceptible to parking knocks. Just like the front panelling, there's a good chance of filler galore in these areas, but single-skinned panels all round make filler spotting easy. Just lift the bonnet or the bootlid and you'll be able to see immediately if there are big dents that have been filled.

Front and rear wings were made of steel originally, but replacements are now available in aluminium. Fitting alloy items will reduce corrosion – both electrolytic and water-induced – but they are more prone to dents, being softer.

TIMELINE

» **1952** Healey 100 debuts at Earls Court Motor Show.

» **1953** Limited production starts in Warwick. Series production starts at Longbridge. The Austin-Healey 100 (retrospectively the 100/4 or BN1) uses Austin's A90 2660cc four-cylinder engine in 94bhp form with three-speed (plus overdrive) gearbox; 10,688 made.

» **1954** Fifty-five 100S (for Sebring) cars built, with alloy bodies and cylinder heads.

» **1955** BN2 supersedes BN1, with four-speed C-series gearbox, stronger brakes and swage line through to the tail; 3924 are built. 100M sees power upped to 100-110bhp depending on camshaft. About 1100 made.

» **1955-'56** Launch of six-cylinder 100-6 (BN4) marks the end of the 100/4.

SPECIALISTS

» **AH Spares** +44 (0)1926 817181

» **Cape International** +44 (0)1676 542464, www.cape.international.com

» **Denis Welch** +44 (0)1543 472214, www.bighealey.co.uk

» **JME Healeys** +44 (0)1926 425038

» **Murray Scott-Nelson** +44 (0)1723 361227, www.murrayscott-nelson.com

» **Rawles Engineering** +44 (0)1420 23212

» **SC Parts Group** +44 (0)1293 847200, www.scparts.co.uk

» **Trevor Hirst Restoration** +44 (0)1425 61477, www.trevorhirstcars.co.uk

CLUBS

» **Austin-Healey Club UK** www.austin-healey-club.com

» **Austin-Healey Club USA** www.healey.org

» **Austin-Healey Club of America** www.healeyclub.org

» **Austin-Healey Sports and Touring Club** (USA), www.austin-healey-stc.org

» **Austin-Healey Club Nederland** http://rsm.healey.nl/

» **Austin-Healey Club of Japan** www.yk.rim.or.jp/%7Ehealey

BOOKS

» *Austin-Healey 100 in detail* by Bill Piggott. ISBN 0 9541063 4 2

» *Austin-Healey 100, 100-6, 3000 Restoration Guide* by Gary Anderson. ISBN 0 7603 0673 7

» *Original Austin-Healey* by Anders Clausager. ISBN 0 7603 1225 7

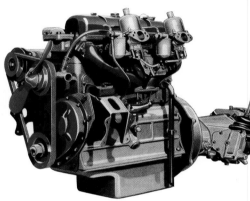

Take a look at the swage line that runs from behind the front wheelarch to the rear wing. If it's not consistent where it meets or leaves the door it's likely the car has been poorly restored.

A worthwhile check is to see how well the doors open and shut if the car is jacked up at its rearmost point. The chassis should be strong enough not to bend at all when subjected to this – so if the door gaps start to close up, the chassis is weak.

Re-importing Big Healeys from the drier parts of the USA was popular 15 years ago. Although such cars may be in good condition bodily, the sun will have taken its toll on the interior. Many 'restored' cars will have bits of trim missing and, although most things are available, much of it is expensive. Also bear in mind that off-the-shelf trim kits don't always fit particularly well, as there are often small differences between one car and another. The only way of trimming a car really well is to make all the carpets and panels to suit the actual car being worked on.

Rear bumpers suffer from corrosion thanks to the exhaust exiting onto them, and windscreen frames are almost impossible to obtain. The supply situation for external trim is otherwise good – but a new (reproduction) grille will set you back £250.

Conclusion

Nearly 90 percent of Big Healeys were built for export to America. Many have found their way back and have been restored with varying degrees of success. If you're at all unsure about what you're looking at, employ an expert to ensure you don't buy a bottomless pit into which you'll end up pouring all your cash.

» **Thanks to Phil Gardner of the Austin-Healey Club UK.**

This page and facing page
100 successfully married handsome roadster looks with reliable Austin running gear; hood drops down neatly behind seats.

£203.10

FOOTMAN JAMES
Insurance specialists. At your service.

1955 Austin-Healey 100 & 3000
Value: £20,000
Quote: **£203.10** (£100x/s unlimited mpa)

AUSTIN-HEALEY SPRITE & MG MIDGET

Fun and affordable, and there's plenty of choice
Words: Richard Dredge, Photography: www.magiccarpics.co.uk

MG Midget Mk1

SPECIFICATION

Engine
1275cc in-line four, eight
overhead valves. Cast-
iron head and block. Two
SU HS2 carburettors

Power
65bhp @ 6000rpm

Torque
72lb ft @ 3000rpm

Transmission
Four-speed manual
Rear-wheel drive

Suspension
Front: Independent with
coil springs, wishbones,
lever arm dampers
Rear: Live axle with half-
elliptic leaf springs, lever
arm dampers

Brakes
Front: 210mm discs
Rear: 178mm drums
No servo assistance
Weight: 721kg (1589lb)

Performance
0-60mph 14.6sec
Top speed 94mph

Value
Cost £683 New (1967)
Value now £500-£5,000

One of the standard modern-day motoring clichés is the desire for a modern-day Sprite – a synonym for an open-topped two-seater that's cheap to buy and run. When Austin-Healey launched its 'Frogeye' Sprite in May 1958 it cost £679, or not much more than a four-door Morris Minor; this really was fun motoring on the cheap. Thanks to a poverty spec (even bumpers were an extra), both weight and price were kept to a minimum, but values have climbed steadily as restoration costs have soared and the number of decent examples has dwindled; the days of students running these cars on a shoestring disappeared long ago.

Whatever you buy, as long as you don't pay over the odds you'll be having a whale of a time. There's not much than can touch the simplicity and purity of a Frogeye, nearly half a century after it first saw the light of day. However, these cars got more and more complex over time.

The most valuable Spridgets are the Frogeyes, with the Midget 1500 worth the least – all the other derivatives fall pretty much equally in the middle. If you're handy with the MIG and you want to give your socket set a good airing you'll be able to buy a project Frogeye for £1500-£2000, but that'll cost a fair bit in parts and will take a lot of your time to get to a roadworthy condition. If you want something that you can use without having to put any effort in you can pick something up for £4500-£5500. Even the best cars are worth no more than £7500, although some are optimistically advertised for closer to £9000.

Although the Midget 1500 is the best to drive and the easiest to live with – as it's the most highly developed of them all – the best examples are worth no more than £4000. Projects start at £200, which means a decent, usable car is around £2000. That leaves all the other derivatives, which start at around £500 for a complete project; the best examples fetch around £5000, with good runners around the £2500 mark. Incidentally, although Sprites have more cachet than Midgets, they're worth no more.

Engine

The Frogeye's engine is based on the A35's, but with twin SU carburettors instead of a single Zenith, plus stronger bearings, valves and springs. Not many Frogeyes still have their original 948cc engine as most have either bigger units or rebuilt items fitted by now; if you're after one with an original powerplant, check if the serial number begins with 9C-U-H. That won't tell you if it's the original engine (you'll need a Heritage trace certificate for that), but you can at least tell if it's the correct version for the car. If your quest is to track down a car that's original in every respect, make sure the carburettors have brass tops, indicating the correct 1 1/8in versions. Later plastic-topped 1 1/4in units are often substituted.

The A-series engine isn't known for its ability to retain oil, and if you're looking at a 948cc version fitted with a scroll-type rear crank seal there's almost no chance of it being oil-tight. Starting from cold the oil pressure should be 60psi – once warmed up expect 40psi at 1000rpm. If there's much less than this you can expect to have to rebuild it before long.

Tappet noise is a part of Sprite ownership, as is a rattling timing chain. If you find the timing chain too noisy a Duplex assembly can be fitted to make it run more quietly. A loud rattle when starting probably comes from a fractured carburettor heat shield; over-enthusiastic tightening can break the rear lug on the manifold.

The A-series engine isn't durable, but it will take hard use without complaint. In 948cc form a set of big end shells may last just 40,000 miles and 1275cc versions will probably suffer from worn piston rings and bores by the time 70,000 miles have been racked up. To check for the early stages of this, run the engine with the oil filler cap removed. If any fumes are evident it'll be time for a rebore before long.

Check for a white emulsion on the oil filler

There just aren't enough seats in an Austin Healey Sprite to carry a crowd. Sometimes this can be an advantage.

cap on 1275cc engines, which are prone to failed head gaskets. Many cars are fitted with electric fuel pumps, most of which were fitted in the 1980s when the correct mechanical pumps were hard to source. It's now possible to get the right bits again, so returning the car to original specification is easy.

The crankshaft of the 1493cc engine can wear badly, as can the pistons and rings. Listen out for rattling when starting up and look for blue smoke as you accelerate through the gears, indicating that the engine has worn. If these symptoms are present, your best bet is to source an exchange rebuilt unit, for which you'll pay around £1100.

Transmission

The MkI Sprite's gearbox and back axle are the same as those used in the A35. There's syncro on second, third and fourth, although early gearboxes had rather weak syncromesh on second gear. Original cars will have a smooth gearbox casing (visible down the back of the engine), which is often substituted for the later ribbed version, offering greater strength and improved syncromesh. If the gearbox is getting worn it'll jump out of gear while you're giving it a test drive – rebuilding the gearbox costs around £200 if you do it yourself. Having it done by a specialist will cost closer to £600.

Halfshafts of early cars are prone to breaking, and with engine upgrades being popular they have an even harder time. A lack of soundproofing makes it easy to hear whines and knocks from the halfshaft splines once they begin to wear.

Suspension, steering and brakes

Front suspension is A35-sourced, but the rack and pinion steering is borrowed from the Minor. If it doesn't feel really precise there's a problem – the steering should be light and positive. If it isn't, the chances are the suspension hasn't been greased regularly.

The front trunnions should have been greased every three months to prevent premature wear. Kingpins are also prone to wear through a lack of regular greasing, so make sure they've been done at the same time. To check if a rebuild is due, jack up the front of the car by supporting it under the front crossmember, and grip the road wheel at top and bottom. Try to rock it – if there's any play it may indicate kingpin wear. To be certain, get somebody to apply the footbrake while you repeat the process. If it's 'cured' a new wheel bearing is needed – if there's still play the kingpin bushes or lower links (fulcrum pins) are due for replacement.

The front lever arm dampers lose their effectiveness very quickly, so check them by bouncing each front corner. The rears are far more durable. Some cars have had a telescopic damper conversion, which is quite involved. The end result doesn't feel any better, but the replacement dampers will be much more durable than the original lever arm units.

Drum brakes were fitted all round on the Frogeye, and these are perfectly adequate for the car's performance. Fronts were taken from the A35 and rears from the Minor. Pedal pressures are a bit higher than with a disc/drum set up, but there should be plenty of feel through the pedal.

»Info

TIMELINE
» 1958: Sprite MkI introduced in May, then modified screen and hood fittings from October
» 1960: Sliding side windows introduced
» 1961: Sprite MkII and MG Midget are launched
» 1964: Midget MkII and Sprite MkIII arrive, with more power, wind-up windows and a revised dashboard
» 1966: The Midget MkIII and Sprite IV go on sale, with 1275cc engine and a folding roof
» 1969: There are now Rostyle wheels, black sills and slim-line bumpers
» 1971: Sprites now carry Austin badges, but the model dies in July; Midget gets round wheelarches in August
» 1972: There's now an alternator
» 1974: Midget gets a 1500 engine, rubber bumpers, square wheelarches and all-synchro gearbox

(Continued overleaf)

»Info

» 1977: Headrests and inertia-reel belts
» 1978: Dual-circuit brakes
» 1979: The final Midget is built in
  November; the last 500 feature a
  black commemorative badge

SPECIALISTS

» Frontline Costello, Bath, 01225
  852777, www.frontlinedevelopments.com
» Spridgebits, Birmingham, 0121 554
  3000, www.pbw-mg-ah.co.uk
» AH Spares, Warks. 01926 817 181,
  www.ahspares.co.uk
» Frogeye Spares Co, Herts. 01923
  464 005, www.frogeyespares.co.uk
» Meacam Spridgets, Wilts.
  01793 845 757
» Moss Europe. 0800 281 182,
  www.moss-europe.co.uk
» Rawles Motorsport, Hants.
  01420 23212,
  www.austinhealeyspecialists.co.uk

AUSTIN HEALEY SPRITE MARK FOUR

Later Sprites used disc brakes at the front; these can also be fitted to the Frogeye. If the swap has already been made make sure the master cylinder from a later Sprite (MkIII/IV) has been fitted, otherwise the brake pedal will require an even greater pressure to pull the car up.

Another complication is the fact that the master cylinder is a dual item, controlling both the brake and clutch hydraulic systems. Check the braking efficiency and look for leaks around the master cylinder, because if one of the bores is damaged or worn you'll probably have to scrap the whole unit and replace it with a new one – at £230.

Bodywork, electrics and trim

The car's monocoque construction can cause tremendous problems with weakening of the structure – by far the biggest problem with these cars is bodywork rot. What looks like a good car may actually be full of filler, so inspect the panelwork very closely and make sure you take a magnet with you to check for filler. Worst culprits are the rear spring mounting boxes in the floor behind the seats. There should be a gap of three inches or so between the top of the rear tyre and the wheelarch. If the gap is much less than this the rear

'There isn't much that isn't available for the Sprite and Midget and running costs are low – so what are you waiting for'

spring box has almost certainly collapsed, which means major surgery – and big bills if you don't want to tackle it yourself.

Sills and A-posts are also prone to corrosion. Check the gaps between the door and both the A-post and the B-post, which should be even. It's common for the gap to be narrower at the top, indicating sag in the bodyshell. If there's any evidence of a weakened structure it won't be cheap to fix. To do the job properly you'll need the use of jigs, time and a lot of patience. Either that or very deep pockets.

The Frogeye's rear-hinged bonnet incorporates the front wings and valance. Both of these tend to rust badly and the area around the bonnet hinges also dissolves readily. While you're in this area inspect the grille surround and the seams between the wings and bonnet top, all of which can get very frilly. Another weak point is the battery

tray, which collects water then rots through. It doesn't stop there, as the combined brake and clutch master cylinder can leak brake fluid onto the surrounding bodywork. As you can guess, this strips the paint then allows the elements to attack the bodywork.

Check the boot floor where it joins the rear panel along with the footwells and area behind the seats. If the car has been fitted with carpets make sure they're not hiding serious corrosion. With the Frogeye, the lack of a bootlid makes checking the boot from the inside a rather tricky proposition. You won't look very graceful peering into the blackness from behind the seats, but putting appearances before your finances could cost you dearly. As if that's not enough, rust can also appear on the join between the boot floor and the rear panels as well as underneath the rear number plate. Also, because there's no bootlid, many Frogeyes

have been fitted with luggage racks. This can lead to distorted rear shrouds due to overloading or poor fitment of the rack.

Many of the main corrosion hot spots aren't particularly difficult to put right, but if the inner sills have rotted badly the repair job will be involved. Similarly, rear wheelarches and lower rear wings can rust badly, and although repair sections are available it's not easy to effect a repair. If the outer rear wheelarch looks as though it has seen better days it's a sure bet that the inner one will be in at least as poor a state. Bodged repairs are common in this area – instead of using the correct pressed panels some 'craftsmen' prefer the traditional art of sheet steel and rivets. Also, new sills are sometimes fitted over the old ones – the old sill must be completely removed and every trace of rust must be cut out. Anything else will lead to an early visit to the body shop. »

Above
Corners are what a Spridget lives for – steering should be super-precise.

Look into the Mark II MG Midget

Top from left
Engine access unrivalled on Frogeye; MkII; Federalised 1500

On the Frogeye, make sure you check all the beading along the length of each front and rear wing. This is used to separate the wings from the shrouds, but it can cause problems when water sits under the head of the beading and rots away the panels. Replacing the beading means separating the panels, which if it needs to be done either side, front and rear is going to be rather time consuming – and expensive if entrusted to a specialist.

There's not much interior trim as the cars were fairly basic. Early cars had rubber mats instead of carpets, but many interiors now have carpets instead, with the original rubber matting very hard to find. Few cars carry the original steering wheel, as even when they were new many were thrown away in favour of a wood-rimmed one. Sourcing original wheels isn't difficult, although few people seem to worry about anything non-original.

The rev counter works via a mechanical drive from the back of the dynamo. Replacements are expensive but the original units are pretty durable. Instrumentation is often incorrect or not working – and costly, so make sure you won't need to buy any.

The electrical system is simple, so there's not much to go wrong. Heaters were initially an optional extra so there's only the car's lighting, wipers and ignition wiring to consider. Despite this, electrical systems are frequently bodged. Its simplicity makes it easy to check, so have a good look round or you could end up with poor reliability and even some auxiliary heating you didn't bank on.

If a Frogeye's rear lights are damaged you can replace them with MGA or TR3 units, as they're the same. Control boxes for the car's electrical system also give up the ghost, but as there are no moving parts it's impossible to tell how much life is left in a unit. Replacements weigh in at around £25.

Conclusion

Where early cars are concerned, originality is important, so don't consider making major modifications unless they can be reversed or you're prepared to make a loss when selling on. The exception to this is under the bonnet – a larger capacity powerplant is okay as long as it's an A-series and is joined by uprated brakes. It's worth knowing if any changes to the car are period or not – contemporary tweaks can be quite desirable – but later ones won't be in keeping. Tuned cars by companies such as Speedwell or Downton aren't worth much more than standard cars, but they're worth tracking down just for their rarity.

There isn't much that isn't available new for the Sprite and Midget, although restoration costs can add up very quickly. What isn't available new is generally available second-hand. The simple construction of the car allows an easy inspection to be made before parting with your cash, so there's really no excuse if you get caught out. Running costs are also very low – so what are you waiting for?

» Thanks to Paul at the Birmingham Spridget Centre for his help with this article

£103.35

1964 Austin-Healey Sprites & MG Midgets
Value: £4000
Quote: **£103.35** (£50x/s unlimited mpa)

DAIMLER SP250

Words: Richard Dredge Photography: www.magiccarpics.co.uk

Above
Odd looks belie unexpectedly good assets, like strong V8 and glassfibre body.

There's no shortage of fast British roadsters from which to choose if you're after a desirable classic. The problem for many is that most decent Brit sportsters are rather predictable, but there are exceptions, and the Daimler SP250 is often overlooked. Perhaps it's because of the rarity; with just 2645 built during a five-year production run, there aren't many to go round.

Whatever the grounds for the SP250 being overlooked, there are plenty more reasons why you want one – not least of all the performance on offer. There's also no body rot to worry about – the glassfibre shell is tougher than most and rarely needs any significant TLC. Unless the car has been really neglected it's unlikely that you'll spend much on keeping an SP250 going – they're strong and with superb parts availability it's never an issue getting the bits you need.

The SP250 made its debut in April 1959 at the New York auto show, where it was unveiled as the Dart. But Dodge had already registered the name and started throwing its toys out of the pram

– forcing Daimler to come up with the rather bland SP250 moniker instead. After some minor bits of re-engineering the car made its debut at the October 1959 Earls Court motor show, where it was announced that 7500 would be sold in the first three years. Production would then settle at the rate of 3000 a year, the bulk of cars going to the US. In the event, fewer than 3000 cars were made in a five-year production span, with just 1200 left-hand drive editions being produced. The car may have been a failure in its day, but it only makes for a less predictable and thoroughly desirable classic now.

Even though many reckon the SP250 is ugly, that doesn't stop demand outstripping supply to a massive degree. Although most buyers want something really nice that needs nothing doing, values of all cars are high. Even a complete box of parts will cost at least £6000; expect to pay at least double this for a usable car that's a bit tatty. Really nice SP250s cost at least £16,000 while a superb example is around the

£25,000 mark. The best (exceptional) cars are now changing hands for around £30,000 – and there's every sign of values creeping even higher.

Engine

Not many of the SP250's rivals could claim to have eight cylinders under the bonnet – and even fewer of those are now affordable. The V8 is a fabulous unit too, with astonishing flexibility and superb durability if properly maintained. While the V8 saloon sometimes suffered from worn engines after surprisingly low mileages, the SP250's powerplant isn't as stressed (as the car is much lighter) so it keeps going for much longer.

It's quite normal for an SP250 engine to cover 250,000 miles between rebuilds, but allowing the unit's coolant or anti-freeze levels to drop will have a dramatic effect on life expectancy. The powerplant features a cast-iron block with alloy heads, so coolant that's too dilute will lead to the cylinder heads breaking up internally and blocking up the whole cooling system – leading to

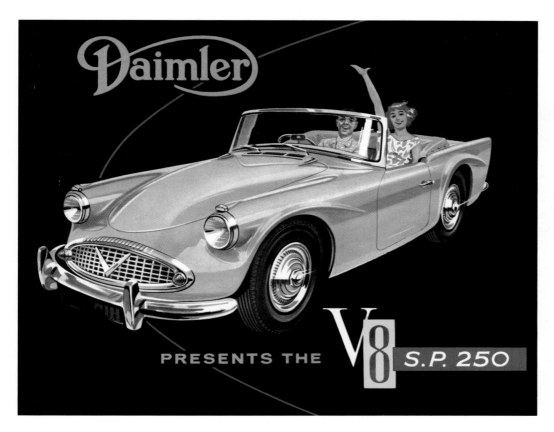

'It's pokey, frugal and well put together. It's great to drive too, thanks to its willing engine, supple ride and agility'

overheating and potentially causing the heads to warp. That's why you need to check for emulsion on the underside of the oil filler cap, signalling that big bills are imminent.

If the top end sounds tappety, it could be that the valve clearances need adjusting, but it's more likely to be problems with the valve guides, which can move in the head. Lumpy running may be down to the exhaust valves sticking, as they can get clogged up with carbon deposits; some Redex in the fuel tank normally sorts this. If it doesn't, it's time for a decoke.

Most SP250 engines have an appetite for oil, with the earliest cars guzzling at the rate of 300-400 miles per pint. The B and C-Spec cars are a bit better, but they'll still get through a pint every 600 miles. To check the health of the bottom end, it's worth ensuring there's at least 15psi on the dial at tickover; expect to see 35-45psi at 40mph.

Transmission

The SP250's gearbox shares some bits with the Triumph TR, although the units aren't interchangeable because the casings are different; the Daimler uses an integral bellhousing while the Triumph doesn't. The gearbox struggles to cope with the V8's torque, and if the car has been driven hard there's a good chance damage will have resulted. Stripped gears are the usual result, with first being especially weak. If the gear has broken there will be lots of clicking; continuous whirring means the teeth have worn. Unusually for such a prestigious car, overdrive was never offered even as an option.

The rear axle is fragile with a worn crown wheel and pinion assembly likely. That's especially so with pre-1961 cars; B and C-spec SP250s featured stronger rear axles with a trio of drain and filler plugs on the casing whereas the earlier cars had just a pair. It's likely that the axle tubes will have started to separate from the casing, as they're not especially well secured. The obvious sign is leaking oil, but there's a good chance there'll be plenty of clonking and wheel wobble.

Suspension, steering and brakes

There's little to worry about at the rear, aside from leaking dampers and sagging leaf springs. At the front though there are potential problems because the trunnions and vertical links can both wear if they haven't been greased every 1000 miles or so. While the trunnions are available new at just £35 each (they're the same as on the TR3/4), the vertical links are only available on a refurbished basis and are a horrific £1350 apiece. You can check for wear by jacking up the front wheels and using a crowbar to check for play between the wheel and the vertical link; any detectable movement means new trunnions and/or links are needed.

All SP250s were supplied with steel disc wheels, although wire wheels were available as an option – and many owners have fitted them since their cars were built. You need to make all the usual checks where the wire wheels are concerned; rusty, worn, broken or missing spokes can all strike. There's

Above
Advertising capitalised strongly on power unit, when a V8 was big news.

Daimler Dart
SPECIFICATIONS

Engine
2548cc V8, 16 overhead
valves. Alloy heads, cast-
iron block. Twin SU HD6
carburettors

Power
140bhp @ 5800rpm

Torque
155lb ft @ 3600rpm

Transmission
Four-speed manual

Suspension
Front: Independent with
coil springs, telescopic
dampers and wishbones.
Rear: Live axle with half-
elliptic leaf springs and
lever arm dampers.

Brakes
Front: 269mm discs
Rear: 254mm discs

Weight
1000kg (2200lb)

Performance
0-60mph 8.9sec
Top speed 124mph

Value
£1489 new (1960)
Value now £12,000-
£25,000

also the spectre of tired splines to contend with, so jack up each corner and try turning the wheel while somebody applies the footbrake. Any detectable movement means the splines are worn.

Unusually, the steel wheels can give problems as they're prone to cracking around the mounting holes – which is why many owners fit Minilites or wires. However, some owners substitute Triumph TR items instead if they're keen to stick with pressed steel.

There are Girling disc brakes at the front and rear, without the aid of a servo. There's not much to go wrong, although you need to check for the usual problems of scored, warped or worn discs along with sticking caliper pistons. The easiest way to check for all of these is to listen for untoward noises under braking while also feeling for juddering from the brake pedal. Sticking pistons will be given away by uneven braking or the brakes sticking on – so see if the car quickly grinds to a halt on a shallow incline. Another clue is feeling to see if one or more wheel centres get unusually hot.

Another reason why the car might come to a halt prematurely is a partially seized handbrake mechanism. The cable needs to be kept greased in its guides, but this is often overlooked. As a result it can stick on when released – although it's nothing that a dab of grease won't fix.

Bodywork, electrics and trim

With its glassfibre bodyshell, visible corrosion isn't something that afflicts the SP250 – although under the skin there are all sorts of potential rust issues. However, while bodyshell rot isn't something to worry about, there are other possible maladies as glassfibre was in its infancy when the SP250 was being produced. The key affliction is crazing of the gel coat, although the SP250's skin is so thick that serious cracking is unlikely. If major fissures are evident it's more likely that the car has been crunched at some point, so check that the inner wings aren't rippled.

If the car has never been in an accident, any crazing will be cosmetic only, and it will affect the bodywork forward of the windscreen the most. However, the plastic around the door handles as well as the boot hinges can also be affected; grinding back and re-gelling will effect a permanent repair if done properly.

Take a look at the bonnet and see it's not damaged; it can fly open on the move for various reasons. As well as its securing latch wearing, the radiator supports can corrode. They're made of steel coated in glassfibre and are structural; if they rot, the nose can flex leading to the bonnet opening as the car is being driven. A caring owner will have fitted a safety latch; they're just £20 or so from the Owners' Club.

The chassis is simple in its construction, but it's unlikely to be completely free of corrosion. You need to start at the front and work backwards, examining every bit of the chassis; putting it up on ramps is the only way of doing this properly.

The tubular crossmember at the front is usually rusty; this houses the mountings for the body as well as the steering box. New crossmembers are available and they're easy enough to replace with four hours usually seeing the job through. Nearby are the front suspension turrets, which rot out when water gets in through the steering column apertures. Whichever turret houses the steering column is less likely to have corroded because the column helps prevent water getting in. Plating is usually perfectly acceptable, but if the corrosion has really taken hold (which is rare), it will be necessary to replace the entire turret. That's not a problem at all – once you've removed the bodyshell to gain access to it…

Even if the metal is untouched by corrosion there's a chance that the welds will have cracked around the mounting brackets for the lower wishbones. Any cracks are easy to spot on a clean chassis, but if it's caked in grime or oil you could miss them. Fixing them properly means stripping the chassis, which involves removing the engine. While in theory it's possible to leave the powerplant in place to

Clockwise from left
Turner-designed V8; many cars now on wires; retrims cost around £3000.

do the work, the reality is that access is restricted and the problem may not be fully eliminated.

Post-1961 cars have a stronger chassis, extra bracing for the B-posts and stiffening beams underneath the door apertures. It's all susceptible to rot, though all the necessary parts are available new. If the whole lot needs renewing you'll have to remove over 50 sets of nuts and bolts first – and if they're all seized up that's not a quick job.

There's a substantial crossmember immediately behind the back axle. This can rust, although it's less likely than the two supplementary strengthening beams behind it suffering from corrosion. At least it's easy repairing these areas – unlike those around the hangers for the rear springs. These corrode and accessibility is an issue unless the bodyshell is lifted; things are made even trickier by precise alignment being absolutely key.

Although the newest SP250s are now over four decades old, until recently it was possible to buy a brand new chassis made on the original jigs. Consequently, it's possible that any car you look at doesn't sit on its original chassis – but as long as the work has been done properly, you could have a frame that's far better rustproofed than anything that ever came out of the factory.

The SP250's electrical system is straightforward, but the wiring may have gone brittle and some of the connections will probably not be that great. While emery will fix the latter, a brittle loom needs to be replaced; new ones cost around £200. Instruments, switchgear and light units are all available – but are unlikely to be needed as it's all so reliable.

As you'd expect of any car wearing Daimler badges, the SP250's interior is luxuriously trimmed, although it's not as expensively finished as the saloons. That still doesn't mean it's cheap to retrim though, and if everything is needed you'll be looking at a bill of around £3000 to put it all right, including a new set of carpets. A replacement soft top costs £350, so check the one fitted is in decent condition. However, fitting an SP250's hood is easier than most, so you won't necessarily have to fork out for labour on top.

Conclusion

It may not be the prettiest sporting classic, but the SP250 has got a huge amount going for it. Affordability and exclusivity are just two of its key attributes, but it's also pokey, frugal and very well put together. It's great to drive too, thanks to its willing engine, supple ride and agility through its light weight. You want more? Well how about great parts back up, with just about everything available off the shelf. It's easy to upgrade too and thanks to that glassfibre bodyshell there's no need to worry about corrosion ever striking. It's one of the most usable classic sportscars going – at any price.

£229.35 FOOTMAN JAMES
Insurance specialists. At your service.
1961 Daimler Dart
Value: £20,000
Quote: **£229.35** (£100x/s unlimited mpa)

»Info

TIMELINE
» Apr 1959: Daimler Dart announced at the New York Auto Show.
» Sep 1959: Car launched in UK; first cars have recesses behind the door handles.
» Oct 1960: A hard top becomes available.
» Feb 1961: Private UK buyers can now specify an automatic gearbox; previously available only to export markets and the police.
» Apr 1961: B-Spec cars on sale with adjustable steering column, front and rear bumpers, reserve fuel tank and windscreen washers. There's also a stronger rear axle, a stronger chassis and revised interior trim.
» Apr 1963: C-Spec SP250 arrives with standard heater, cigarette lighter and built-in trickle charger socket.
» Sep 1964: Production ends.

SPECIALISTS
» Autotech (mechanicals), Middlesex. 020 8423 3752
» Barry Thorne (parts), Surrey. 01306 711789, 07885 882 416
» Brian Purves (trim), West Sussex. 01342 315065, www.bryanpurves.co.uk
» David Manners, West Midlands. 0121 544 4040, www.davidmanners.co.uk
» Graham Frost, Kent. 01322 522958

CLUBS
» Daimler and Lanchester Owners' Club, 02380 766372, www.dloc.org.uk
» SP250 Owners' Club. 01322 522958

BOOKS
» Daimler SP250 by Brian Long. Veloce, ISBN 1-874105-24-3
» Daimler Dart SP250 Parts Manual by Mercian Manuals. ISBN X-1676-0221-6

(1973-1980)
FERRARI 308GT4

It offers everything you could want from a classic car – except, some would say, desirability. But don't let that put you off considering a 308GT4 for your garage

Words: Richard Dredge Photography: www.magiccarpics.co.uk

Above
Don't let anyone tell you 'proper' Ferraris must seat only two and be designed by Pininfarina.

The Holy Grail of most car enthusiasts is a toy in the garage with a Ferrari badge on its nose. Failing that, most of us would settle for anything with a V8 engine, or just a small powerplant in the middle to offer that perfect balance.

So what about a model that combines all these things – surely that would be the ultimate prize for the car nut? You'd think so, but the 308GT4 does indeed combine all the essentials (although strictly speaking not always the Ferrari badge), yet it's a machine that's frequently scoffed at. As a result, you can pick up one of these mid-engined V8s for £10,000 – and there's even space in the back to bring the kids along for the ride. Well, as long as they're very small.

There are two reasons why the GT4 has always been seen as a lesser Ferrari; those Bertone lines and the fact that it's

a four-seater. 'Proper' Ferraris don't have space for four and have to be designed by Pininfarina – or that's what 'they' would have you believe. But don't believe the hype – this car looks great, handles brilliantly and is as fast as you are ever going to need. Yet a decent one will cost you no more than a two-year-old repmobile – which will continue to shed value faster than yesterday's newspapers.

The GT4 superseded the 246GT and was launched to take on Porsche's 911 – hence the 2+2 seating layout. It was criticised from the outset for that wedgy profile, and after the beautifully curvaceous 246GT it was certainly different – but it was far from ugly. Whatever your views on the looks, you can't argue with the power, the noise, the handling or the heritage. If we're honest, values aren't likely to go

stratospheric any time soon, but don't let that put you off buying one now.

If you've already been swayed that you need a GT4 in your life, don't be tempted to spend much less than £12,000 or you'll constantly be paying out on repairs. It's best to fork out closer to £16,000 for a tidy example, although you could spend up to £20,000 on one of the best GT4s in existence.

Engine

With its 7600rpm red-line, the GT4's 2926cc V8 is a gem of an engine as long as it's in fine fettle. Tough and reliable, the powerplant will cover 100,000 miles between rebuilds if looked after. But it won't take much in the way of abuse before it starts to give serious (and costly) problems.

One of the easiest ways to hurt a

‘There are two reasons why the GT4 has always been seen as a lesser Ferrari; those Bertone lines and the fact that it’s a four-seater’

Ferrari V8 is to rev it hard from cold, causing piston ring and valve wear. Blue smoke from the exhaust gives the game away, but don’t fret too much if there’s a steady stream of white smoke; they all do that! If a full rebuild is needed, you’ll spend around £10,000; if just the top end needs fettling, this figure is halved.

Each camshaft is driven by a toothed rubber cam belt, and these need to be renewed every 25,000 miles or two years – although most specialists reckon every 16,000 miles is a safer bet. If the belt breaks, the pistons and valves will get intimate and you’ll be staring down the barrel of a full engine rebuild.

Head gaskets are prone to problems, and while it’s worth doing the standard test of looking for a white emulsion on the underside of the oil filler cap, you can also check the oil itself, on the dipstick. However, a common tell-tale is the temperature gauge shooting up to maximum soon after starting the car, even when the engine hasn’t got up to temperature. If either of the gaskets has failed, expect to pay £3000 on a fix. This covers the cost of replacing both, as they should be done in pairs even if one is apparently healthy.

Setting up the quartet of Weber twin-choke carbs can be costly and time-consuming, so if the engine runs unevenly suspect everything is out of balance. It’s worth doing a compression check on each combustion chamber; you’re looking for 150psi each time.

Transmission

You can tell the GT4 is a genuine Italian supercar by the way it refuses to allow you to select second gear until the transmission has fully warmed up. However, if this ratio is still hard to get once everything is at temperature, it’s because the synchromesh has worn. By the time this happens, the whole gearbox usually needs rebuilding – at a cost of up to £5000, although it can be less.

Clutches don’t last long: if the car isn’t driven too hard you’ll get 20,000 miles out of one if you’re lucky. When replacement time comes round, expect to pay £750 to have the work done. Other than that it’s just a question of making sure there’s no vibration because of a propshaft that’s out of balance, and no whining because the diff or gearbox are past their best. Universal joints can also wear, leading to clonks as the drive is taken up – but even if this work does need doing, it’s not difficult or costly.

»

'Don't believe the hype – this car looks great, handles brilliantly and is as fast as you are ever going to need'

From above left
1970s' splendour: leather trim, bold lights, classic dash and V8 power equate to a bargain Ferrari.

»**Info**

TIMELINE

» 1973: The 308 GT4 breaks cover at the Paris Motor Show. It's the first production V8 Ferrari and the only Modenese motor to be penned by Bertone.

» 1975: For the Italian market only, there's the tax-break special 208GT4, with a 170bhp 1991cc engine.

» 1976: There are now Ferrari badges on the bonnet, wheels and steering wheel, replacing the previous Dino items. A fresh grille is also introduced. At the Turin Motor Show there's a one-off GT4, in the form of the Bertone 308GT Rainbow.

» 1980: The GT4 is replaced by the Mondial, after 2826 examples have been built.

SPECIALISTS

» AE Performance Engineering, Cheshire. +44 (0)1565 625 612, www.aeperformance.co.uk
» Bob Houghton, Glos. +44 (0)1451 860 794, www.racecar.co.uk/bobhoughton
» Damax, Silverstone. +44 (0)1280 851 004, www.damax.co.uk
» DK Engineering, Herts. +44 (0)1923 287 687, www.dkeng.co.uk
» Emblem, Bournemouth. +44 (0)1202 722 247, www.emblemsportscars.com
» Eurospares, Essex. +44 (0)1787 477 169, www.eurospares.co.uk
» JMH Automotive, Cheshire. +44 (0)1477 534499, www.j-m-h.co.uk
» Nick Cartwright, Derby. +44 (0)1629 56 999, www.racecarnewmedia.co.uk/nickcartwright
» Superformance, London. +44 (0)208 500 7127, www.superformance.co.uk
» Verdi, Middlesex. +44 (0)20 8756 0066, www.verdiferrari.biz

CLUBS

» Ferrari Owners' Club (UK), www.ferrariownersclub.co.uk
» Ferrari Owners' Club (US), www.ferrariownersclub.com

Suspension, steering and brakes

In true supercar fashion, at each end of a GT4 you'll find double wishbones with coil springs and telescopic dampers. That's why the car should handle so fabulously, although bits do wear if a grease gun hasn't been used every two or three years. Without proper lubrication, the various ball joints suffer (there are four of them), while the rubber bushes can also perish, which will lead to wayward handling.

All GT4s were supplied with alloy wheels, and these can look the worse for wear if there's been too much intimate contact with kerbstones. Also check that the lacquer isn't peeling off; in both cases, if the damage is superficial, it's cheap and easy enough to get the rims reconditioned. Expect to pay no more than £50-60 per corner to get the wheels looking as good as new.

There are two possible brake problems, but it's unlikely that any one car will be afflicted with both. The first is the seizing up of components from a lack of use; many of these motors sit from one month to the next without turning a wheel. As a result the handbrake can start to give problems, although it's nothing that a bit of grease won't cure – and even when working properly it can struggle to hold the car. The other likely malady is a set of brake discs that are scored from hard use; some owners drive their GT4s brutally, and while the stoppers work fine in normal conditions, they don't take abuse very readily. A fresh set of discs all round costs £750.

Bodywork, electrics and trim

The GT4 may have been costly when new, but it's still a 1970s Italian car so don't be surprised if the one you're inspecting is riddled with rot. Superb examples abound – but there are some complete sheds out there as well.

Start by opening the doors, bonnet and boot, and looking at all the panel edges to make sure they haven't begun to corrode. The bonnet and bootlid are made of aluminium, but the rest of the panels are steel, over a stretched 246GT spaceframe chassis (which can corrode, so check it thoroughly). If the car has been crashed, unless it's been rebuilt by someone who knows what they are doing, the bodyshell is likely to be twisted. However, you could struggle to spot this unless the panel fit is very poor and there's rubbing of the door, bonnet or bootlid edges with the surrounding panels.

The rear wheelarches are especially likely to be 'lacy', along with most of the lower panels such as the sills, valances and back quarters. It's the same story where the bottom edges of the doors are concerned; their drain holes clog so they rot from the inside out. The door frames and skins are both constructed from metal that's too thin for its own good, so once corrosion gets started the whole lower part of the assembly will soon be history.

Other common rot spots include the tops of each front wing, so check that these haven't already been bodged with glassfibre repairs – a magnet is an essential tool for anybody who is thinking about »

Ferrari 308GT4
SPECIFICATIONS

Engine
2926cc V8, four overhead camshafts, 16 valves. Alloy heads and block. Four Weber 40DCNF carburettors

Power
250bhp @ 7700rpm

Torque
210lb ft @ 5000rpm

Transmission
Five-speed manual
Rear-wheel drive

Suspension
Front: Independent with coil springs, double wishbones, telescopic dampers, anti-roll bar
Rear: Independent with coil springs, double wishbones, telescopic dampers, anti-roll bar

Brakes
Front: 257mm ventilated discs
Rear: 257mm ventilated discs
Servo-assisted

Weight
1327kg (2923lb)

Performance
0-60mph: 6.9sec
Top speed: 154mph

Value
Cost new: £9442 (1976)
Value now:
£10,000-£20,000

buying a Ferrari. You also need to wield said magnet around the door hinges; any bodging here is likely to lead to giveaway sagging doors. Finish off by inspecting the top of the rear window, where the ventilation slots corrode.

Your final check should be that neither of the two fuel tanks is leaking – which they will do if they are rotten. They sit just ahead of the rear wheels and cost £1200 apiece to change, including labour.

Leather upholstery was the order of the day for the GT4; at first the seats were trimmed with a combination of suede and hide, but towards the end of production this became leather throughout. Whatever the car you are looking at has make sure there are no tears or splits, as retrimming a GT4 interior is costly.

It's cliché time again, because the Ferrari's electrics are typically Italian in that they throw a wobbly at the drop of a hat. One of the most temperamental components is the fuse box, which can create all sorts of strange happenings as it gradually overheats and blows fuses in the process. A new unit (at £150) is sometimes the only solution because the connections are too far gone to be revived.

Another common ailment is an oil-pressure gauge sender that makes up readings as it goes along. Start the engine

and see if the gauge is erratic; if it is, budget on spending £100 for a new sender unit. Also check the headlamps go up and down okay; each unit has a cam to stop it popping up when it shouldn't. When these wear, the bill can run to over £200 per side.

Conclusion

We reckon the GT4 offers fabulous value for money – but it also gives virtually unrivalled opportunities for hefty financial shocks. Buy a good one and you'll need to budget significant sums to keep it in fine fettle. Buy a bad one and you could end up with a car that costs more to put right than you'll ever get back if you have to sell.

That's why it's essential that once you have found a model which appears to be sound, you get an expert to ensure that it's as good as it seems. If it is, snap it up and enjoy it before fun on the roads is banned entirely!

£197.85

FOOTMAN JAMES
Insurance specialists. At your service.

1974 Ferrari 308GT4
Value: £16,000
Quote: **£197.85**
(£100x/s unlimited mpa)

»Info

BOOKS

» The Complete Guide to the Ferrari 308, 328, Mondial by Wallace A Wyss. Dalton Watson, ISBN 0-901564-91-5*

» Ferrari 308, 328, Mondial by Geoff Willoughby. Osprey, ISBN 0-85045-832-3*

» Ferrari Dino 246, 308 & 328 Collectors' Guide by Alan Henry. MRP, ISBN 01-899870-76-8

» Ferrari Dino 308 & Mondial Gold Portfolio 1974-1985 by Brooklands Books. ISBN 01-85520-358-8

» Original Ferrari V8 Restorer's Guide by Keith Bluemel. Bay View, ISBN 01-870979-78-8

» Ferrari Dino by Anthony Curtis. Crowood, ISBN 1-86126-065-2

FIAT DINO (1966-1972)

Put thoughts of baby Ferraris out of your head: Fiat's Dino is just as desirable as its supercar cousin, and these days rarer, too. Good ones are scarce but well worth seeking out

Words: Richard Dredge Photography: www.magiccarpics.co.uk

Mention you've got a Dino to someone and they'll coo over the fact that you're lucky enough to own a mid-engined baby Ferrari. That's always been the Fiat Dino's problem; ever since it was unveiled more than four decades ago, it has lived in the shadow of its more glamorous cousin. But it's a double-edged sword, because you can buy this enigmatic sportscar with the same engine as Ferrari's Dino, for a fraction of the price. Even better, you can choose from open or closed variants while also enjoying greater levels of rarity with consequently lower levels of familiarity. Perhaps the Fiat Dino is no consolation prize after all.

It came about thanks to a Formula 2 rule change in the mid-1960s. Any car racing would have to use an engine of which no fewer than 500 units were built. Ferrari wanted to be represented in the Formula but didn't have the factory capacity. Instead, a tie up with Fiat was arranged. Ferrari had a suitable engine;

penned by Vittorio Jano in 1956, the highly stressed racing V6 was redesigned by Aurelio Lampredi to ready it for road use. He increased the initial displacement of 1596cc to a production capacity of 1987cc, and later expanded it to 2418cc.

Design and production would be outsourced; the dropheads were styled and built by Pininfarina, while Bertone was responsible for the fixed heads. Although the spider was unveiled first, Bertone had been working on its coupé since 1963, intending it to replace Fiat's 2300S. While the spider is something of an acquired taste, the understated lines of the coupé are universally admired. It's less fussy, and the proportions are better too thanks to a stretched wheelbase to accommodate full-sized rear seats. The drophead has a 2+2 configuration instead, which in reality means space for two people plus a bit of extra luggage room.

Dino production lasted six years until 1972. By then, just 1557 spiders and 6043

coupés had been built – all left-hand drive. Of these, 1133 spiders and 3629 coupés featured the smaller engine. Over the years many have been scrapped, but it doesn't happen any more; they're too sought after, if not especially valuable. The estimated 30 spiders and 70 coupés in the UK are generally united by one factor; Dino nut Mike Morris. He set up the Dino Register 25 years ago; it now covers nearly 2000 examples around the globe. Having written the definitive book on the car, there isn't much that Mike doesn't know about the Dino.

He says: 'There are nothing like enough Dinos to go round – especially when it comes to really good examples. There are few truly superb Dinos; those that do exist are retained by fastidious owners. Restoration projects

'This isn't a poor man's Ferrari;
it's a rich man's Fiat'

almost never come onto the market, so that leaves just average examples that need a bit of tidying. The best cars are in Switzerland and Germany; owners there are meticulous with their cars.'

The Dino's rarity was guaranteed from the outset; with a homeland list price higher than for an Aston Martin DB6, it's no wonder few were sold. That was before local taxes too, so it's no surprise the car was never available in the UK. Now it's 36 years since the last Dino was built, the cars are much more affordable. Renowned motor sport photographer Bernard Cahier owned a Dino for a while; he loved it but was moved to comment that if it wasn't for the badge on the bonnet, the car would be worth three times as much.

Mike Morris confirms Cahier's views: 'People are starting to overlook the badge; 2.4 Spiders were designed and trimmed by Pininfarina and built in Maranello – the same as a 246. Each has the same ZF box and Girling brakes, so they're not that far

apart. The 2.4 Spider is most valuable; it's also rarer than the Ferrari. You'll pay £15-30,000, while a 2-litre car is worth only £10-16,000. Coupés go for even less; a 2.4 edition is £7-14,000 and 2-litres fetch just £5-10,000. These prices are for running, roadworthy examples: they're criminally cheap, and values can only go up. But remember, while purchase costs are low, running costs are in Ferrari territory – and buyers often overlook this. It isn't a poor man's Ferrari; it's a rich man's Fiat.'

Engine

Whether you're looking at a 2-litre car or a 2.4, the potential problems are much the same, although the latter tends to be more reliable. The most likely issue is with the camshafts, which can readily wear – especially if the engine hasn't warmed up properly before piling on the revs. Things are made even worse by ignoring the valve clearances, which must be checked every 6000 miles. It's a time-consuming, fiddly

job that's frequently put off, which can prove expensive. There's the potential for a lobe to get knocked off; that's when things can get costly. Genuine Ferrari cams are around £1200 each (remember there are four), but Superformance does a set for £970, offering better mid-range torque.

Listen out for worn, rattling timing chains; fresh ones cost around £850 if replaced by a specialist. On 2-litre engines the chain itself is less problematic than the tensioner, which must be adjusted every 6000 miles. Failure to do so can result in the chain jumping a cog and wrecking the engine.

Also watch out for blue smoke when accelerating, betraying worn bores. This is especially likely on a 2-litre unit, but all Dino engines suffer from unreliable sender units for the oil pressure gauge. Expect 50psi at 3000rpm: if it is not indicated it could be a worn engine or faulty dials.

The Dino was the first car ever to get electronic ignition; the Dinoplex system

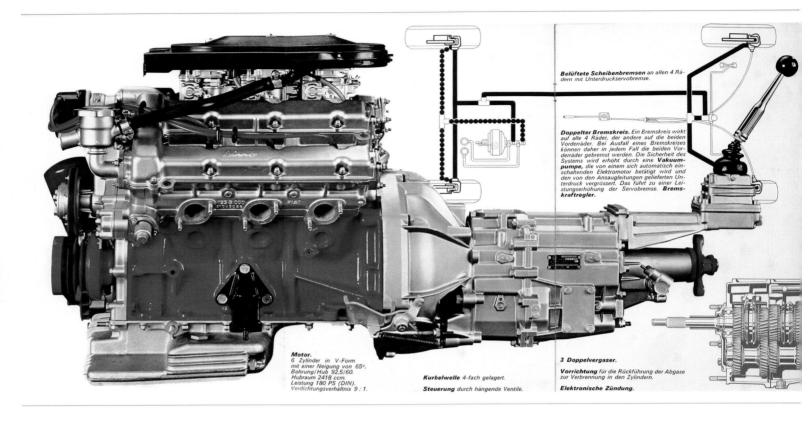

Motor.
6 Zylinder in V-Form
mit einer Neigung von 65°.
Bohrung/Hub 92.5/60.
Hubraum 2418 ccm.
Leistung 180 PS (DIN).
Verdichtungsverhältnis 9 : 1.

Kurbelwelle 4-fach gelagert.

Steuerung durch hängende Ventile.

Belüftete Scheibenbremsen an allen 4 Rädern mit Unterdruckservobremse.

Doppelter Bremskreis. Ein Bremskreis wirkt auf alle 4 Räder, der andere auf die beiden Vorderräder. Bei Ausfall eines Bremskreises können daher in jedem Fall die beiden Vorderräder gebremst werden. Die Sicherheit des Systems wird erhöht durch eine *Vakuumpumpe*, die von einem sich automatisch einschaltenden Elektromotor betätigt wird und den von den Ansaugleitungen gelieferten Unterdruck vergrössert. Das führt zu einer Leistungserhöhung der Servobremse. *Bremskraftregler.*

3 Doppelvergaser.

Vorrichtung für die Rückführung der Abgase zur Verbrennung in den Zylindern.

Elektronische Zündung.

'Coupé or Spider? The former is more of a cruiser, with more compliant suspension, greater refinement and higher comfort levels'

was once state of the art but is now fragile and costly to fix. That's why most systems have been swapped for modern Bosch units; a cost-effective solution. Less easy to mend cheaply is the distributor, which wears easily. They're not easy to revive, with a rebuild costing around £250.

The 2.4-litre engine potentially suffers from a few afflictions that don't affect the smaller unit. The first is broken exhaust valves, which are brittle sodium-filled items that can be quite fragile. Core plugs are also prone to weeping, and if left this can lead to the coolant level dropping to the point where the motor overheats.

Engine upgrades are popular on both variants, with displacement increases possible on the 2-litres. Bigger valves, uprated camshafts, high-capacity oil pumps and oil cooler kits all may have been fitted, along with a lightened flywheel and uprated radiator – all things that make the car more usable.

Transmission

There's little to worry about with the transmission of a 2.4-litre Dino. Clonking universal joints or a whiny diff should be the extent of any problems. It's a different matter for the 2-litre car though, whose gearbox and differential are both weak. In the case of the former, the initial

things to go will be the synchromesh on second and third. Putting it right costs at least £1750, as long as no gears are needed.

Suspension, steering and brakes

Independent front suspension by double wishbones means the Dino is a fabulous car to drive – as long as it's in fine fettle. Unfortunately it sometimes isn't, with worn ball joints common. They are sealed units that rapidly deteriorate once the rubbers split, but replacing them is easy enough. They're cheap too at less than £20 each; even a full suspension bush kit is under £100. A lot of the parts are common to the 124, 125 and 2300, which means many are available from specialists, if not especially plentiful at an autojumble.

The worm and roller steering is sharper than you'd think. It's reliable too, although its damper sometimes loses an oil seal, leading to all the lubricant leaking out. Steering kickback over bumps betrays the fact that there's no oil in the system; fitting a new seal is an easy task.

All Dinos feature discs at each corner and have no weak spots as such. Check for sticking cylinders, leaks and worn pads or discs, and be aware that each variant has its own disc specification.

Bodywork, electrics and trim

It's that old Italian chestnut; poor-quality steel and minimal rustproofing. The Dino is as badly afflicted by rot as most of its cousins – and replacement panels have long been extinct. Of the two, the spider is the more vulnerable; filler was routinely used on the production line if panels didn't fit, whereas the Bertone-built coupé was built to slightly more exacting standards.

The A-posts and sills are most likely to corrode, both of which are essential to the car's strength. For the former, open the doors and check the shuts along their forward edges. Also look at the back of the inside of the wheelarch; this is where the metal starts to corrode when it gets battered by debris from the front wheels.

Tatty outer sills indicate that the inner and intermediate panels are history, with repairs being involved and costly. Rotted sills could compromise the car's structure, so check that the doors close and fit properly. This is particularly important on the Spider, whose floorpans suffer as a result of water leaking into the cabin.

All cars can have rotten jacking points and outriggers, but checking these out is easy enough. It's the same with the door bottoms. The coupé's trailing edge of the bootlid and leading edge of the bonnet

»Info

TIMELINE

» 1966: Dino Spider debuts at Turin Motor Show
» 1967: Coupé version appears at Geneva Motor Show
» 1968: Production of 2-litre Dino ends
» 1969: Production of 2.4-litre cars starts; all cars now assembled at Maranello
» 1972: All Dino production ends

SPECIALISTS

» Superformance, Essex. +44 (0)208 500 7127, www.superformance.co.uk
» Rosneath Engineering, East Sussex. +44 (0)1892 770 032, www. rosneathengineering.co.uk
» Eurospares, Essex. +44 (0)1787 477 169, www.eurospares.co.uk

CLUBS

» Fiat Dino Register. Mike Morris, +44 (0)1553 829 685, mmikedino@aol.com
» Dino Owners' Club (Germany). www.dino-owners-club.de
» The Other Dino. Brian Boxall, brian.boxall@maxxium.com, http://autos.groups.yahoo.com/group/fiatdino/

BOOKS

» Les Ferrari de Turin by Jean-Pierre Gabriel. Editions du Palmier, ISBN 2-914920-25-3 (French/English text)
» Fiat Dino – Ferrari By Another Name, by Mike Morris. Out of print but available on CD-ROM for £14.95 from Mike; see 'Clubs' for details.

need close inspection; on the spider, these panels are made of aluminium.

Scrutinise the rear valance, because rust eats its way into the structure and repairs are complicated. The same is true of the front bulkhead, so lift the bonnet and make sure there's no corrosion or bodges. Things aren't helped by rust often breaking out in the windscreen surround; the paint was frequently damaged here when the glass was originally fitted.

Bodge-free electricals aren't inherently unreliable. Some parts are difficult to find, but much of it – including instrumentation and switchgear – was common to other Fiats. The exterior lighting wasn't, though; the rear clusters are very hard to locate and are handed, too. Persevere and you'll track down what you need – and if you can put a Fiat 125 or 130 part number to something instead of its original Dino one, you'll invariably pay a lot less.

Conclusion

Coupé or Spider? The former is more of a cruiser, with more compliant suspension, greater refinement and higher comfort levels. Which engine you choose is also important; the larger unit being more usable and reliable. The 2-litre is freer-revving however, while the car is less prone to understeer thanks to the lighter

nose – this is an all-alloy block while the 2.4 is cast-iron. The earlier cars make do with the live rear axle and half-elliptic leaf springs of the 2300 coupé. The 2.4-litre cars are blessed with the independent set-up of the flagship 130.

All cars let you delight in the sounds of the quad-cam V6 and, ultimately, your decision may rest with what you can find.

The biggest challenge is finding a Dino that's been properly restored or genuinely cherished all its life. Restoration costs are way beyond what the car will be worth in the foreseeable future, leading to bodges. However, there are good cars out there; you must just be patient and prepared to see several before you buy. Once you've found a minter, look after it and its value can only increase – but you're unlikely to make your fortune from it. ⚠

Fiat Dino 2.4 Coupé
SPECIFICATIONS

Engine
2418cc V6, twin overhead camshafts, 12 valves. Alloy head, cast-iron block. Three Weber 40DCNF carburettors

Power
180bhp @ 6600rpm

Torque
159lb ft @ 4600rpm

Transmission
Five-speed manual

Suspension
Front: Independent with coil springs, double wishbones, telescopic dampers, anti-roll bar. Rear: Independent with MacPherson struts, semi-trailing arms, anti-roll bar

Brakes
Front: 270mm ventilated discs Rear: 280mm ventilated discs Servo-assisted

Weight
1400kg (3087lb)

Performance
0-60mph: 8.2sec Top speed: 127mph

Value
Cost new: c£5000 (not sold in UK) Value now: £7-14,000

(1961-1974)
Jaguar E-type

At least as beautiful as a contemporary Ferrari
or Aston, the E-type is still a relative bargain – but
prices for good cars are rising as more and more
buyers jump on the bandwagon

Words: Richard Dredge Photography: www.magiccarpics.co.uk

'All those
clichés
about
setting the
world alight
are true;
the Jaguar
E-type
really did
rewrite the
rulebook'

Nine out of ten cool cats who expressed a preference reckon this is the most glamorous, sensual car of all time. And is that any wonder? There aren't enough superlatives in the dictionary to do the E-type justice; if grown men had car posters on their bedroom walls, this Jag would grace most of them.

All those clichés about setting the world alight are true; this car really did rewrite the rulebook. With looks, pace, power, engineering and heritage, the Jag also offered an extra quality – relative affordability. While Aston Martin, Ferrari, Porsche *et al* had worthy rivals, they were much more costly. That price differential has remained; a superb E-type can now be valuable, but an equivalent DB4 or 250GT will cost rather more.

Jaguar historian Philip Porter runs the E-type Club. He owns several examples himself, and says: 'There's a huge spread of values from £5000 up to £200,000 – or £1million for a genuine Lightweight. At

one extreme you can buy a 2+2 project and at the other a superbly restored, heavily upgraded Series 1 roadster. Fixed-heads used to be around half the price of roadsters but that gap has narrowed considerably. Series 1 FHC projects are still £9-12,000, while roadsters are £10-17,000. Influences on values include structural integrity, completeness, engine displacement (unless a very early car, the 4.2s are worth a shade more at present), matching numbers and LHD or RHD.

'For a usable car that hasn't been fully restored or upgraded, pay £20-28,000 for a coupé and £26-33,000 for an open car. Really superb original or restored models start at £32,000 for coupés and £38,000 for roadsters. Some reputable dealers charge considerably more, as a proper professional restoration costs at least £80,000 and upgrades can add far more.'

Value rises of recent years have put the cars out of reach for many. However, while everyone clamours for the earlier six-pot

models' greater design purity, the Series 3, or V12, can get overlooked – despite being more usable thanks to its longer, wider body and superior engineering.

It may not be as beautiful as the Series 1, but if you're on a budget the V12 is the car to go for. However, although fuel consumption isn't an issue unless you plan to cover a significant mileage each year, maintenance costs can be high.

Low-mileage V12s abound, but check the history because clocked cars aren't rare. Similarly, restored examples are sometimes claimed as original, but with so many truly cherished models out there, many run on a money-no-object basis, finding something worth buying isn't hard.

You can buy a usable 2+2 for £10,000 – but it won't be all that shiny. Even the nicest 2+2s rarely fetch more than £25,000, while you can add around 50 per cent for a roadster. Transmissions don't generally affect values, but while buyers of fixed-heads don't mind an auto, it's the stick

'Fixed-heads used to be half the price of roadsters but, quite rightly, that gap has narrowed considerably in the last year or two'

shift that roadster fans usually want. Commemorative cars rarely surface for sale; minters have touched six figures.

Engine

The 1961-1971 E-type's iconic XK unit is renowned for its durability as long as it's looked after. Capable of giving 150,000 miles between rebuilds, the straight-six isn't especially stressed unless regularly thrashed – and few owners drive hard.

Get it up to temperature before testing; listen for any knocks or rattles. Check for oil leaks as well as exhaust smoke; expect a few wisps on start-up, but things should soon settle. Once fully warm, look for at least 40psi on the pressure gauge with the engine turning over at 3000rpm.

Make sure the cooling fan cuts in on tickover. If the temperature gauge needle keeps climbing, the engine may well have overheated once: evidence of a blown head gasket is white 'mayonnaise' on the oil filler cap. If the motor is smoking badly

or it's very rattly, it'll need total rebuild – but don't panic. You can rebuild one at home for around £2000, or pay double this to get it done professionally. If you go DIY, the XK engine is the easier to revive of the pair.

The V12 that arrived in 1971 is an all-time great; properly kept it'll do 200,000 miles. Poor maintenance leads to overheating, so idle the engine for a few minutes and watch the gauge. Harshness points to previous overheating having distorted the long block and heads. These are alloy, so anti-freeze must be maintained otherwise internal corrosion is guaranteed, leading to a less-efficient cooling system that ensures even worse overheating.

Low oil pressure at idle isn't a problem, but check for at least 45lb (preferably 55lb) at 2500rpm. Leaks are common at the rear crankshaft seal; once it's failed, a full rebuild is needed. A specialist charges £4000+, or you could do it yourself for £600 – if you're skilled. Cars that have

been run infrequently are especially likely to suffer from this, as the seal dries out then wears more readily.

The V12 has 20 rubber coolant hoses; the replacement of perished ones is very involved as the water rails and carbs have to be removed. They must also be to the correct reinforced spec; the coolant system runs at 15lb psi (earlier E-types are just 4lb psi). A full set is £143.50.

The original rubber fuel lines will now be brittle, while the Zenith-Stromberg carbs go out of tune when their diaphragms perish. Rebuilt carbs are the best solution; there are four at £350 each. Incidentally, the V12 happily runs on unleaded, as hardened valve seats were factory fitted.

Transmission

There's little to worry about here, but listen for clonks that signify worn universal joints or whining that betrays a dodgy diff. Fixing the former is straightforward; the latter is less easy and rather more costly with a

Above
Even American safety regs – side repeater lights, uncowled headlights and wrap-around bumpers – couldn't ruin the E-type's sex appeal.

➤➤

'Frankly, if all is well with the body, the car is unlikely to give any insurmountable problems elsewhere'

replacement diff costing £750. Gearboxes are also strong, but the recalcitrance of the Moss unit on 3.8-litre cars is legendary. It's noisier than the later one, too, so don't expect a box that's especially easy or pleasant to use, particularly when selecting first or reverse. Expect to pay £900 for a rebuilt transmission, whether it's a Moss unit or a later one.

Most V12s have a three-speed Borg Warner Model 12 auto, yet the Jaguar four-speed manual is more sought after. They're both durable, but the latter can suffer from weak synchro on second and third; check for difficulty selecting gears when cold. Expect to pay £400 for an exchange unit.

If ratio changes are jerky on the auto, or there's any slipping, a service involves fresh fluid, filters and band adjustment. For an overhaul, budget £1100. Clutches, diffs and driveshafts are durable, but check for vibrations, clonks or whines.

Suspension, steering and brakes

Jack up each wheel and rock it diagonally, feeling for wear in the bushes and bearings. If there is no play at the rear, the bearings have been set too tight and will probably overheat and fail. There are some in the hub as well as the lower fulcrum; a little play in each of these can lead to what feels like an alarming amount of movement at the wheel, but it should be no more than an eighth of an inch or so.

Remove the rear wheels and look at the axle cage mountings, which can perish or break. If you've already driven the car by now and it feels rather lively at the back, it could be due to rear-wheel steering as a result of the wear. While you're under there, ensure there's no oil leaking from the diff onto the inboard rear brakes. Any signs of trouble and it's an axle-out job to sort.

If there are creaks from the rear suspension, it'll be because the lower hub pivots have corroded; if not greased regularly they wear rapidly or seize.

At the front there shouldn't be nearly as much play, but don't be surprised if you can detect a small amount. If it's bearing wear, that's easy to sort, but it might be worn lower wishbone balljoints. These act directly on the wishbone, which can be shimmed only so much before replacements are needed at a little over £100 per side.

The rack-and-pinion steering is reliable, but wear in the column joints is normal; replacement is easy at just £65 for the pair.

The brakes should feel very strong, but imbalance is usually caused by that oil on the discs we mentioned. The handbrake can also give problems; the self-adjusting mechanism often seizes through lack of

greasing. Try to roll the car on a level surface and see if it quickly grinds to a halt; if it does, fixing is simply a case of freeing off and lubing.

Although steel wheels were standard, chromed wires are now fitted to many V12s. The usual checks for damaged spokes and worn splines are essential; this is especially important with a V12 because of the torque generated.

Bodywork, electrics and trim

Buying an over-priced, dressed-up shed could leave you out of pocket to the tune of tens of thousands of pounds. Properly restoring an E-type is a hell of an undertaking, and many people get it wrong. Frankly, if all's well in the body department, the car is unlikely to give any insurmountable problems elsewhere – but check all is what it seems.

If a vehicle has been restored, poor body repairs are one thing you may have to contend with. E-types can rot just about anywhere, so check every square inch of metal – twice over. Lift the fuel filler flap and see what's lurking beneath; if it's a mess, other bits will have been missed as the car was clearly restored with no attention to detail.

Gapping should be tight and even,

especially where the bonnet butts up against the bulkhead. With this panel accounting for nearly half the car's length, it's tricky getting things to line up properly – which is why they often don't. Also check all the seams as well as the front valance, which frequently harbours rot.

Coupé tailgates rarely rust but bootlids do, along with door bottoms. In the case of the latter there should be a polythene sheet inside the door casing; it's usually missing. The door fills up with water as a result and, with the drain holes often blocked, the water has nowhere to go.

Don't overlook the frame ahead of the front bulkhead, which supports the engine, steering and suspension. Its tubes can crack and corrode, and it's not easy to check as it's rather overcrowded in there. For work to be done, everything ahead of the bulkhead must be removed for access.

Locks can give problems so operate and open each door from inside as well as out. Electrics-wise, unrestored cars suffer from poor earths or brittle wiring, easily fixed with emery paper or fresh looms. On V12s, the heater motor can suffer failed circuitry or seizure through lack of use, but access is easy as it's next to the battery. Also check that the thermostatic cooling fan cuts in; it's not always reliable and failure can lead to major bills.

Jaguar E-type 3.8 Coupé

SPECIFICATIONS

Engine
3781cc in-line six, twin overhead camshafts, 12 valves. Alloy head, cast-iron block. Three SU HD8 carburettors. Compression ratio 9:1, 87mm bore and 106mm stroke

Power
265bhp @ 5500rpm

Torque
260lb ft @ 4000rpm

Transmission
Four-speed manual

Suspension
Front: Independent with transverse wishbones, torsion bars and telescopic dampers, plus anti-roll bar
Rear: Independent with lower transverse tubular links, twin coil springs each side, telescopic dampers

Brakes
Front: 279mm solid discs
Rear: 254mm inboard solid discs
Servo-assisted

Weight
1202kg (2644lb)

Performance
0-60mph: 7.1sec
Top speed: 149mph

Value
Cost new: £2160
Value now: £30,000-150,000

*Out of print

»Info

SPECIALISTS

» Classic Motor Cars, Shropshire. +44 (0)1746 765 804, www.classic-motor-cars.co.uk
» David Manners, West Midlands. +44 (0)121 544 4040, www.davidmanners.co.uk
» Eagle, Kent. +44 (0)1825 830 966, www.eaglegb.com
» Jaguar Daimler Heritage Trust. www.jdht.com
» Lane's Cars, West Midlands. +44 (0)1922 749 244, www.lanescars.co.uk
» Martin Robey, Warks. +44 (0)2476 386 903, www.martinrobey.com
» Racing Green Cars, Hants. +44 (0)1252 894 844, www.racinggreencars.com
» SNG Barratt. +44 (0)1746 765 432, www.sngbarratt.com
» Woodmanton Classics, Herefs. +44 (0)1885 410 396, www.woodmantonclassics.co.uk

CLUBS

» E-type Club. +44 (0)1584 781 588, www.e-typeclub.com
» Jaguar Drivers' Club. +44 (0)1582 419 332, http://jaguardriver.co.uk
» Jaguar Enthusiasts' Club. +44 (0)1179 698 186, www.jec.org.uk
» Jaguar Clubs of North America (umbrella organisation), www.jcna.com

BOOKS

» E-type, End of an Era by Chris Harvey. Haynes, ISBN 0-946609-16-0*
» Jaguar E-type (Great Cars) by Nigel Thorley. Haynes, ISBN 0-1-85960-813-2
» Jaguar E-type, Definitive History by Philip Porter. Haynes, 0-85429-580-1
» Jaguar E-type by Jonathan Wood. Crowood, ISBN 0-1-86126-147-0
» Jaguar E-type 3.8 & 4.2-litre, Essential Buyer's Guide by Peter Crespin. Veloce, ISBN 0-1-904788-85-8
» Original Jaguar E-type by Philip Porter. Bay View, ISBN 1-870979-12-5

'Few cars at any price are as rewarding to own or drive as a properly restored E-type'

Jaguar E-type V12 2+2

SPECIFICATIONS

Engine
5343cc 60° V12, single overhead camshaft per bank, 24 valves. Alloy head and block. Four Zenith-Stromberg carbs

Power
272bhp @ 5850rpm

Torque
304lb ft @ 5600rpm

Transmission
Four-speed manual or three-speed auto

Suspension
Front: Independent with wishbones, torsion bars, tele dampers, anti-roll bar
Rear: Independent with fixed-length driveshafts, lower transverse links, radius arms, twin coil spring and tele damper units, anti-roll bar

Brakes
Front: Discs
Rear: Discs
Servo-assisted

Weight
1527kg (3361lb)

Performance
0-60mph: 6.4sec
Top speed: 146mph

Value
Cost new: £3387 (1971)
Value now:
£10,000-£25,000

All trim is available, but it'll get costly if everything needs doing. Brightwork can be replaced; mazak such as door handles and tail-lamp housings tend to pit. A fresh mohair soft-top is £700, with fitting the same again.

Conclusion

It's easy to overlook the differences between the various iterations of E-type, but they're highly significant. Buy the wrong car and you'll wonder what all the fuss is about. Also, don't get taken in by the glamour of the roadster when the coupé is more affordable and every bit as good to drive.

Original right-hand-drive cars are a lot rarer than you'd think. Around 85 per cent of production was exported, so many right-hand-drive cars have been converted from left-hand drive at some point. Just ensure the car you buy is what it claims to be. Check it has the correct engine and that it's not a roadster which left the factory as a coupé. The Jaguar Daimler Heritage Trust is invaluable in providing details of the car's original spec. Philip Porter's book *Original Jaguar E-type* (details in books listing), will highlight any inconsistencies in the specification.

If the car does need work there's no need to fret about parts availability, because everything is available to revive an E-type, no matter how tired. With the right tools and enough time, a competent home mechanic can tackle just about any job that's likely to crop up.

Crucially, there's no such thing as a bargain E-type. It's quite common for someone to buy an example that's priced at £20,000 below what would be expected. Then the new owner starts delving and discovers that to get the model up to the standard they were expecting, it needs £50,000 spent on it.

Few cars at any price are as rewarding to own or drive as a well-restored E-type. And there's the rub; it must be properly renovated if it is to give any pleasure – and there's a huge amount of enjoyment to be gained from E-type ownership. ◬

£199.95

FOOTMAN JAMES
Insurance specialists. At your service.

1969 Jaguar E-type coupé
Value: £25,000
Quote: **£199.95**
(£250x/s unlimited mpa)
JEC member

With a 21-year production run, there are plenty of XJ-S coupés to choose from. Consider your choice carefully, buy the right one and you won't regret it.

Words: Simon Goldsworthy

JAGUAR XJ-S

Go on, treat yourself. You know you deserve it. For the cost of a service on the Ferrari, you could go out and buy the kind of power that you can't even begin to justify with a straight face, packaged with such sensual grace that it leaves a deliciously-guilty feeling every time you run a hand over the panels. Yes, the XJ-S has the lot. But can you make a case for using one as a daily driver?

In part, that comes down to what kind of driving you do every day. The XJ-S was conceived as a true Grand Tourer, capable of devouring huge distances while cocooning the occupants in the utmost luxury. Which, to be quite honest, couldn't be more different from the average school run or office commute.

But stay with it for a moment. Just because the run to work is dull, that doesn't mean you want it to be uncomfortable. Surely borrowing a little glamour from an imaginary cross-continental jaunt can only leave your energy levels higher when Monday morning rolls around?

»

100% Genuine heritage

![JAGUAR]

a breed apart

Uniquely engineered through 86 years experience.

Visit Jaguar Classic Parts online and discover our uniquely extensive cataloguing system, boasting over 21,000 part number references for XJ12 Series III, XJ6 and XJ12 (XJ40) and all XJ-S. Additionally, you can browse through a number of special offers and parts news. Experience our easy-to-use ordering system, with delivery direct to your door or 'postage free' to your local Jaguar dealer. All parts are covered by a one year Jaguar warranty.

Maintain the prestige – buy your genuine Jaguar parts from the definitive source.

www.JaguarClassicParts.com

Jaguar Classic Parts operates in partnership with JDHT. For further information regarding other Jaguar Classic products and services email – parts@jaguarclassicparts.com

JAGUAR DAIMLER
Heritage Trust

Part shown: Boot Badge – BEC22058

'Driving a car with so much torque that it can accelerate to over 140mph from rest in top gear alone may get addicitive'

Above
Luxurious interior will cosset you; complicated engine bay will just blow your mind...

And if the school run is an integral part of your morning, then it stands to reason that most of your passengers will be rather short in stature and so ideal for the pint-sized plus-two seating out back. But every indulgence comes at a price, and there is no getting away from that dreaded Jaguar curse of prodigious thirst. The XJ-S was more aerodynamic than the E-type, but the first cars struggled to get into double figures under all but the gentlest of use. That's hardly surprising when you consider the long, wide and very sturdy bodywork sitting on a modified version of the XJ6C floorpan. Combine this with a lusty 5.3-litre V12 engine and, although driving a car with so much torque that it can accelerate to over 140mph from rest in top gear alone may get addictive, paying for the privilege at the pumps will always be painful.

Fortunately, there are ways of mitigating this problem. The most obvious is to buy a post-1981 car with a 5.3HE tag on the back. That stands for High Efficiency, and refers to the adaptation of Michael May's head design for the combustion chambers. Combine this with the fuel injection and you get the same power, a torque curve that comes in usefully lower down the rev range and a 20% improvement in economy.

Heck, with that you can even push towards 16mpg. Or, if you are confident enough in your own abilities not to need the reassurance of 12 cylinders, go for the 3590cc AJ6-engined models that arrived in 1983. They'll still do 142mph thanks in part to the five-speed Getrag gearbox, but can squeeze up to the psychological 20mpg barrier. With either of these later cars, you'll also get facelifted interiors with the wood paneling that the cars' elegance somehow seems to demand. There were subtle but extensive changes to the panelwork in 1991, but those distinctive flying buttresses remained. If you really can't live with them, there is always the Convertible option available from 1988.

But whichever you choose, don't think about trying to run an XJ- S on just loose change – it takes all the fun out of the experience. Buy one that is sound and has been regularly serviced. Leave some money over for the occasional hefty repair bill, then relax and enjoy the experience. As we said, you deserve it.

Buy one that is sound and has been regularly serviced. Leave some money over for the occasional hefty repair bill then relax and enjoy the experience. ⚠

JENSEN HEALEY (1972-1976)

It had a tough early life, but find a good Jensen Healey now and you won't regret it

Words: Richard Dredge   Photography: www.magiccarpics.co.uk

Above
Roadsters far more numerous than Jensen GT estate (opposite).

Take a two-seater sports car and equip it with a Lotus 16-valve engine. Give it distinctive styling and bestow it with two of the most charismatic automotive names available; Jensen and Healey. The car couldn't possibly fail – or could it? Although the Jensen Healey had the makings of something brilliant, teething problems conspired against it, cutting short its life. Despite generally very favourable press reviews, and effective fixes quickly being found for its various initial afflictions, the mud stuck.

While the earliest cars were plagued with problems, by the time of the introduction of the MkII in September 1973, there was no reason to be afraid. But people were afraid, buying MGs and Triumphs instead, ultimately leading to the downfall of Jensen Healey.

In a bid to widen the car's appeal, a sports estate was launched in July 1975. Called the Jensen GT, there were no Healey references because Donald Healey had quit the company around the time the first Roadsters had been delivered to their customers. By this stage there were so many Roadsters stockpiled, that the GT effectively replaced its open-topped sibling on the production lines, if not in the showroom.

By the time production ended in April 1976, just 473 GTs had been built, plus 10,453 Roadsters. Survivors are still being scrapped though; if you want one of the few cars left you'd better start looking soon as demand is already starting to outstrip supply.

If you do want a Jensen Healey, bear in mind that while the GTs are rare, they're also hard to sell because everyone wants a Roadster. As a result, values don't vary between open and closed cars. Restoration projects are sometimes given away; expect to pay £4000 for a usable car. Nice examples

cost £5000+, while the very best cars sell for £8000 – although they very rarely come onto the market and usually change hands within the club.

Engine

The all-alloy twin-cam engine is very tough if looked after, but it won't tolerate neglect. MkI engines were notoriously fragile, but a much stronger casting was designed for MkII cars. With its more rigid structure, the oil leaks that plagued the first cars were banished to history. Having said this, even a molly-coddled powerplant won't last more than 80,000 miles between rebuilds – and 50,000 miles is more typical.

It's the bottom end that wears first; by the time this is making rumbling noises it'll be time to revive the top end as well. Expect to pay £3000 or so to have the engine restored to its former glory; do the work yourself and it'll cost you little

'The Jensen Healey has an almost unrivalled mix of qualities – which is why it's worth tracking down a really good one'

more than half this figure. If you're rebuilding a MkI engine it's worth using a MkII powerplant as your start point; a unit fit for rebuilding costs £250.

If the oil isn't replaced every 6000 miles and the anti-freeze concentration levels maintained at 25 per cent, trouble is guaranteed. It's also good practice to check valve clearances regularly as well as to get the engine up to temperature before venturing towards the top end of the rev range. Because of the twin-cam engine's origins, any decent Lotus specialist will be able to maintain it without any problems – although their rates are usually rather high.

It's worthing changing the cam belt every 24,000 miles or three years to avoid disaster. If it breaks, pistons will hit valves and you'll be landed with a £3000 bill for a complete rebuild. A new belt costs just £27.50 and replacement is straightforward.

Flat spots at just over 2000rpm are common on cars fitted with Dell'Orto carburettors, as the accelerator pumps on these are prone to seizing. This is cured by lubricating the lever mechanism and replacing the two pump diaphragms, which cost £10 each.

Transmission

The earlier Chrysler (four-speed) gearbox is nicer to use than the later Getrag (five-speed) version, but it's weaker too. During spirited driving it's possible to break the gearbox; if it's on its way out it'll jump out of gear as you so accelerate through the ratios. The five-speed unit is a much stronger 'box and soldiers on forever, but don't be surprised if the gearchange is baulky.

Difficult gear selection on a four-speed car means the mainshaft locknut has worked loose. That entails removing the gearbox; while it's not difficult, it is

time-consuming. This gearbox was taken from the Rapier H120, although the Chrysler and Jensen Healey units aren't interchangeable because the input shafts and gearlever mounting extensions are different.

Once a four-speed gearbox has worn, it's best to fit a five-speed unit, complete with bellhousing. There aren't many around, but decent ones are £350. If there isn't one available it's possible to have a four-speed unit rebuilt; the parts are getting ever harder to find with the current cost around £250.

The Salisbury back axle, from the Vauxhall Magnum 2.3, is very strong and lasts for well over 150,000 miles without problems. Don't expect the unit to be quiet though – they whined and rumbled when new. Nobody ever rebuilds them, because they tend to just keep going – if the noise becomes unbearable, fit a used unit for around £100.

Above
Neat styling almost unspoilt by impact bumpers – except on GT proposal, left.

Jensen Healey Roadster
SPECIFICATIONS

Engine
1973cc in-line four, twin overhead camshafts, 16 valves. Alloy head and block. Two Dell'Orto DHLA carburettors

Power
140bhp @ 6500rpm

Torque
130lb ft @ 5000rpm

Transmission
Four-speed manual

Suspension
Front: Independent with coil springs, double wishbones, telescopic dampers.
Rear: Live axle with coil springs, trailing and semi-trailing links, telescopic dampers.

Brakes
Front: 254mm discs
Rear: 229mm drums
Servo-assisted

Weight
965kg (2128lb)
Performance
0-60mph 7.8sec
Top speed 119mph

Value
Cost £1810 new (1972)
Value now £4000-£8000

If the rear axle has been swapped, make sure the correct one is fitted as they're interchangeable. The five-speed diff has a ratio of 3.45:1, giving 23.7mph/1000rpm for more relaxed cruising; four-speed cars were fitted with a 3.73:1 back axle instead.

Propshafts also differ between four and five-speed cars, with the earlier unit being a single-piece item. This doesn't give problems, but the rubber coupling in the middle of the later two-piece unit perishes, causing vibrations. New couplings aren't available, but complete repro propshafts are £200 each.

Suspension, steering and brakes

The front suspension and steering are taken from the Magnum 2.3, without modifications. Original-spec springs can go soft, leading to the car leaning to one side; it's usually the offside that sits the lowest for some reason. It's also important to check for oil contamination of the front suspension mountings, thanks to engine leaks. The mounting rubbers rot once they've been soaked in engine oil, and replacements cost £11-16 each; there are three on each side. Some people fit polyurethane bushes instead, but the standard rubber ones give the car a much better ride, and they're generally pretty durable.

All Jensen Healeys were fitted with the same design of alloy wheel, now unavailable new but used examples are around £15 apiece. There's a good chance that wheels at this ultra-low price will need refurbishing, but that's a job that's easily and cheaply sorted with one of the many specialists.

The Girling braking system is straightforward, with a servo-assisted disc/drum set-up. The only common problem afflicts post-November 1974 models, with Lockheed self-adjusting rear brakes. These stop adjusting themselves, so you'll need to free them up and file the teeth of the adjusting mechanisms, so they engage properly. Swapping to the earlier system isn't advised because it means changing everything, including the backplates.

Bodywork, electrics and trim

Many a Jensen Healey has been relegated to scrapper status because of lacy bodywork; the pressed-steel monocoque can rot badly anywhere. Few original cars are left, so you must check the quality of work already done; the low values of Jensen Healeys means they're often bodged.

Checking the outer panels is easy, but repairing them isn't necessarily straightforward. It's underneath that you need to really analyse – these are also the trickiest areas to put right. Things aren't helped with most cars being open-topped, as they can leak badly. While it's possible to buy new floorpans, fitting them is tricky because so much dismantling is necessary.

Start by checking the sills and front chassis legs, located just ahead of the front footwells; repairing these areas is difficult. Restoring the sills entails removing the front and rear wings, although they're bolted on. The leading edge of the sill corrodes first, the rot spreads and by the time it's reached the back, things could be terminal. It's also common for the sill to corrode from the top down; the rot starts behind the wings and by the time it's visible, the corrosion is advanced. Patching the sills isn't possible; with fresh panels, welding and labour the bill will be at least £500 per side. If heavy corrosion has spread to the floors, it's time for a major rebuild – which costs far more than the car will ever be worth. Rot in the chassis legs means an MoT failure, and the engine, gearbox and front suspension have to be dropped to get to the affected area.

Outer panels also corrode, especially the forward edge of the bonnet. Front wings rot along the lower, top and leading edges – and round the wheelarches. New wings are available from the original tooling and it's an involved job getting them to fit properly.

Rear wings fare little better, as they rot along their top edge, after water has got into the joint between the inner and outer panels. There's some beading here, between the wing and the hood closing panel. This

Clockwise from left
Dashboards survive well; wheels unique to model; seats originally vinyl; even room for golf clubs!

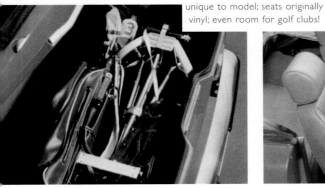

perishes and allows water in, causing the inner wing to corrode unseen, accelerated by corrosion from the underside. Also open the boot and check the state of the metal from inside – any sgnificant rot means major work. The boot floor rots away, as does the trailing edge of the lid itself – so while you've got everything open, take a close look at all the metalwork.

Check the bottoms of the doors, as they rot from the inside out. By the time the outer skin has started to corrode, there will probably be nothing left of the lower part of the frame. New doors are now available to special order only (and priced at over £250) while a decent used one will set you back £100+.

The electrical system is simple and reliable, but if a complete rewire is needed because of a perished or damaged loom, a new harness will cost £250. The instrumentation is stock Smiths, so it's generally available, but getting harder to find. The switchgear can be fragile, but it's now all being remanufactured, with new rocker switches costing £21-28 apiece.

A new vinyl roof costs £150, but fitting it typically doubles the bill. A hard top is a desirable extra, especially if a factory-produced item. This is double-skinned and better built than the more rounded version made by Lenham. Used factory hard tops cost £100-300 depending on condition, while the Lenham alternative is worth around half as much.

Apart from the strips on the factory hard top, all exterior brightwork is available. Unfortunately none of the interior trim is available new and it's now hard to find decent used items. By the time a car is broken for spares, its interior trim is usually beyond redemption.

The trim panels have a hardboard backing that absorbs water then disintegrates. The vinyl-trimmed seats split and carpets wear through; early MkIs featured rubber mats with the Jensen Healey logo embossed in them, but these are all long gone. At least the dash surround is pretty robust.

Conclusion

The best Jensen Healeys change hands within the Jensen Owners' Club. However, if you want a restoration project you should be looking at cars worth £1500 rather than £500. You'll ultimately save far more than £1000 by the time the restoration is complete.

If you're after a road-ready example, check carefully before buying or you'll be agreeing with all those pub bores who reckon the Jensen Healey was always a dog. However, if you track down a car that's been cherished, you'll forever be defending the Jensen Healey. At every opportunity you'll be pointing out how great it is to drive, how affordable it is – and how you don't see rows of them at car shows. The Jensen Healey has an almost unrivalled mix of qualities – which is why it's worth tracking down a really good one before word gets out. △

TIMELINE

» March 1972: Jensen Healey Roadster introduced at the Geneva motor show, with 1973cc twin-cam engine
» July 1972: First cars delivered
» September 1973: MkII version goes into production (from chassis 13350), with indicator flashers on front wings, full length bright trim strip and wood-grain finish for dashboard. Refinement improved with extra soundproofing. A one-piece hard top becomes available and there's a heavily revised engine.
» November 1974: A Getrag five-speed gearbox replaces the previous Chrysler four-speeder (from chassis 18950). Self-adjusting rear brakes are also fitted, a hard top is now standard issue and impact bumpers are fitted.
» July 1975: Four-seater Jensen GT goes on sale, with two-door estate bodyshell; note there's no reference to Healey in the name now. Standard equipment includes electric windows, walnut dash and five-speed gearbox.

SPECIALISTS

» Appleyard Parts, Derbys. 0115 932 5320, www.jensen.co.uk
» Cropredy Bridge Garage, Oxon. 01295 758444, www.jensen-cars.co.uk
» David Booth, Chester. 01244 336331, www.jensenhealey.co.uk
» Rejen, Hants. 01489 878805, www.rejen.info
» Martin Robey, Warks. 02476 3860903, www.martinrobey.co.uk

CLUBS

» Jensen Owners' Club. 01625 525 699, www.joc.org.uk
» Jensen Healey Preservation Society (US), www.jensenhealey.com

BOOKS

» Jensen by Keith Anderson. Haynes, ISBN 0-854-29682-4 *
» Jensen and Jensen Healey by Keith Anderson. Sutton, ISBN 0-7509-1808-X *
» The Jensen Healey Stories by Peter Browning and John Blunsden. MRP, ISBN 0-900-54921-1 *
» Jensen Healey Limited Edition by Brooklands Books. ISBN 1-85520-494-0

LANCIA (1975-1982) MONTECARLO

Not what immediately springs to mind when Italian exotica is mentioned, but this Beta-based sportscar can still get your pulse racing

Words: Richard Dredge Photography: www.magiccarpics.co.uk

Above
Those sharp Pininfarina styling lines and mid-mounted engine make Montecarlo a great Italian sportscar buy.

Mid-engined Italian two-seaters tend to have rather large price tags attached; if you want something with Italian flair but your budget is modest, the Lancia Montecarlo could be just the ticket. Part of the ill-fated Beta family, the Montecarlo suffered from the same poor reputation as its less-glamorous siblings, ensuring that values remain on the low side. However, thanks to that mid-mounted engine, sharp Pininfarina lines, crisp handling and surprising rarity, the Lancia makes a great left-field classic buy.

Even a minted-up Montecarlo is worth no more than about £8000 – and to command that much money it has to be something pretty special. A merely 'nice' example that you won't be afraid to take out of the garage is worth more like £5000, but a usable Montecarlo that's a little dog-eared around the edges can be bought for just £3000. If a great driving experience is higher on your list of priorities than ultimate practicality, there's not much that can touch it for the money.

Engine

The Montecarlo's lusty four-cylinder twin-cam powerplant is its biggest asset, although there are potential problems. But as is often the case, most of these stem from inadequate maintenance – look after these units and they'll easily despatch 200,000 miles without murmur.

Although the twin-cam unit is based on the Fiat unit of the same configuration, only the cylinder block is interchangeable. That's because the head was modified by Lancia to up the power, but it does carry over a free-revving nature, which is no bad thing.

Within the last 30,000 miles the cambelt should have been changed, as if it breaks the valves will come into contact with the pistons. The result is a bill for £400 to have the cylinder head rebuilt. Also be wary of blown head gaskets; after 60,000 miles, the head retaining bolts stretch. Look at the inside of the oil filler cap to make sure there's no mayonnaise-like substance to give the game away. It's usually a case

of just replacing the gasket and the retaining bolts, but the face of the head will need to be checked for flatness. If the engine doesn't run very happily, suspect dirt in the idle jets of the Weber carburettor. Fixing it is easy enough, as long as you know your way around.

Don't be too worried about an oily engine bay as the powerplant is notoriously tricky to seal. Cam cover and head gaskets are the most likely culprits. Lubricant shouldn't be pouring out, but you should expect to see signs of it in the engine bay.

Transmission

The gearbox is tough, but a neglected car might give the impression that there are major issues that need addressing, the key one being difficulty in getting the gears. If fifth or reverse are hard to select it's because the selector shaft needs greasing – an easy job. There's also some sideways adjustment of the gearshift linkage available, which often gets overlooked. As the box moves slightly over time (due to softening

Lancia Montecarlo series 2

SPECIFICATIONS

Engine
1995cc in-line four, eight overhead valves. alloy head, cast-iron block. Single Weber 34 DATR carburettor

Power
120bhp @ 6000rpm

Torque
126lb ft @ 3400rpm

Transmission
Five-speed manual
Rear-wheel drive

Suspension
Front: Independent with MacPherson struts, coil springs, dampers, lower wishbones
Rear: Independent with MacPherson struts, coil springs, dampers, lower wishbones

Brakes
Front: 257mm discs
Rear: 257mm discs
No servo assistance
Weight: 970kg (2139lb)

Performance
0-60mph: 9.8sec
Top speed: 119mph

Value
Cost new: £8355 (1981)
Value now: £1500-8000

'If a great driving experience is more of a priority than ultimate practicality, there's not much that can touch it for the money'

mountings), the gearchange gets increasingly notchy. All that's needed are a few adjustments of the linkage and everything can be restored to normal.

Make sure you get to drive the car from cold, paying attention to the change up from first to second as well as down from third. The synchromesh on second gear is always the first to go, and when the box is cold it can be a pain getting the ratio at all. You can either learn to live with it by selecting the ratio slowly or you can fit a used box – expect to pick one up for around £150 with replacement taking a day.

Suspension, steering and brakes

The Montecarlo has independent suspension all round, with MacPherson struts and lower wishbones front and rear. All cars featured a front anti-roll bar; early series 1s also had a rear anti-roll bar. There aren't any particular weak spots, apart from the struts, which can leak. Any hydraulic fluid that has escaped from the dampers will be immediately obvious if you look into the wheelarches – replacement is

the only fix, with a new pair of dampers costing £275. Although wheel bearings aren't an especially weak point, renewing them takes ages.

While the braking system of a series 2 car is efficient enough, the series 1 wasn't very well thought through. The problem with these earlier cars is that the servo acts on the front wheels only, and it has a habit of locking up early – which is why it's very much advised to disconnect the servo of a series 1 Montecarlo, if it's still fitted.

The brakes don't take kindly to being left idle for long periods; caliper pistons seize, along with handbrake cables. As a result you need to roll the Lancia on some level ground and see how quickly it comes to a halt. If the car stops quickly, the system will need to be freed off. Depending on how much dismantling and lubricating is needed, this can get pretty involved.

If the brake pedal is very spongy it's because the system hasn't been bled properly. The Montecarlo has a dual-circuit braking system, and both circuits have to be bled together – something that many owners overlook.

Bodywork, electrics and trim

Rust can be a major issue, but any Montecarlo that has lasted this long, and is still in good condition, should continue to survive in decent nick for many years yet. And that's why you have to be on the lookout for tarted-up cars. Taking your magnet when going to buy a Montecarlo is absolutely essential.

Post-1981 cars were better rust-proofed, but all need careful checking. If significant corrosion is evident, your best bet is to find a better example, because although you can get pretty much any panels you're likely to need, the costs will quickly add up if your example is rotten.

Start by looking at the bonnet, which gets stone-chipped, with holed metal the usual result. There are three layers of metal in the corners of this panel, and it's not possible to properly rustproof. Moisture gets trapped in the seams and the corrosion then starts on the inside; things aren't helped by a layer of sponge that lines the bonnet's underside. By the time any rust is evident, it's too late. But these

Above
Leather trim from new is rare: many restored cars have been upgraded. Most models were ordered with vinyl or cloth.

»

»Info

TIMELINE

- » 1972: Beta saloon launched at Turin Motor Show.
- » 1973: Beta coupé launched at Frankfurt Motor Show.
- » 1975: HPE (High Performance Estate) arrives and Montecarlo launched with a 2-litre engine; there's a choice of coupé or spyder editions.
- » 1976: Montecarlo debuts in the US, but it's called Scorpion as Montecarlo tag is already in use by Chevrolet.
- » 1977: UK imports start.
- » 1978: Montecarlo production temporarily ceases.
- » 1980: A revised Montecarlo is launched, with a new grille, bigger wheels and revised suspension.
- » 1982: The final Montecarlo is built, and it's sold in the UK the following year.

SPECIALISTS

- » The Monte Hospital, Wilts. +44 (0)121 288 2160, http://montehospital.com
- » Richard Thorne, Berks. +44 (0)118 983 1200, www.rtcc.co.uk

CLUBS

- » The Montecarlo Consortium, www.montecarlo.org.uk
- » Betaboyz, www.betaboyz.co.uk
- » Lancia Motor Club, www.lanciamotorclub.co.uk
- » Club LanciaSport, www.lanciasport.com

BOOKS

- » Lancia Beta Montecarlo: Cars That Made History by B Vettore. Giorgio Nada, ISBN 0-88-7911-355-0
- » Lancia Beta – A Collector's Guide by Brian Long. MRP, ISBN 0-947981-62-4
- » Lancia Beta Gold Portfolio 1972-1984. Brooklands, ISBN 1-85520-195-X

areas are only cosmetic – it's under the bonnet that you need to have a really good look. Especially important are the MacPherson strut mountings and the inner wings, crucial to the car's structure. These can rot and allow the suspension to push straight through.

The front wings can corrode very badly where they meet the sills, as well as along their tops. Don't forget to look at them closely from underneath, although post-1980 cars had wheelarch liners fitted.

See what state the underside of each door is in – then check its condition at the base of the quarterlight. The quarterlights themselves can rot and even if the doors are okay, the A-posts to which they're attached can corrode badly if the front wings have also rusted. Once this happens the A-posts lose their strength, so see if the doors are dropping; this is impossible to disguise.

Moving towards the back of the car, inspect the whole length of each sill, which has three sections including a centre membrane. All can dissolve, usually from the inside out, so press firmly and feel for the metal giving way. Then take a look inside each wheelarch, paying close attention to the seam between the inner and outer arch. There's a mastic used here which hardens then cracks, allowing moisture in and leading to bad corrosion. Finish off by checking the rear valance and the quarter panels along with the back wings and the rear strut towers; this last area is best inspected from inside the engine bay.

Check that all the electrics are working properly, especially things like the power-operated windows. The main problem is poor earthing through corrosion of the terminals, along with worn motor bearings, and

although fixing things probably won't cost much tracking down what the problem is can be a pain.

Various materials were used to trim the Montecarlo; all series 1 spiders had vinyl, most other cars had cloth but a few used leather. None of the trim should pose any problems as the original materials were generally very durable and you can source pretty much anything on a second-hand basis. It's even possible to get some new bits through specialists such as the Monte Hospital.

Conclusion

While everyone is flocking to major British marques such as Triumph and MG, you don't have to follow the herd. Affordability, great handling and a lusty engine are three great reasons to buy a classic – and the Montecarlo can offer all of those. Even better, you can buy anything you're ever likely to need to rebuild one or simply to keep it on the road. However, finding a good example is getting harder, which is why you must join the Montecarlo Consortium before you commit. Its members are always keen to advise on buying a Monte. △

» Thanks to David Griffiths of the Montecarlo Consortium.

LOTUS ELAN (1962-1973)

It's a giant of British sports car history, but what can this little Lotus do for you? Words: Richard Dredge Photography: www.magiccarpics.co.uk

Below
Iconic Lotus Elan blends light weight, peppy engine and fabulous handling to give the classic car ride of your life.

If you're trying to find a classic that's guaranteed to put a smile on your face every time you open the garage door, then look no further. Forget drugs – this is the ultimate anti-depressant and it should be available on prescription. With its light weight, zesty engine and virtually unparalleled handling, there's no wonder this Lotus has taken its place in the iconic cars hall of fame. But the best bit is that you can buy one of these four-wheeled wonders without having to break the bank – for just £8000 you could have your own usable Elan.

This was the car that saved Lotus, the company having made a loss on every Elite it sold. When the Elan was first shown at the 1962 Earls Court Motor Show it featured a 1499cc Ford-based engine, but it wasn't long before the classic 1558cc unit took its place – a motor that was to power the Elan until its demise just over a decade later.

Although there was relatively little development of the Elan throughout its decade of production, there are a surprising number of variants on offer. You can choose between convertibles and coupés as well as the rather ugly +2 derivatives that aren't as sought after but are more practical. Not that the Elan is about practicality in the load-lugging sense...

The same engine powered all Elans, but it was available in varying states of tune. The standard Elan's 105bhp is ample because the car is so light, but if you want more there's always the Special Equipment (SE) which offered 115bhp. If this still isn't enough you'll be looking at a Sprint, complete with 126bhp and two-tone paintwork. However, it matters not which version you opt for – you are guaranteed to find every journey a blast. Elan +2s are worth less than a two-seater example, but otherwise there's no variance in values across the models – apart from at the very top, where S1s and S2s are typically worth around £3000 more. A +2 restoration project is £2000 – two-seater Elan equivalents are double this. A usable example of the latter is £8000-9000; similar +2s are £7000. The best +2 is worth £18,000 while the nicest Elans cost £25,000 – but to command this latter sum it has to be very special indeed.

Engine

Don't listen to those around you who are keen to relate tales of doom about the Elan's twin-cam four-pot. If problems occur it's because the car hasn't been properly looked after – and when things do go wrong they can be extremely pricey to fix. That's why it's worth looking to see if the engine has been rebuilt. Technology is now far better than when the cars were made, and a reworked unit should soldier on for 140,000 miles or more.

The engine's coolant needs to retain a decent concentration of anti-freeze (at least 25%) to ensure the alloy cylinder head doesn't corrode. This will lead to the radiator getting clogged up, which in turn causes to the engine to overheat – expect to see 90-95 degrees on the temperature gauge once the car has had a run. From the S3 onwards the

Lotus Elan Sprint
SPECIFICATIONS

Engine
1558cc in-line four, twin overhead camshafts, eight valves. Alloy head, cast-iron block. Twin Weber 40DCOE carburettors

Power
126bhp @ 6500rpm

Torque
113lb ft @ 5500rpm

Transmission
Four-speed manual, rear-wheel drive

Suspension
Front: Independent with coil springs, double wishbones, telescopic dampers, anti-roll bar
Rear: Independent with coil springs, double wishbones, telescopic dampers, anti-roll bar

Brakes
Front: 241mm discs
Rear: 254mm discs
Servo-assisted

Weight
718kg (1580lb)

Performance
0-60mph: 7.0sec
Top speed: 118mph

Value
Cost new: £1706 (1971, in component form)
Value now: £5000-£17,000

'Forget drugs – the Lotus Elan is the ultimate anti-depressant and it should be available on prescription'

cooling system was marginal, and it is even less efficient after 30 years' use. If in doubt it's worth fitting a new radiator for £200 or so – that way, you'll know the powerplant isn't going to get cooked. If you want to take the belt-and-braces approach it's possible to install an alloy radiator for £500, but it's only really necessary if the car is likely to get stuck in traffic frequently.

Overheating problems will be made worse if the water pump is past its best, so feel for play in the unit and look for leaks. If a pump needs replacing it means removing the cylinder head, with the job typically taking at least 10 hours. That'll mean a bill of £700 (the pump is £90 on its own), so make sure it's not on its way out. If the fan belt is overtightened the pump's life will be sharply reduced – there should be half an inch of travel on the longest run.

The only other likely malady is a timing chain that needs replacing. If the chain is whining it's because it is too tight; its demise will be speeded up as a result. If there's a chattering noise from the front of the engine it's because the chain is too

loose. Check the adjustment bolt on the motor's front plate; if all the travel is taken up there's no adjustment left and a new chain and tensioner are needed at £35 for the pair.

Various carbs were fitted, with twin Webers on most cars. Yet some Sprints and late S4s featured Dell'Ortos, while Strombergs were fitted to some early S4s. They are generally reliable, but the Strombergs can ice up in cold weather.

Transmission

The Elan's four-speed gearbox is taken from the Ford 2000E, and it doesn't give many problems because it's tough. The five-speed unit fitted to the Plus 2 S 130/5 has its internals sourced from the Maxi, and it's a model of imprecision even when in perfect condition. There's no way of sharpening things up, so just console yourself that it's 'character'. However, if it is noisy or gear selection is really difficult, prepare yourself for the worst. Gears and bearings wear out all too readily, and rebuilding the unit costs anywhere between £1000 and £1500 depending on how bad things are.

Although the differentials look like Lotus parts, the oily bits inside are sourced from the Ford Cortina. They're durable enough, but listen out for whining that suggests some TLC may be imminent. If a rebuild is needed you can expect to pay up to £1000.

On the test drive, turn the steering between locks as the car is moving, to transfer the weight from side to side. As you do so, listen for chattering from the rear wheels, indicating that the bearings have worn out; new ones are less than a tenner.

If the car still sports Rotoflex suspension (which incorporates rubber doughnut joints) there's a chance that the couplings will have started to break up. The best way of checking for wear is to inspect them closely to see if they're perished and cracked. If both sides need doing a specialist will charge over £400 to do the whole job, although the parts on their own (couplings and bolts) are just £160 or so.

Conversions are becoming increasingly common to remove the rubber couplings from the system. There are three types available; each of a different design. They're

Above

A properly looked after or rebuilt engine should see 140,000 miles before needing expert attention.

'It is not easy to put a market price on the pleasure an Elan can offer'

Above
Most parts can be bought for Elan, including replacement bodyshells and chassis.

all more durable than the original set-up, with the cost of conversion around the same as a rebuild of the standard system.

Suspension, steering and brakes

The Elan's steering rack is based on a Triumph Herald unit; the main difference between the two is that the Elan's has lock stops fitted and shorter outer tie rods to prevent the wheels rubbing against the anti-roll bar. Make sure there's been no contact between wheels and suspension; if there has, the Herald item needs to be swapped for an Elan one. Exchange racks are available at £170 each.

One of the keys to the Elan's sublime driving experience is its suspension, and as long as it's maintained in good order it's more than capable of delivering the goods. Make sure the car doesn't pull to one side when accelerating or braking, and also get underneath and check that nothing is bent. If the Lotus has been kerbed, or if the chassis is damaged from any sort of impact, everything will be out of line – and it'll soon be apparent when you drive the car. It's worth getting a four-wheel suspension alignment check done because the geometry needs to be exactly right. If the Elan has had a new chassis doing this is especially

worthwhile because everything needs to be set up from scratch – and often isn't.

As well as the chassis being out of true, the wishbones can be bent if the car has been kerbed badly. If this has happened the Elan obviously won't drive as well as it should, but the easiest way to check for damage is to get underneath and see if there are any kinks in the metal. If the car tries to steer itself under acceleration, it's because the wishbone bushes have worn; a new set costs under £15.

Give the Elan a bounce test at each corner by pushing down and seeing how quickly it settles; you need to do this at least three times to get an accurate picture, though. If the car carries on bouncing it needs new shock absorbers at £100 apiece for Koni units. If the springs have sagged, new ones are £50 each.

Bolt-on pressed steel wheels were standard fare for all Elans, although the SE and Sprint featured knock-ons from the factory. These were optional for all other models, while the +2 S was available with alloys. Wheels should be painted silver, although the Sprint's were finished in black. Look for cracks around the mounting holes, as the metal fatigues. New wheels aren't available to original spec, although much heavier items are on the market that look the same.

Right from the start the Elan was equipped with disc brakes all round, with Herald units being used at the front – the rears were made specially for Lotus. The system works well, helped by the car's lightness. If there's any pulling to one side it's because a caliper piston is sticking; rebuild kits cost £25-£50, while exchange calipers are £60-£120 depending on model. If the handbrake fails to hold the car on a hill it's probably because any play has been taken up at the lever end of the system. The most effective adjustment is done at the wheels, although the handbrake is notoriously poor on the Elan anyway, so don't expect much.

Bodywork, electrics and trim

The good news with the Elan's glassfibre bodyshell is that it doesn't rust. Despite this, it still needs very careful inspection from stem to stern because there are plenty of potential problem areas. Accident damage is the key thing to look out for, not least of all because proper repairs are something that can be carried out only by somebody who really knows what they're doing. And often they don't!

Even if the car has never been shunted it's likely that the glassfibre will be looking the worse for wear. That's because the Elan's bodyshell flexes, leading to star cracks in the

LOTUS ELAN S.4

»Info

TIMELINE

» **1962:** Elan 1500 Roadster launched at Earls Court Motor Show, priced at £1499 fully built or £1095 in kit form. Ford-based 1499cc DOHC engine gives 100bhp and 114mph. Disc brakes all round and all-independent suspension with rack-and-pinion steering. Three separate light units per side at the rear.

» **1963:** Engine size increased to 1558cc. Hard-top now available as an option.

» **1964:** Series 2 is launched with larger front brake calipers, full-width wooden dash and single-piece rear light clusters.

» **1965:** Series 3 fixed-head coupé arrives. Electric windows now standard across range and close-ratio gearbox can be ordered. Tweaks include longer bootlid (to cure leaks) and boot-mounted battery.

» **1966:** Special Equipment model available with 115bhp engine, close-ratio box, servo-assisted brakes. Also gets side repeaters on front wings and centre-lock wheels. Series 3 convertible appears with the same amendments as the fixed-head coupé.

» **1967:** Elan +2 goes on sale. Available as fixed-head only, it's an Elan with a longer, wider body to offer 2+2 seating. Also features a power hike to 118bhp.

» **1968:** Series 4 coupé and convertible arrive, with flared wheelarches and new rear light clusters (as per the Elan +2). Fascia revised (now with rocker switches), power bulge in bonnet. Also, the Plus 2S supplements the standard car, with better-built interior and standard foglights. It's the first Elan not to be offered in kit form.

» **1969:** Elan +2 'dies', but Plus 2S remains.

» **1971:** Elan Sprint now here, with 126bhp big-valve engine, stronger transmission and two-tone paintwork. Elan Plus 2S 130 gets the same engine and a silver roof.

» **1972:** Five-speed gearbox now available on the Plus 2S 130. Cars with this option fitted are badged Plus 2S 130/5.

» **1973:** Elan S4 is discontinued, but Elan Plus 2S 130 stays until 1974.

panels which are time-consuming to put right. These flaws can appear anywhere, but the most likely locations are around the door handles, boot hinges and badge mountings. Panel edges can also succumb, and you should make sure the headlamp pods are okay; these can also be pitted with stone chips, much like the rest of the nose.

A pristine car has probably been restored at some point. If this is the case you must find out who did the work – and also ask for evidence of the job having been carried out properly. It's not difficult to tart up a tatty Elan, but keeping it looking mint is much harder. No corners can be cut, and the renovation work needs to have been done by an expert.

Pinpointing who did any work is especially important if the car has been restored (or even simply repainted) within the last two years or less. If a paint job still appears great after this time the chances are it'll keep looking good. What's common is for a respray to look superb for a few months, but then the cracks in the glassfibre start to reappear and it's back to square one. As a result, in many ways you're better off buying a car that looks rather tatty – at least that way you know exactly what you're getting. Also establish whether just a respray was carried out or if the glassfibre was restored at the same time. Fresh paint over old guarantees problems later – all the old paint has

to be stripped away (which takes at least 80 hours), the glassfibre revived, then new colour applied. If no restoration photos are available, look for signs of overspray such as around the door handles and on the rubber seals. The engine bay should be black – see if there's body-colour paint around its top edges.

Because of imperfections in the original moulds, filler was used (sparingly) on the production line to tidy things up. Some restored cars have dimples ahead of the doors, which originally contained filler to smooth things out. Also, don't be alarmed if the door fit isn't great. Sometimes the bottom rear corners can stick out by as much as half an inch; just like when the car came off the production line!

It may be that a new bodyshell is the most cost-effective way of restoring an Elan – by the time a car has been stripped and several panels have been attended to, it's usually cheaper to just buy a new shell. Naturally this means a complete rebuild will be necessary rather than just patching up here and there. However, with shells costing 'just' £4350 (including panels such as the bonnet, boot and doors) it frequently makes financial sense.

Any chassis produced after 1980 is galvanised, so if there's zinc-plating on the one you're looking at it's not the original. Fitting a new one typically costs £4000, as brakes and ancillaries are normally done at the same time. The chassis alone is £1195, »

'It's possible (but not necessarily desirable) to replace everything in the Elan's cockpit'

or you can opt for a tubular chassis from Spyder that can also be bought with fittings for improved suspension and a modern Zetec engine.

The age-old problem of rotting from the inside out claims most Elan chassis. Key areas to check are the front suspension pick-up points, where the drain holes get blocked. Even if the frame isn't rusty, stress cracks and fractures are inevitable on a car that's done 70,000 miles or more. The area around the engine mountings is usually the first to go, and once cracks appear it's time for a replacement, as welding isn't recommended.

You need to check that each electrical component is working properly, because there's no shortage of wiring in an Elan. That's because the glassfibre bodyshell means each item has to have two wires going to it – a live and an earth. Although the system is usually pretty reliable, there's plenty of scope for loose or broken connections. Infrequently-used cars also suffer from duff relays – they're Lucas 6R units that can bought for £15 each. Everything is available to effect any repairs, and often all that's needed is the cleaning of some contacts.

The Plus 2 is a more luxurious car, with higher levels of standard equipment, including more instrumentation. Again, you need to check it's all working, just like the electric windows that were fitted from all Elans from the S3 (1965) onwards.

It's possible (but not necessarily desirable) to replace everything in the Elan's cockpit. If you're purchasing a complete basket-case you'll have no

Above & right
Interiors are better made than you might expect; Plus 2 is longer than Elan and a little ungainly.

choice, but it's often better to restore than to buy new. Originality counts for a lot in Elan circles, and sometimes replacement parts don't look the same as the originals. Dash tops, for example, are now vacuum formed then foam filled, although they do look very similar to the originals. However, there are noticeable differences, which is why it's best to retain the Lotus part if possible.

Carpets weren't fitted until the Series 3 of 1965 – although most cars now have a set. You also won't find much chrome trim on an Elan, so there's not much to check. Door handles are pricey for the S1 and S2, at £130 each, but other cars' handles are just £20 apiece.

Conclusion

A sorted Elan isn't cheap, but you're not going to find many cars that offers as many smiles per mile. It's not one of those models that appeals to the person who knows the price of everything but the value of nothing; it's not easy to put a price on the pleasure an Elan can offer. That's if you buy a good one; purchase badly and it'll be a money pit that could break you!

£134.85

FOOTMAN JAMES
Insurance specialists. At your service.

1965 Lotus Elan RWD
Value: £8000
Quote: £134.85 (£50x/s unlimited mpa)

LOTUS ELAN (1989-1996)

Traditionalists didn't open their arms to the all-new Elan, but the Brit roadster is now a sought-after classic

Words: Richard Dredge Photography: www.magiccarpics.co.uk

Below
Critics of the new front-wheel-drive Elan soon changed their mind when they climbed behind the wheel

A front-wheel drive Lotus? Sacrilege! Whatever next; a diesel engine? That was the verdict of many Lotus traditionalists when the covers were pulled off an all-new Elan in 1989 – one propelled by a Japanese engine that fed power to the wrong set of tyres. Such critics were quickly silenced though as soon as they got behind the wheel; it may not have rear-wheel drive, but that doesn't stop the Elan being an absolute blast. The new car, codenamed M100, had been a long time coming.

Although the response was universally positive, the project was beset with problems. While UK sales were reasonably strong, it was much harder to find customers in the US because the car was priced level with the Corvette – V8 power and all. Then Isuzu pulled the plug on its 1.6-litre twin-cam engine, and re-engineering the model with a new powerplant would have been prohibitively expensive. However, when Bugatti bought Lotus in 1993, it put the car back into production before then selling the project on to Kia, which also reintroduced it – with very limited sales success.

Just 3855 Series 1 Elans had been built by the time production was wound up, with another 800 Series 2s being constructed. A mere 500 of the first batch went to the US, and while many other cars were exported, most examples built were sold to UK buyers.

You can now pick up a high-mileage Elan (with around 100,000 miles on the clock) for £5000-6000. It's surprising how many of these cars are around; the front-wheel-drive model is so usable that many owners rack up high annual distances. There aren't many normally-aspirated examples about, but if you do find one you can expect to pay a little less than for an equivalent turbocharged (SE) edition. Most cars for sale will be priced at £7000-£10,000; the latter figure will net a 50,000-mile example from a specialist. Really exceptional Elans can fetch over £11,000.

Engine

The 1588cc Isuzu 4XE1-MT engine was chosen through GM's links with the Japanese company; Lotus was owned by the conglomerate at the time. Although it initially seemed an odd choice, it shown to be a shrewd move as the unit has proven to be compact, light, powerful and durable. Although there were normally aspirated as well as turbo editions available, it's the latter that everyone wants because it delivers 165bhp and 148lb ft of torque compared with the standard version's 130bhp and 105lb ft.

A thoroughly modern powerplant (at least for a classic), the 1.6-litre engine will just keep going as long as it's properly serviced. One owner has even covered around a quarter of

> 'It may not have rear-wheel drive, but that doesn't stop the Elan being an absolute blast'

Above
With its snug cabin and zippy Isuzu engine, the Lotus sports car makes a perfect wind-in-the-hair cruiser

a million miles without the motor needing a rebuild. As with any engine – and especially a turbocharged one – the secret is regular oil changes. A refresh every 5000 miles is ideal, and even better if a fully synthetic lubricant is used.

Many owners have chosen to upgrade their engine by having the ECU remapped (chipped), to take power up to anywhere between 175bhp and 210bhp or so. It's a project undertaken by renowned Lotus guru Paul Matty, and it's nearly a decade since the first conversions were offered, with no ill effects yet – but stronger brakes are needed if the wick is turned up to the max.

In typical Japanese fashion, the cambelt needs replacing regularly if disaster isn't to strike. The original service schedule reckoned every six years or 60,000 miles was frequent enough, but it's generally understood that every 30,000 miles is a better idea – especially as most cars are now just occasional toys – so it's the six-year limit that'll usually be the decider.

The IHI turbocharger will last for as long as the engine if the oil is changed frequently; its lifespan will be increased significantly if the motor is allowed to idle for a few minutes before being turned off, to let the turbocharger and its bearings cool down more evenly.

There's just one weak spot with the Isuzu unit, and that's the Cam Angle Sensor, which fails and causes the fuel-injection system to malfunction. Sometimes the engine warning light illuminates when this happens, but not always – it's not the end of the world though, as a new sensor is just £150 and fitting it is easy enough.

Transmission

Because it's so strong, there's little chance of the five-speed manual transmission causing problems, even if the engine has been chipped to give more power. Hard-driven cars may be suffering from a clutch that's past its best, but you simply need to feel for slipping as you accelerate hard through the gears. Also, check that the clutch doesn't reach its biting point towards the top of the pedal travel.

Although the box itself is tough, the gear linkage is not, with failures all too common. The ball link on the end of the cable will break away, leading to difficulty in getting some of the gears; you'll still be able to drive the car, you just won't have all five ratios at your disposal. Fixing the broken linkage is cheap and easy though.

Suspension, steering and brakes

The Elan's suspension is as tough as the rest of the car, with springs and dampers generally not causing any

»

»Info

problems. However, the latter can leak, but a swift visual check will soon establish whether replacements are due or not. If one is leaking, remember you'll need to renew both sides at the same time; replacement shock absorbers cost £175 apiece.

Some early cars have shown signs of corrosion on the rear suspension wishbones, and because this tends to occur on the top face, it's difficult to spot as the vehicle sits so low. Replacement wishbones are £50 each; those for Series 2 cars are three times as much, but they're not prone to corrosion so replacements shouldn't be needed.

There's a multitude of suspension bushes which can perish, but unless the car has been driven really hard, it's unlikely that you'll need to get your wallet out. Once again, if any new bits are needed they're available off the shelf.

Of more concern potentially is suspension that's out of alignment; this is guaranteed to lead to wayward handling and uneven tyre wear. It may be because the car has been in a shunt, but more likely is simply some heavy kerbing. However, if this has taken place, the wheel(s) will also be looking the worse for wear.

Series 1 Elans were fitted with 15-inch alloys, although American cars got 16-inch wheels instead. Whichever side of the Atlantic the car was sold on, the rims featured seven spokes and were made by OZ. Are these still available? Many cars with the smaller wheels have since had the larger items fitted, as they fill out the arches better; those the Series 2 were

equipped with are even larger as they're half an inch wider, and once again, they're a popular aftermarket fitment for many owners.

There's nothing to fret about with the Elan's braking system, as it's completely conventional and there aren't any serious weak spots. Indeed, the only thing that's likely to go wrong is the rear discs corroding if the car is stored outside, but thanks to the spoked design of the alloys you can see at a glance what state the discs are in.

Bodywork, electrics and trim

For most cars in this guide, this is the longest section and highlights the greatest number of potential problem areas. Not for the Elan though, thanks to a chassis that was galvanised when new, and which so far has shown no inclination to corrode.

It's a similar story for the glassfibre bodyshell, which has so far proved itself to be remarkably durable. Until the Elan arrived, most Lotuses were built in two halves (upper and lower sections), but this car changed all that. Instead, there were 63 different composite panels, with a further 17 being used for versions of the car sold in markets other than the UK. While the panels at the front are simply bolted on, those at the rear are glued together, and as they're not load-bearing, they're a mere 2mm thick — although most of the panels such as the door casings, bumpers and bulkheads are much thicker. There's little chance of cracking or crazing. And apart from stone chips on the

Lotus Elan
(1989-1992)
SPECIFICATIONS

Engine
1588cc in-line four, twin
overhead camshafts,
16 valves. Alloy head,
cast-iron block. Multi-
point fuel injection,
turbocharged

Power
165bhp @ 6600rpm

Torque
148lb ft @ 4200rpm

Transmission
Five-speed manual
Front-wheel drive

Suspension
Front: Independent with
coil springs, double
wishbones, telescopic
dampers, anti-roll bar
Rear: Independent upper
link and lower wishbone,
coil springs and dampers,
anti-roll bar

Brakes
Front: 256mm
ventilated discs
Rear: 236mm discs
Servo-assisted

Weight
1020kg (2249lb)

Performance
0-60mph: 6.7sec
Top speed: 137mph

Value
Cost new: £19,850 (1989)
Value now:
£5,000-£10,000

nose you're unlikely to encounter anything worth worrying about. One note of caution, though; if you're looking at a car finished in red, and the colour has faded, the only long-lasting solution is a complete respray.

Unfortunately, the electrics are more likely to cause problems; things aren't helped by that plastic bodyshell. The Elan's electrical problems aren't just down to poor earths though; motors for the windows and headlamps can also play up. Most replacement parts aren't especially expensive, but if you're incapable of attempting any fixes yourself calling in the professionals might end up costing you dear as some of the repairs can be time-consuming.

The interior can also give problems, while it also doesn't take much to start looking tatty. The Vauxhall switchgear seems cheap and the materials used throughout the construction of the cabin weren't really in keeping with the car's price. Most owners opted for a full leather interior (standard offering was a leather/cloth mix), but even this doesn't wear very well so it needs to be treated regularly if it isn't to look down-at-heel. A common fault is a sagging driver's seat, but it's easier to fix than you might think. All you need to do is buy some fresh clips to hold the base cushion in place, turn the cushion over, and away you go.

Expect plenty of rattles from the interior trim; they're something most owners just learn to live with, although with time and patience it is possible to eradicate them. Something that's much harder to sort is a damaged roof; they're strong so likely to need replacing only if vandals have struck. However, the folding roofs never effectively sealed the cabin from the elements so don't expect any roof to be totally watertight – although at least Series 2 cars

were better in this respect. If a new roof is needed, expect to pay £500 – and another £700 for a fresh set of seals. Ouch...

Conclusion

The front-wheel-drive Elan was so over-engineered that Lotus never really stood a chance of making any money on it. Indeed, just to break even the firm would have needed to sell twice as many cars each year as it actually did. The whole episode was partly responsible for General Motors getting rid of Lotus in 1993 and the restart of production under Bugatti. Such over-engineering is great news if you fancy dipping your toe in the Lotus waters, but don't want something older and potentially more fragile.

However, don't assume that the Elan is unbreakable; cars that haven't been cared for won't feel at all together when you test drive them, which is why you need to try a few to work out what a decent one feels like. You should also compare Series 1 and Series 2 cars, as they're engineered differently. Unsurprisingly, they're quite different to drive, too; the earlier car is more comfortable, with softer suspension and a good chance of roof leaks; the Series 2 featured a modified set of rubbers here to reduce water ingress.

£222

1990 Lotus Elan FWD
Value: £8000
Quote: **£222** (£100x/s unlimited mpa)

LOTUS ELISE AND EXIGE (1996-2000)

It'll knock your socks off to drive – but what's the Lotus baby like to own? Words: Richard Dredge Photography: www.magiccarpics.co.uk

The Elise might just be the car that offers more fun per pound than any other ever built. 'Just add lightness,' was Colin Chapman's famous maxim, and that's exactly what Lotus did with the Elise. Quite possibly the best-handling car ever made, the Elise redefines the term agility and also offers surprising economy. During four years of production, there was a bewildering array of Series 1 Elises – all of which are great to drive and are just as capable on a track around town.

Unless you've piloted a highly-focused driver's car before, you're guaranteed to have your socks blown off by the experience that the Elise offers. Thanks to its mid-mounted engine, the car is beautifully balanced, with its light

Below
A Lotus Elise is all about the drive: uncompromising, noisy at times, but amazing fun.

steering verging on the telepathic. While most modern sportscars tend to have controls that are overdamped, the Elise is a tactile delight that connects the driver directly to the road.

There are several keys to the Elise's astonishing abilities, but the most important one is the low weight. The core of the car is a chassis that consists of several aluminium extrusions, bonded and riveted together. The result of all this technology is a frame that weighs all of 70kg – and the whole vehicle is little more than 700kg as a result. That's around 35 per cent less than an MGF, a car with which the Elise shares the 1.8-litre K-series engine.

The whole point of this Lotus is the

driving experience that it offers – try carrying people or luggage in the car and it will fall at the first hurdle. But there is only so much you can say about the driving experience, and no words will ever be a substitute for getting behind the wheel. That's why you need to try one out before attempting to establish whether the car is for you or not.

There's a downside to the raw excitement that the Elise offers though, and that's a lack of comfort on long journeys. Compared with a Seven it's a revelation, but unless your previous toy was a pre-war car you're going to find this model noisy and pretty uncompromising.

Early Elises begin at £7500, yet don't assume that because this is the start

'Quite possibly the best-handling car ever made, the Elise redefines the term agility and also offers surprising economy'

point, any car priced at this level will be a money pit. This will buy you a perfectly good Elise, but it won't have had much in the way of upgrades. This might be a good thing; unmolested cars are the ones that have probably led the easiest lives, as some of the more heavily upgraded examples will have seen masses of track action.

Your best bet is to find £9000-£10,000 for a really nice, relatively low-mileage car, built towards the end of production. However, if you want something truly special you can pay up to £13,000 for one of the last models made, with a low mileage – at this money you can also buy an early Series 2 car, which is arguably the way to go.

If you'd prefer an Exige, you'll have to dig pretty deep as just 500 examples of the S1 were made and they've held their value very well. It's easy to spend

£20,000 on one; indeed you'll be doing well to pick up a decent low-mileage example for any less. And remember, mileage is important with these because of that highly-stressed engine which often doesn't last long. It's the same with the 340R, with just 340 examples built: values are the same and so is the caveat about engine life.

Cars that have had official Lotus Motorsport parts fitted are usually worth more than completely standard examples. However, an Elise decked out with parts produced by unknown aftermarket suppliers will normally be worth less than a standard car because the quality is so variable.

Engine
The K-series engine is famous for its ability to overheat, partly because of its design and partly because of the small

coolant capacity. However, in the Elise it's less prone to giving problems, but you still need to make sure there are no signs of it previously having overheated, so check for that tell-tale mayonnaise-like substance on the underside of the oil-filler cap.

Also take a look at the level of the coolant, because Elise radiators can be rather fragile. That's why even if the liquid is up to the mark, you still need to check for signs of coolant at the base of the radiator.

Standard Elise powerplants are pretty reliable, but those fitted to the more high-performance derivatives can be worn out within 50,000 miles if the car has been driven really hard. The models affected are those such as the 190 VHPD, 340R and Exige, so you should look for signs of oil being burned (blue smoke from the exhaust under

Above
Elise was updated in 2000 to S2 form, with neater styling and, remarkably, even better handling.

»

'Unless you've piloted a highly-focused driver's car before, you're guaranteed to have your socks blown off by the experience that the Elise offers'

» 1996: Elise goes on sale, with a 118bhp 16v fuel-injected K-Series engine. Alloys, immobiliser and cloth are all standard, with leather and metallic paint optional.

» 1998: First official high-performance model arrives; the 190 VHPD (Very High Performance Derivative), with 187bhp. It's more for track than road, with race seats and harnesses, roll cage and adjustable suspension. In the same year comes the 340R; perhaps the most raw and focused driver's car ever to come out of Lotus. Initially planned as a regular production model, just 340 examples are built.

» 1999: Elise Sprint on sale, but few are built as it goes on to become the 111S, a regular production car with a 143bhp version of the VVC K-Series engine. Six-spoke alloys, bolt-on rear spoiler and wider rear tyres. Sport 135 appears at same time, a 50-off special edition with uprated brakes and suspension.

» 2000: Sport 160 joins range, with 160bhp from non-VVC version of K-Series engine, a higher rear wing and metallic grey five-spoke alloys. Around same time, the Exige goes on sale: effectively a fixed-roof version of the Elise, with 177bhp and much more downforce thanks to a huge rear wing. With a 0-60mph time of just 4.7 seconds and a 136mph top speed, the Exige is fast – but harsh to live with day-to-day.

» We've mentioned only the key Elise derivatives here; along the way there were also versions such as the Type 49, Type 79 and GT1. All of these were built in tiny numbers, offering the same pure driving experience of the regular car. By the end of 2000 the Series 1 had been superseded by the Series 2.

Lotus Elise Series 1
SPECIFICATIONS

Engine
1796cc in-line four, overhead camshafts, 16 valves. Alloy head and block. Multi-point fuel injection

Power
118bhp @ 5500rpm

Torque
122lb ft @ 3000rpm

Transmission
Five-speed manual
Rear-wheel drive

Suspension
Front: Independent coil springs, double wishbones, telescopic dampers, anti-roll bar
Rear: Independent coil springs, double wishbones, telescopic dampers

Brakes
Front: 282mm ventilated discs
Rear: 282mm ventilated discs

Weight
723kg (1591lb)

Performance
0-60mph: 5.5sec
Top speed: 124mph

Value
new: £18,950 (1996)
now: £7000-£10,000

acceleration) suggesting that the piston rings and cylinder bores have worn.

Transmission
The transmission is strong, and thanks to the car's low weight there's no reason for a high-mileage car to be suffering significant problems if it's been driven with any skill. Differentials will whine if the Elise has been subjected to too many emergency starts, while gear selection will be tricky if the synchromesh has worn. However, don't confuse the latter with a badly-adjusted gear linkage; if you struggle to select ratios even when you take things slowly, it'll be because the linkages are all out of kilter.

Elise clutches can also take a beating, especially if there has been too much full-bore acceleration. Make sure the clutch isn't slipping, by accelerating hard through the gears and seeing if the engine revs increase while the road speed doesn't.

Suspension, steering and brakes
The ball joints in the front suspension wear out after 35,000 miles, while shock absorbers will usually last just 20,000 miles or so. Once these need replacing, the car's dynamics suffer badly, so budget on spending £100 per corner for the new dampers, and another £23 for each of the

ball joints. Steering racks typically wear out within 35,000 miles, so check for play in the system to see if a new one is needed. They're not as cheap as you might think; at £350 for a fresh unit, plus the fitting, it's a cost you could do with not having to bear.

Make sure the alloy wheels haven't been damaged, as replacements are no longer available for the Series 1. Used or aftermarket items can be tracked down however – and are often fitted anyway. If the wheels are badly kerbed, there's a good chance the suspension will have been knocked out of true – so make sure the tyres haven't worn unevenly. If there's a fresh set of boots on the car, be wary; they might have been fitted because it's the cheapest way of masking a twisted chassis.

Brake discs wear if the car is driven hard, and they rust if it isn't used very often. Either way, check their condition as they may need renewing. Replacements cost £100 apiece for standard original-equipment items; if you're tempted to take the grooved alternative, bank on spending just £55 for each disc.

Bodywork, electrics and trim
If the car has been in an accident, the chassis will show signs of an impact. Once the Elise's frame has been distorted in any way the whole thing has to be replaced. If it isn't, not only is »

Clockwise from left
High-performance fixed-roof
Exige; minimal interior; S1s had
optional headlamp covers.

the car's structure adversely affected, but it'll never handle as well as it ought to. Building a car round a new chassis is major money; don't pick up a 'bargain' then find you've been duped.

Just as bad as an obviously damaged chassis is one that's been repaired. Put the car up on a ramp and look for evidence of buckling or rippling, mismatched adhesives or any signs of welding. Inspect the aluminium floor for signs of damage. If it's rippled or buckled it's because of an impact at some point. Also ensure the metal hasn't been clouted by road debris.

Your final check from underneath is to make sure that the steel subframe which carries the engine hasn't corroded. It's the only significant piece of steel used in the car, and it has been known to rust. It is replaceable, but the part on its own is £500.

All Elises tend to sit pretty close to the ground, so you need to look for damage to the car's underside as well as the front valance, headlamps and nosecone. The Exige features a front splitter, prone to knocks which can push it out of shape or cause cracks, so check it's intact.

Repairing damaged glassfibre is a specialised business, so if the car has been shunted it will need to have been repaired by an expert. If it hasn't been properly reworked, there'll be sunken paint, possibly microblistering and perhaps even cracks in the panels.

The roof is surprisingly complex considering how basic it appears, and it can also tear all too easily. Whatever the weather is doing, make sure you remove and refit the top, to check that all the components are present and correct.

Conclusion

With that peach of a chassis and reasonable reliability, it's possible to live with an Elise every day – as long as you don't cover huge mileages. Few people use it daily, keeping it instead as a toy, but as a regular plaything the Lotus is hard to beat. It's as comfortable on the track as it is blasting around deserted B-roads.

There are few totally standard cars out there, yet that's no bad thing as some minor modifications will make it even more enjoyable. What's more important is that the structure is in perfect condition.

Some of the really low-volume specials make great investments but tend not to be so usable on an everyday basis. These include the Exige and 340R, the latter model being especially raw. But track down a good standard example and everything else you ever drive will pale into insignificance – it really is that good.

A decent service history by someone who knows what they're doing is essential. Look for evidence of maintenance having been carried out every year or 9000 miles – though the 190 VHPD, Sport 160, Exige and 340R need attention every 6000 miles. ⚠

£300.75 **FOOTMAN JAMES** insurance specialists. At your service.

1997 Lotus Elise
Value: £10,000
Quote: **£300.75** (£100x/s unlimited mpa)
Club Lotus member

»Info

SPECIALISTS
» Christopher Neil, Cheshire.
+44 (0)1606 41481,
www.christopherneil.co.uk
» Fibreglass Services, West Sussex.
+44 (0)1243 554422,
www.fibreglassservices.co.uk
» Hangar 111, Suffolk.
+44 (0)1473 811811,
www.hangar111.com
» Kelvedon Lotus, Lincs.
+44 (0)1775 725457,
www.racecar.co.uk/kelvedonlotus
» Paul Matty, Worcs.
+44 (0)1527 835656,
www.paulmattysportscars.co.uk
» Spyder Engineering, Cambridgeshire.
+44 (0)1733 203986,
www.spydercars.co.uk
» Sue Miller, Suffolk.
+44 (0)1728 603307

CLUBS
» Club Lotus, www.clublotus.co.uk
» Lotus Drivers' Club,
www.lotusdriversclub.org
» Lotus Enthusiasts' Club,
www.seloc.org
» Lotus on Track,
www.lotus-on-track.com

BOOKS
» Elise, Rebirth Of The True Lotus
by Alastair Clements.
Haynes, ISBN 1-85960-857-4
» Lotus Elise and Derivatives 1996-2004
by Paul Robinshaw.
ISBN 0-9528086-4-1
» Lotus Elise, The Complete Story
by John Tipler. ISBN 0-1-86126-213-2
» Lotus Elise: The Official Story Continues
by Jeremy Walton.
ISBN 0-1-902351-15-0

LOTUS/ CATERHAM SEVEN(1957-1988)

They're so simple that buying one is straightforward, and driving a Seven is just pure fun!

Words: Richard Dredge Photography: www.magiccarpics.co.uk

Above
Classic S3 Lotus –
Caterham-built
cars were identical
from '74

If imitation is the sincerest form of flattery, Colin Chapman would be pretty chuffed to see how many copies of his Seven are now available. Aside from the Cobra, his oversized rollerskate must be the most copied car ever, and it's for a good reason – it gives you a chance to put the fun back into motoring. Ever since the first Seven was shown in 1957, for relatively little money it's been possible to have some real fun behind the wheel, and the chance to go on a track day then drive home without having to swap cars is as appealing a prospect as ever.

Because of the car's kit nature, engines and gearboxes came and went while Lotus was building the Seven, and it was the same when Caterham took over production in 1973. But whether you buy Caterham or Lotus, factory-built or kit, you'll have a hoot every time you get behind the wheel. Short of buying

a motorbike, you'll struggle – for the money – to find anything that offers such an adrenalin rush.

You can get into a tatty early 1980s Caterham for £5000, although £7000 is more usual for a reasonable live-axle car. £10k gets a decent De Dion-equipped car while newer cars will command up to £20,000 – or much more for some of the mega machines built in recent years. Post-1988 cars are the easiest to find – most early cars were exported.

A good Lotus will cost £15,000 for a Series 1 and £12,000 for a Series 2 or 3. Series 4 values are lower, with £4000 bagging an okay example. Restoration cases are very rare; a full rebuild on a Series One will cost over £15,000 and the best cars are worth only £20,000.

Engine
Engines wear out eventually, especially as they tend to get used hard, but

whichever unit is fitted it will have had a relatively easy life because the Seven weighs so little. But some units are also very highly tuned because of the type of use to which they're subjected, and as a result you need to make sure that they haven't been overstressed.

Lotus cars used Ford, BMC and Coventry-Climax powerplants as well as their own, but these cars rarely come onto the market – and even more infrequently with their original engines as most Lotus Sevens have had their powerplants updated along the way. Nicest of the early engines is the Coventry-Climax unit, but these suffer from internal corrosion and cracked cylinder heads. The 1340 Cosworth in the S2 is also sought after, but equally rare and temperamental thanks to its three-bearing crank, which leaves you with the 1500 (in both Cosworth and non-Cosworth forms) as the most likely

'Short of buying a motorbike, you'll struggle – for the money – to find anything that offers such an adrenalin rush'

powerplants you'll track down, other than a twin-cam. This is the nicest of all the units fitted to the Lotus cars, but if neglected it'll soon be down on power. They're intolerant of low-maintenance regimes, and it doesn't take too much for the unit to need an overhaul once things have started to deteriorate. Rebuilding one of these is very expensive and if the cylinder head needs replacing you're looking at over £3000 for a new casting.

For most of the first 20 years of its Seven production, Caterham relied on the Ford Kent engine, sometimes fettled by Cosworth. Displacements ranged from 1.3 (for one year only) to 1.7 litres with 1.6-litre units also common. The Kent engine isn't especially durable but it is

easy to rebuild and tune, even if some parts such as heads, crankshafts and blocks are now getting hard to find.

Transmission
Gearboxes tend not to give problems, whether they're of the three-speed Ford or four-speed BMC types. Up to 1980 Caterham used a Corsair four-speed unit which was superseded by one from the Escort Mk2. Five speeds weren't available until 1986 and whichever 'box is fitted it's just a question of looking for oil leaks – none of the units has any inherent problems.

Lotus cars used Nash Metropolitan axles until 1960, when the Standard Companion unit took over. Neither is very

strong, so many have been swapped for Marina or Escort items. Caterhams have been fitted with Escort and Marina/Ital axles but the De Dion system fitted as an option from 1985 used a Sierra diff, as strong as you're ever likely to need.

Suspension, steering and brakes
All Sevens have rack and pinion steering, except for the very first few which had a worm and nut system. In 1958 a Morris 1000 rack was adopted but the following year this was superseded by a Triumph Herald unit and later a Spitfire MkIV unit. A Mini rack arrived in 1984 and quick racks are available if you like your drive even more sporting.

»

LOTUS SEVEN

THE EXCITING LOTUS SEVEN 1500

The Super Seven is supplied with the Ford 116E 1500 c.c. engine fitted with a single twin-choke Weber 40/DCOE carburettor and special Lotus Manifolds. In this form the engine yields much improved power and torque at lower revolutions. The Ford 116E type four-speed gearbox with syncromesh on all forward speeds is standard equipment. Girling disc brakes are fitted to the front wheels. Drum brakes are retained at the rear and provide a very effective handbrake. The hood and sidescreens are made in attractive Vynide material with a large rear window to give excellent all-round visibility. Additional items of equipment included in the speci-fication comprise dipping sealed-beam headlights, electric tachometer, woodrim steering wheel, an electric cooling fan and Elan type 4½J road wheels.

Available in easy to assemble component form, the Super Seven gives high-performance motoring at a price you can afford. The powerful 1500 c.c. Ford engine with Weber Carb., all syncromesh four-speed gearbox and front wheel disc brakes combined with the almost legendary Lotus suspension create a real opportunity for you to enjoy your driving.

COMPONENT FORM PRICE STRUCTURE		
LOTUS "Super" SEVEN 1500		£645
LOTUS "Super" SEVEN Less engine and gearbox		£485

OPTIONAL EXTRAS		
Tonneau cover (unfitted)		£8 3s. 9d.
Heater		£17 10s. 0d.
Exhaust extension		£2 9s. 0d.
Workshop Manual		£3 0s. 0d.
Oil cooler kit		£17 10s. 0d.
Close-ratio gears		£50 0s. 0d.
Radial Ply S.P. 41 tyres		£8 10s. 0d.

LOTUS CARS (SALES) LIMITED, NORWICH, NORFOLK, NOR 92W. Tel: WYMONDHAM 3411

67/02R

LOTUS SEVEN

»Info

TIMELINE
The most significant changes over 28 years
» **1957** Lotus 7 launched with Ford 100E engine, 15in wheels. Later known as 7F
» **1958** Super 7 arrives with Coventry Climax FWA 1100cc engine – 7C
» **1959** A-series engine: Lotus 7A
» **1960** 7 America with Sprite engine, flared wings, glassfibre nose and tubular bumpers
» **1961** Ford 105E engine
» **1962** Super 7 1500 on sale, with Cortina power. Fuel tank up from 5.5 to 8 gallons
» **1963** Flared wings replace cycle wings
» **1967** Series 2¹/₂; Ford 1600 crossflow
» **1968** Series 3 arrives with 1300 or 1600 Crossflow engines, front disc brakes.
» **1970** Series 4; glassfibre bodyshell and spaceframe chassis, negative earth electrics
» **1972** Lotus Seven production ceases
» **1973** Caterham resumes S4 production
» **1974** ... and replaces S4 with revised S3
» **1980** 1600 Sprint appears.
» **1982** Long cockpit chassis goes on sale
» **1985** De Dion rear suspension available

SPECIALISTS
» Arch Motors (chassis), Huntingdon. 01480 459661, www.archmotor.co.uk
» Redline Components, Surrey. 01883 346515, www.redlinecomponents.co.uk
» James Whiting, Middlesex. 01784 241466, www.jameswhiting.com
» Ratrace Motorsport, Herts. 020 8216 5567, www.ratrace-motorsport.co.uk
» The Seven Workshop, Herts. 01992 470480, www.7workshop.com
» UK Sports Cars, Kent. 01227 728190, www.uksportscars.com
» Woodcote Sportscars, Surrey, 01737-645213, www.racecar.co.uk/woodcote
» Caterham Cars, Surrey, 01322 625804, www.caterham.co.uk
» Caterham Cars, Midlands, 01455 841616, www.caterham.co.uk

CLUBS
» Lotus Seven Club. 07000 572582, www.lotus7club.com

BOOKS
» The Magnificent 7 by Chris Rees. Haynes: ISBN 1-85960-848-5
» Lotus Seven, a collector's guide by Jeremy Coulter. Motor Racing Publications: ISBN 0-947981-71-3
» Lotus Seven restoration, preparation and maintenance by Tony Weale (out of print). MBI: ISBN 1-85532-153-X

There are 22 bushes in the suspension, and they all wear out at differing rates. Replacing them is cheap and easy, as is the one that locates the A-frame for the rear suspension. This perishes because of oil contamination from engine and transmission leaks, and can be treated as a consumable. Swapping it is a quick job, and transforms the handling.

Apart from Series 1 cars which used 15-inch wire or pressed-steel wheels, Sevens were fitted with 13-inch pressed-steel wheels – either Triumph (Herald) or Ford (Cortina). If wires are fitted the splines and spokes will need to be checked, but otherwise there shouldn't be any problems.

Because the Seven is so light, its brakes have a relatively easy time. Cars with de Dion rear suspension usually had four-wheel disc brakes while all live-axle cars had rear drums. Upgrading to ventilated discs is easy, but it's not necessary unless the car is going to be hammered regularly.

Bodywork, electrics and trim
It's the chassis that needs the most careful inspection when buying a Seven. Replacement sections and even complete chassis are available for all Sevens, but it's rarely a DIY job. Replacing the chassis wholesale can cost £4000, but Arch Motors, which built some of the original Seven's chassis, still builds all the frames for Caterham.

Chassis rust will normally only be a problem if the car has been shunted and poorly repaired, unless you're looking at a Lotus S4. These featured a bodyshell that was bonded to the chassis. Not only is the car much more prone to rust, but it's also harder to inspect the chassis and much more tricky to properly repair any corrosion.

At least it's easy to see most of the chassis of any Seven other than an S4. Badly repaired accident damage is the most likely problem, with frontal impacts being the normal state of affairs. Look for

Lotus Seven Series 3

SPECIFICATION

Engine
1598cc in-line four, 8 overhead valves. Cast-iron head and block. Single Weber 32DFM carburettor

Power
84bhp @ 6500rpm

Torque
91lb ft @ 3500rpm

Transmission
Four-speed manual, rear-wheel drive

Suspension
Front: Independent with coil springs, double wishbones, telescopic dampers, anti-roll bar. Rear: live axle with A-frame, radius arms, coil springs, telescopic dampers, anti-roll bar

Brakes
Front: 229mm discs
Rear: 203mm drums

Weight
549kg (1210lb)

Performance
0-60mph 7.7sec
Top speed 104mph

Value
Cost £1600 new (fully built)
Value now £8000-£16,000

Above and below
Sevens have always been offered as kits. Left is S1.

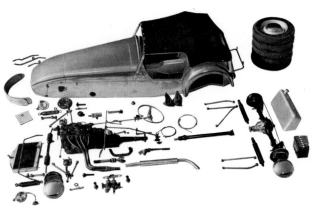

'You can get into a tatty Kent-engined Caterham for £5000, or £10,000 gets a decent de Dion-equipped car'

bent tubes or badly let in replacement sections. To get the best view you'll need to remove the bonnet and nosecone and when you test drive the car make sure it's not pulling to one side.

Because the Seven's bodywork is made of aluminium and glassfibre, rust isn't an issue, although dented alloy panels are. Unpainted alloy panels can also become pitted if they haven't been kept clean, and glassfibre can become cracked and crazed. But the latter is cheap and easy to replace, although Lotus S4 cars are harder to fix because the rear wings, dash and scuttle are integrated.

Replacing clamshell front wings with the cycle type (which are more popular nowadays) will leave a line of holes along the body sides, although it's possible to swap fairly easily the other way, as the holes will be covered up.

The only other bodywork issue is the aluminium fuel tank, which sits behind the two occupants. These can rub at the

mounting points when the rubber wears thin, and may start to leak; replacement means the removal of the roll bar, if one is fitted. Buying a new one will set you back around £130. If the unit is leaking, it'll be obvious from the smell.

Like any car you need to make sure the trim that's there is intact. But there's so little of it that even the tattiest interior is going to be cheap and easy to put right, unless it's a Lotus and you're keen to retain its originality. Even then, the chances are that the car will have been updated anyway, with changes to the steering wheel and perhaps even the instruments.

Interior trim panels are just trimmed cards and as long as the seats, carpets and weather protection are intact, there isn't much to have a look at inside the car. The outside is much the same – brightwork is minimal and it's easy enough to replace.

There's so little equipment fitted to the Seven that the wiring loom is about as simple as it's possible to get. Consequently,

checking that everything works takes no time at all, and neither does inspecting the loom for damage or bodgery.

The biggest problem is with earthing – anything that isn't working is normally easily fixed. But if you're looking at a Lotus, don't underestimate the task of finding original parts – simple things like the headlights can be devilishly tricky to source.

Conclusion

Whatever the car is worth, the grin factor doesn't vary by that much. You'll enjoy plenty of smiles per pound spent, whichever version you buy. It's also hard to find a tatty one, as they're almost always cherished and pampered, although badly repaired cars are out there.

More than 10,000 genuine Sevens have been built, but only around 30 per cent of those were from Lotus. As these are also the oldest cars, it's no surprise that by far the most common (and affordable) Seven is one that wears Caterham badges. But most early Caterhams were exported so you'll probably end up buying something from the early 1980s or newer. That's no bad thing, because development of the car has led to better engines, brakes, handling and even weather protection

– the newer the car, the better all these will be. Until 1984 all Caterhams were built from kits, using all new parts. After this date it was possible to use some second-hand bits, and any car in that category will carry a Q-plate, which can't be replaced.

Demand has always outstripped supply, so values are very high; consequently, provided you buy carefully, you'd be pretty unlucky not to get back what you paid for the car when it comes time to sell it on. And unless you're upgrading, the chances are you won't ever want to sell. △

» **Thanks to Steve Winterberg of the Lotus Seven Club.**

Above

S4 is cheapest; used one-piece glassfibre body over more substantial steel chassis.

MAZDA MX-5 (1990-1999)

A modern classic that is affordable, fun and easy to own: what else do you need to know?
Words: Richard Dredge   Photography: www.magiccarpics.co.uk

Above
Baby Mazda revived the fortunes of the two-seater roadster, paving the way for models such as the open MR2 and MGF.

We'd never try to dissuade you from buying a rear-wheel-drive Lotus Elan, but owning one can be fraught with problems. Sure the handling is sublime, but they can be fragile and expensive: what you need is a tougher, cheaper alternative. Cue the MX-5. Okay, we'd be stretching the point if we were to say that the Mazda is as good as the Elan on an empty B-road, but you'd be amazed what a close-run thing it is – and when you think you can buy a perfectly decent early MX-5 for little more than two grand, suddenly the British sportster starts to look a tad expensive.

It was all thanks to Mazda that the affordable two-seater rag-top was revived in the late 1980s; without the MX-5 there's a good chance we'd never have seen the likes of a fully-open MR2 or the MGF. With its rear-wheel drive, double-wishbone suspension all round and an ultra-low weight, the MX-5 was genuinely a true masterpiece; a turning point in the evolution of the car. Yes, it was only reviving a concept seen decades earlier, but as the 1980s were

becoming the 1990s, everyone assumed the world had changed too much for such a model to be commercially viable. Mazda proved the doubters wrong. With its slick gearchange, perfect poise and beautifully-weighted steering, the Mazda showed potential rivals a clean pair of heels before they were even out of the starting blocks.

Believe it or not, the earliest MX-5 are nearly two decades old, and with thousands sold in the UK there are plenty to go round. Although there are frequently MX-5s for sale at about the £1000 level, you really need to spend double this to get something decent – and even better if you have closer to £3500 to spare. The most recent low-mileage cars can still sell for £6000, but the car has to be really good to command that sort of money.

The number of special editions is also bewildering; some are more worthwhile than others so don't pay over the odds for a car that differs from standard simply by having an unusual paint job. The bottom line is that any MX-5 in fine

fettle will be a hoot to drive – and you don't need to spend a fortune to secure something worth keeping.

Engine
You'll struggle to find an engine more durable than an MX-5's; it just keeps on going as long as it's serviced properly, with 200,000 miles no problem at all. However, even if everything seems spot on, take a look at all the fluid levels, which will give some indication of how much care the previous owner has taken.

Also ask when the last service was performed; Mazda recommended maintenance every 9000 miles or annually, but a caring owner will have done it every 6000 miles instead. If flushing oil has also been used at every service, there's little likelihood of the hydraulic tappets chattering on start-up; lift the bonnet and listen for a noisy top end as the engine is started.

The servicing regime should have taken the condition of the coolant into account; because the MX-5's cylinder head is made of alloy, it's essential that this is kept in tip-top condition, with anti-freeze concentrations maintained. The cambelt should also have been renewed within the last five years or 60,000 miles; any car should be on at least its third by now, even if it's covered barely any distance. However, if the belt does break, the pistons and valves won't collide with each other, so all is not lost.

The earliest engines, which are also the most desirable, are the only ones likely to be suffering from any kind of malady. The motor itself is fine; it's the ancillaries that are the problem – specifically the water pump. These tend to wear, so lift the bonnet and, with the engine ticking over, listen for a knocking noise. If the pump has worn, it's a good idea to get the cambelt replaced at the same time, as it'll probably need doing before too long anyway. A fresh water pump is available for £40, while a specialist will typically charge £120 to do the work, plus the cost of fitting a cambelt (usually £200 on its own).

Some of the earliest cars had a problem with the crankshaft pulley's

woodruff key groove wearing; it can potentially wear to the point where the crankshaft is wrecked. Most cars have been sorted by now, but some will have escaped the system so take a look at how many slots there are in the crankshaft pulley. The potentially faulty units will have just four slots; if there are eight, the stronger type of pulley has already been fitted.

MX-5 powerplants also tend to weep oil, but it shouldn't be all over the engine bay. The culprit is the cam sensor's O-ring at the rear of the engine; fixing it is simplicity itself and even a specialist shouldn't charge more than £50 to do the work.

Exhaust systems can give a few problems. First, they all had a catalytic converter fitted, and you need to make sure it's working properly; the best way of doing this is to put the car through an MoT and see if it passes its emissions test. The rest of the system can corrode, but you don't have to go to Mazda for a replacement; you're better off looking to one of the many aftermarket suppliers

who can provide something sportier, cheaper and made of more durable stainless steel.

Because the exhaust sits close to the road, there's a good chance it's been grounded at some point, so get underneath (which is easier said than done!) and see if it's been bashed about. If the car sounds very rattly from beneath on start-up, it's probably because the exhaust's heat shields have worked loose; they're easily screwed tight again.

Any MX-5 that's had a BBR turbo conversion tends to get through exhausts more quickly than a standard car, because of the increased exhaust temperatures; again, the fitment of a stainless steel system is the perfect fix in this scenario.

Finally, if you're looking at a model on an M or N-plate, check the state of the downpipe and listen for blowing. A welding fault on cars built at this time can lead to the metal separating, resulting in blowing and the need to fit a new downpipe. Mazda fixed most under warranty, and any car that's lasted this long should be fine – but you never know. ››

Mazda MX-5 1.6 (1990-1993)

SPECIFICATIONS

Engine
1598cc in-line four, DOHC, 16 valves. Alloy head, cast-iron block. Electronic fuel injection

Power
114bhp @ 6500rpm

Torque
100lb ft @ 5500rpm

Transmission
Five-speed manual
Rear-wheel drive

Suspension
Front: Independent with double wishbones, coil springs and telescopic dampers, anti-roll bar
Rear: Independent with double wishbones, coil springs and telescopic dampers, anti-roll bar

Brakes
Front: 236mm ventilated discs
Rear: 231mm discs
Servo-assisted

Weight
995kg (2193lb)

Performance
0-62mph: 8.7sec
Top speed: 121mph

Value
Cost new: £14,249 (1990)
Value now: £2000-£5000

'With its rear-wheel drive and an ultra-low weight, the MX-5 was genuinely a true masterpiece; a turning point in the evolution of the car'

»Info

TIMELINE

» **1990:** MX-5 goes on sale in 1.6-litre form. There are just three exterior colours to choose from (red, blue and white) and two optional extras; metallic silver paint and a hard-top.

» **1991:** An officially-approved Brodie Brittain Racing (BBR) turbocharger conversion becomes available, pushing power up to 150bhp and torque to 154lb ft. Anti-lock brakes are standardised, while the limited editions also start being released: in 1991 there are the British Racing Green and Le Mans specials.

» **1992:** Special Edition goes on sale.

» **1993:** Another Special Edition arrives – this time it's black both inside and out. Side-impact bars are also fitted from this year.

» **1994:** A 1.8-litre engine replaces the previous 1.6 unit, with 130bhp on tap. There's a standard car or a 1.8iS edition, with power-steering, a radio, alloy wheels and electric windows.

» **1995:** A 1.6 litre car is available once again, but now with just 88bhp. There are also a couple of special editions released; the California and Gleneagles.

» **1996:** There are more special editions this year, in the form of the Monaco and the Merlot.

» **1997:** This year's limited editions are the Monza, Dakar and Harvard

» **1998:** A new MX-5 goes on sale, dispensing with the pop-up headlamps of the original. However, before the Mk1 disappears there's still time for another limited edition, the Berkeley.

Transmission

There are so many great things about the MX-5 that it's hard to single out any one item. However the gearchange might just be the highlight of the driving experience; it's ultra-sweet and beautifully direct. Over time it can get a tad sticky through a lack of lubrication of the linkages, so go up and down through the box on a test drive and make sure all's well – pay particular attention to the change between second and third gears. If any lubing is needed, the job is easy for the DIY mechanic as long as you know which end of a screwdriver to hold!

All UK-supplied models were fitted with a five-speed manual gearbox, but those built for the Japanese market (badged Eunos) were offered with a four-ratio auto. Buy such a car and you'll miss out on one of the most satisfying aspects of piloting an MX-5, but if you really feel the need to take the slush-box route, at least there shouldn't be any reliability issues.

Suspension, steering and brakes

For a rear-wheel-drive sportscar, the MX-5's suspension components are surprisingly durable. Shock absorbers and springs should easily last 100,000 miles, although many owners will have fitted aftermarket recalibrated parts well before that mileage has been racked up. Bushes aren't quite so long-lived, but they should still last at least 60,000 miles. Any car that's needed fresh bushes well before this has probably been thrashed to within an inch of its life at every opportunity – so ask the seller how many sets of bushes have been fitted. A four-wheel alignment check pays dividends in handling.

Not all cars were equipped with power-steering, and while there aren't many established classics which feature such a system, you're much better off buying an MX-5 that has it. Few assisted systems offer the feedback of the Mazda, which is why you should be prepared to pay a premium of up to £500 for the right car with it.

Because there isn't much power available and the kerb weight is very low, the Mazda doesn't tend to get through tyres very quickly. However, many owners get rid of their car just as a new set of boots is due, so make sure there's still plenty of tread on each corner.

Most (but not all) of these early MX-5 were equipped with alloy wheels; many that were initially supplied with steel rims have had alloy replacements by now. Whatever is present, check the state of the finish – especially if the original Mazda items are fitted. Over time these tend to suffer from pitting after the wheels have got caked in brake dust then just left. It's just a cosmetic thing, though; reviving tired alloys is a straightforward job at around £35 per wheel.

Bodywork, electrics and trim

Unless an MX-5 has been involved in a prang there's very little to worry about as far as the bodywork is concerned as the panels are galvanised. It's worth checking the underside of the front wheelarches, though, and make sure the drain tubes that exit in front of the rear wheels are clear. Early cars can suffer from corroded door jambs, because the kick plates originally fitted allow water to collect underneath and stagnate. Mazda quickly realised there was a problem and revised the design with a rubber pad underneath,

yet there's still a chance that you end up looking at a car affected by rust. The company sorted most claims under warranty, but if you're in doubt simply remove the piece of trim in question; it's held in place by a pair of screws so it doesn't take long to have a look.

Because the boot is so shallow, some owners try to cram in too much then slam down the bootlid, damaging it in the process. The bulge that results is very obvious and not easy to remove.

The electrics are generally reliable, but check that the pop-up headlamps are working properly; their motors sometimes stick. If you're looking at a Eunos, ask if it has air-conditioning fitted, as it's an option that was frequently specified by the first owner. If it is, make sure it's working properly. Also check that the electric windows work properly, as the motors can burn out. They're easy enough to sort; expect to pay £80 per side for replacement units.

Although interiors are generally durable, there are one or two weak spots. The first place to check is the driver's seat, which wears down the side; it's a natural consequence of the owner getting in and out. Decent standard used seats and aftermarket items aren't hard to find, but it's still a useful bargaining point.

Also check the condition of the hood, which tends to last reasonably well but which suffers if the MX-5 has been cleaned badly (especially in a car wash) or not at all. The rear screen tends to get scratched; unzip before stowing it or it'll get creased. Also have a look at what state the zip is in; they often get broken by ham-fisted owners. If the worst comes to the worst, replacement hoods aren't that expensive at £160 for a vinyl one; you can even get a mohair replacement

complete with a glass rear screen for just £349. However, don't forget that fitting a fresh roof can be laborious and costly; if the frame is damaged as well, the bill to put things right won't be small.

Conclusion

Blissful to drive, well screwed together, durable and cheap to both buy and run, the Mazda really has got the lot. As long as you don't need to cart much stuff about the MX-5 makes perfect sense even if you need to do the weekly shopping in it.

Pick of the bunch is the early 1.6-litre car, as it's better balanced than the 1.8 that superseded it and more powerful than the later 1.6. Don't be put off by a grey import; to satisfy demand in the early days, many cars were brought over from Japan. These have Eunos badging and a smaller number plate plinth in the bootlid. UK-supplied cars' chassis numbers start JMZ while Japanese editions kick off with NA.

In many cases the Japanese editions are better equipped. However, you do need to make sure there's a decent service history available with the car; many grey imports don't have much paperwork with them, so you could end up buying a liability. ⚠

»Info

MG T-SERIES (1936-1955)

A Brit classic through and through – but just what is it that makes this archetypal MG so appealing?

Words: Richard Dredge Photography: www.magiccarpics.co.uk

Above

When Britain was great: MG's T-Series is one of the most cherished classics from the empire's golden automotive era.

Looking for somewhere safe and fun to put your cash? Then how about an MG T-Series? Buy well and you're guaranteed to get your money back should you need to move on – not that you'll ever want to. One of the most cherished British classics ever made, the T-Series sums up everything that was great about England from a time when Britannia ruled the waves.

Oozing quintessential British charm, the T-Series lasted two decades and encompassed five distinct derivatives – along with all sorts of other variations on the theme. From the narrow-tracked TA to the Morgan-esque TF with its integrated headlamps and wider bodyshell, all these models have their charms and are well supported by specialists around the country.

Thanks to that octagon badge and the T-Series' charm, these cars have always been sought after. In recent years they've increased in value significantly, to the point where the best examples

are now fetching £30,000 on a regular basis. However, with a full professional restoration costing £30,000-£50,000, that's not poor value – especially as a price crash is unlikely.

TCs and TF1500s are the most valuable; a decent runner is worth £14-18,000 while an equivalent TD is £12-15,000. In the middle are the TA, TB and TF1250, fetching £12-17,000. Incomplete restoration projects are worth anywhere between £2000 and £4000 depending on condition and model – if everything is present and correct, these costs immediately double. Incidentally, there's little difference in values between left and right-hand-drive cars nowadays – and remember that the TA, TB and TC were never built with left-hand drive anyway.

Engine

Most Ts were fitted with the same XPAG engine, albeit to varying specifications. However, the TA featured a 1292cc

Wolseley Ten-based powerplant, which can prove frustratingly troublesome in standard form. One of the key problems is a tendency for the cylinder blocks to crack, so check everything carefully for hairline fractures.

Oil and water can also mix, because both the head and the block are prone to cracking; in the case of the latter, it's usually on the pushrod side, behind the tappet cover. Because this is out of sight, it can be tricky to spot; the strength of the metal isn't helped by the cylinder head studs passing straight through the water jacket. Look for white emulsion on the oil filler cap as well as on the dipstick, signalling problems.

As if that's not enough, oil pressures are much higher than most engines are used to, with 100-120psi quite normal during everyday running. To top it all, there are white metal bearings, which ensure engine rebuilds are more costly than a similar shell-bearing unit.

The Morris Ten-based 1250cc engine

'Oozing quintessential old-world charm, the T encompassed five distinct derivatives'

fitted from the TB onwards is a more straightforward unit, with shell bearings. However, the crankshaft has been known to break across the front web while the valves can drop into the combustion chambers, when their heads break off. As if that isn't bad enough, the cam followers can wear quickly – but any engine rebuilt in recent years should have had improvements incorporated to reduce headaches.

These will focus on modifying the valve springs, as many of the failures prevalent in the XPAG engine are down to the springs originally specified. As a result, it's best to fit softer items when the motor is rebuilt, to increase the lifespan of the valve gear while reducing the likelihood of dropped valves.

None of the T-Series cars featured especially powerful engines; if you fancy at least 20 per cent more muscle you could fit a supercharger. It's not cheap at around £2000 – but it'll sound great and give the car a lot more 'go'

Transmission

It's the earlier gearboxes that are the most durable, the later units being fitted with smaller, weaker components that create a somewhat fragile transmission. Consequently, while you're unlikely to have any concerns where the TA, TB and TC gearboxes are concerned, you need to listen very carefully to a TD or TF transmission before buying.

The gears and layshaft create the most problems, so make sure the car doesn't jump out of gear and that there's no significant whining – or you'll have to fork out up to £1000 for a rebuilt gearbox before long. The rest of the transmission is long-lived, with clutches, rear axles and driveshafts all able to cope with the relatively small amounts of torque on offer. The TA, TB and TC each use the same type of rear axle, but the TD and TF feature one altogether, borrowed from the Wolseley 4/44.

For more relaxed cruising, a five-speed gearbox can be fitted to any T apart from

the TA and TF1500. To buy all the parts you'll pay around £700; get a specialist such as Andy King to fit it as well and you'll typically pay another £500.

Suspension, steering and brakes

As you'd expect, the primitive suspension fitted to all these cars needs plenty of TLC on a regular basis if wear isn't to occur. The first three generations of T featured cart springs, while the TD and TF have independent front suspension. The earlier system is generally vice-free, although the TA and TB feature sliding trunnion spring mountings at the rear. The steel tube, classed as a chassis repair, which carries the phosphor bronze bushes, has a habit of wearing to the point where it can be dangerous, but it's easy enough to fix with a repair kit available for around £45 per side. The only other real weak spot is the axle location; the mounting bolts can pull through, leading ➤➤

Above

All models have their appeal and are well supported by specialists scattered around the country.

M G MIDGET

SERIES 'T.C.' TWO-SEATER

The all-weather equipment gives complete protection from wind and rain for driver and passenger alike. Side curtains of special design fit snugly and rigidly into position. For long-distance night driving the 13½-gallon petrol tank is an M.G. MIDGET feature which is widely appreciated.

to some pretty severe problems; sometimes it can be welded up, other times a repair panel is needed, so costs can vary significantly by up to £200.

Although the TD and TF have independent front suspension, they're not immune from problems. The phosphor bronze upper and lower trunnions are prone to wear, and if they've been replaced by steel MGA items they'll be even more worn. Regular lubrication with a mix of oil and grease will have slowed down the wear rate – but it can't be eradicated completely.

The TA, TB and TC featured a worm and peg steering box, which usually wears rapidly and is often over-adjusted in a bid to remove the play. This only makes things worse and ensures the box has to be replaced. The steering racks fitted to the TD and TF are durable; if there is any play, it's probably because of slackness in the adjustable inner ball joints on the tie rods – which is easy to fix.

If you find the steering too heavy, it's possible to fit a Datsun steering box conversion – although this applies only to the TA, TB and TC. However, because even the Datsun parts are now getting hard to find, it's more usual to fit a VW system, for around £450.

Brakes can also give problems; pressed-steel drums are fitted to the TA, TB and TC, and they're prone to warping if allowed to get too hot. If this has happened it'll be obvious; as soon as you apply the brakes there will be juddering galore. Original-style brake drums are available at just under £100 apiece; it's always worth ensuring the best units are fitted at the front, as they take most of the braking effort.

Although the TC and TD were fitted with cast iron drums, problems can still arise – often through a lack of maintenance. Because they are integral with the

hub, they're difficult to remove – which is why preventative maintenance is frequently overlooked. This might not be so bad if the alloy wheel cylinders weren't prone to seizure, so check the car pulls up straight when you dab that middle pedal.

TA, TB and TC brakes can be upgraded to TD/TF spec for £750, to give much better stopping power. However, if you still want more, it's possible to fit Alfin drums, at a cost of £500 for a set of four.

Bodywork, electrics and trim

All these cars feature a separate chassis, with the TA, TB and TC sharing one design and the TD/TF being different. The earlier chassis gives few problems, although any kind of an impact will probably have twisted the frame out of true. Also, cars built before 1948 may exibit cracks in the metal in line with the underneath of the front seats. That's because the reinforcing went only this far back, and the subsequent strain put on the channelling can lead to stress fractures.

The later chassis is less durable than its predecessor, because it is box section rather than channelling. As a result, it rots from the inside out – and things aren't helped by the fact that it's made from thinner-gauge steel than previously. There's also the spectre of accident damage to deal with – fixing a box-section chassis is even more fraught with problems than a channelled unit.

Although the bodyshells varied between the various T-Series derivatives, they're all built in the same way and have the same weaknesses. All rely on wooden framing, although the TF featured more metal than the others, to add stiffness to the structure. It's the wood »

»Info

TIMELINE

» 1936: The TA is announced, with production starting at 20 examples per week.

» 1938: A Tickford TA coupé is made available, with folding hood and wind-up windows; they're now very rare and highly sought after.

» 1939: The TB enters production after 3003 TAs are made, but manufacturing lasts just four months, with a mere 379 cars being produced. The TB is the rarest T of all, but it's nothing more than a re-engined TA.

» 1945: The postwar TC makes its debut. Although it is merely a widened TB, it's a very significant car because it marks MG's entry into the North American market – a milestone reached in 1947.

» 1947: The TD arrives after 10,000 TCs have been built. The new car brings a fresh frame and bodyshell along with redesigned front suspension; it goes on to become the most popular of all the T-Series models, with 29,664 examples constructed before it 'dies' in September 1953.

» 1953: The arrival of the TF brings a more modern look, with faired-in headlamps. Despite its more contemporary appearance though, the TF is really nothing more than a TD with a modified bodyshell. There wasn't even a fresh engine on offer, although this would arrive within little more than a year.

» 1954: The TF1500 goes on sale; the most usable of all the T-Series MGs, just 3400 of these bigger-engined TFs are built, compared with 6200 examples of the TF1250.

SPECIALISTS

» Andy King, Leics. +44 (0)1949 860 519, www.mgsparesandrestorations.com

» Barry Walker, Stratford-upon-Avon. +44 (0)1789 400 181, www.barrywalker.com

» Brown & Gammons, Herts. +44 (0)1462 490 049, www.ukmgparts.com

» Leacy MG, Birmingham. +44 (0)121 356 3003, www.leacymg.co.uk

that causes the greatest problems, and most of it is hidden. However, there's an exposed crossmember under the dash; if this is rotten the rest of the woodwork will be as well.

It's much easier to inspect the outer panels, as there aren't any box sections. Corrosion around the edges of each wing is par for the course, while the seams between panels can harbour rust, thanks to the beading absorbing water then promoting corrosion. It's also worth checking that the wings haven't been replaced with glassfibre items; unlikely, but it has been known.

Other corrosion hot-spots include the rear bulkhead (behind the front seats) and the fuel tank; inspect the latter especially carefully. Problems here can be traced to the felt pads used to locate the tank; they absorb water and it's just a matter of time before the metal starts to dissolve.

All T variants were upholstered with leather, although vinyl was used for the door trims. Most cars will have had at least some retrimming carried out by now, but if any further work is needed it's easy enough to get everything that may be required. When checking it all, don't forget to assemble the hood and sidescreens; you might find the material damaged or even that some of the necessary fittings are missing. At least it's all available, but some original parts can be tricky to find and costs quickly add up.

If you're buying a restoration project, ensure that all the instrumentation and switchgear is present and correct. Again, you can ultimately track everything down should you need to, but some parts have now become very expensive.

Conclusion

Thanks to the cars' simplicity and the fact that they're always in demand, it's easy to keep any T-Series going as long as you've got the cash. That's not to say that individual parts are expensive, but if serious rot sets in, putting everything right won't be cheap.

That's why you must check for rotten wood, corroded steel, worn mechanicals and damaged or missing trim; buy a car suffering from all these things and you'll never get your money back. However, the T is one of those machines that you don't mind lavishing cash on, as you can't put a price on the fun you'll have behind the wheel.

MG TC

Engine
1250cc in-line four, eight overhead valves. Cast-iron head and block. Twin SU carburettors

Power
54bhp @ 5200rpm

Torque
64lb ft @ 2600rpm

Transmission
Four-speed manual, rear-wheel drive

Suspension
Front: Beam axle with half-elliptic leaf springs, Luvax hydraulic lever arm dampers
Rear: Live axle with half-elliptic leaf springs, Luvax hydraulic lever arm dampers

Brakes
Front: Drums
Rear: Drums
No servo assistance

Weight
789kg (1735lb)

Performance
0-60mph: 22.7sec
Top speed: 75mph

Value
Cost new: £375 (1945)
Value now: £10,000-£30,000

£163.20 **FOOTMAN JAMES**
Insurance specialists. At your service.

1946 MG TC
Value: £17,000
Quote: **£163.20** (£100x/s unlimited mpa)

»Info

CLUBS
» MG Car Club. +44 (0)1235 555 552, www.mgcc.co.uk
» MG Owners' Club. +44 (0)1954 231 125, www.mgownersclub.co.uk

BOOKS
» MG T-Series In Detail by Paddy Willmer. Herridge and Sons, ISBN 0-9541063-6-9
» MG T-Series, The Complete Story by Graham Robson. Crowood, ISBN 978-1-861269-09-6
» Original MG T-Series by Anders Clausager. Bay View, ISBN 1-870979-06-0 (out of print)
» MG TA & TC Gold Portfolio 1936-1949 by Brooklands Books. ISBN 000-1-85520-315-4
» MG TD & TF Gold Portfolio 1949-1955 by Brooklands Books. ISBN 000-1-85520-316-2
» MG T-Series Restoration Guide 1936-1955 by Malcolm Green. Brooklands Books, ISBN 000-1-85520-211-5

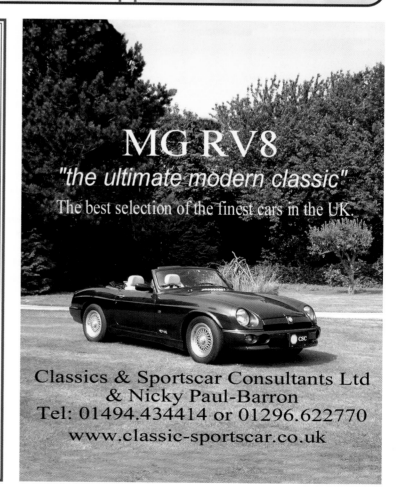

MG RV8 (1992-1995)

Against other 1990s sports cars, the RV8 doesn't compare dynamically. But as a rust-free classic with a tough, powerful V8, it's now finding more and more fans

Words: Richard Dredge, Photography: www.magiccarpics.co.uk

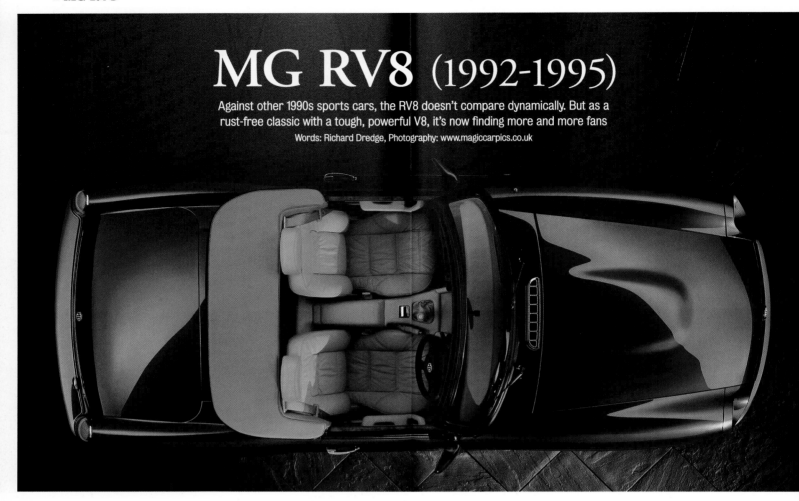

Above
Basics are pure MGB yet most panels were altered, interior was new and engine gave a good 190bhp.

When the MG RV8 was new in 1992, its most common adversary in magazine group tests was the TVR Chimaera. But that's not how those who developed the car saw things – MG reckoned its natural rivals were speedboats, swimming pools and even oil paintings. This wasn't merely an automobile; it was a leisure pursuit that happened to have four wheels. Welcome to the world of disposable income.

The RV8 wasn't really intended to be an everyday car; it was a toy to be taken out on high days and holidays. But whatever it was, there were plenty who suggested that MG should have taken heed of the maxim that you should quit while you're ahead.

While the B had long been revered, the RV8 was frequently reviled – usually by those who had never seen one, never mind driven one. It didn't help that the car market had changed hugely in the 12 years between the B's demise and the RV8's arrival – reskinning an old warhorse that dated back to the early 1960s was seen as a cynical exercise that did little except cash in on MG's rich heritage. A decade after the last RV8 was built, things are now

viewed somewhat differently.

The RV8 came about thanks to Rover's Heritage division, which had recently started to remanufacture MGB bodyshells. MG needed to get a roadster to market in a hurry, and reworking its classic model was quick fix; the MGF wouldn't be along until the end of 1995. However, the metamorphosis from B to RV8 was no minor task as 95 per cent of the panelwork was new.

The 3.9-litre V8 was also a massive improvement over the B-series unit of the original car, and to improve handling there was a wider track (covered by flared wheelarches) and upgraded suspension. The whole vehicle was more butch too, and the interior was streets ahead – even if it was olde worlde. All this updated the B pretty well, but the RV8 still drove like a 1960s car. As a result, many who bought one were disappointed; they expected it to be a 1990s sportscar, but it was no TVR.

Despite its deficiencies, the RV8's classic status was assured from the day it was unveiled, and with a mere 1982 built between 1992 and 1995, the cars are now

sought after. Although 1583 examples went to Japan, many of those have now returned to the UK to join the 307 originally sold here. No RV8s were ever bought in the US, and according to Nicky Paul-Barron (of Classic & Sportscar Consultants, which sells more RV8s in the UK than anyone else), it's still Japan that is the best source of mint examples.

Engine

The 3.9-litre Rover V8 doesn't give many problems unless it's done a high mileage and has been neglected and/or thrashed. The other killer is short journeys, so be aware that an ultra-low mileage car isn't necessarily good news.

Frequent long jaunts will see an engine deliver 300,000 miles of faithful service, but occasional short journeys leads to the camshaft and followers wearing rapidly – perhaps within 30,000 miles if oil and filter changes have been lacking. Listen for ticking from the top end that gives the game away; putting it right costs £250 for the parts and the same again for the labour. If the car isn't used regularly, the

'MG needed to get a roadster to market in a hurry, and reworking its classic model gave it a quick fix'

Above
The 3.9-litre Rover V8 is relatively trouble-free – but low-mileage cars are not necessarily brilliant news.

oil and filter need to be changed much more often than the standard service schedule suggests – as frequently as every 2000 miles or so.

One of the few maladies you need to check for is blown exhaust manifold gaskets. There are four separate gaskets fitted across the exhaust ports (they're in pairs), so you might have to replace more than one. Specialist Clive Wheatley has had higher-quality replacements made and they're less than £13 for a full set. Lift the bonnet and listen for blowing from the manifolds – it'll be immediately obvious if there's an issue.

The exhaust itself can give problems as it's rot-prone – despite being made of stainless steel. There's a good chance that by now a replacement will have been fitted, but if a new system is required you can choose from a single-box set-up (£235) or twin-box (£270).

The Lucas fuel injection is reliable; it's the same as what you'll find under the bonnet of a Range Rover or Discovery. As a result, it's uncomplicated but effective – much like the engine-management system.

As with any alloy motor it's essential that

a decent-quality anti-freeze is used, and that it's kept up to strength. Check that the engine doesn't overheat when left idling – if it does, it may be because the radiator has got partially blocked by debris as a result of the cylinder head breaking up inside.

Transmission

All RV8s were fitted with a five-speed manual gearbox. At first, Land Rover's LT77 unit was used, and from commission number 641 (production started at number 251) the same company's R380 went in. The box in earlier cars, which is more durable and cheaper to rebuild, has reverse located next to first and then it moved to below fifth. The later transmission suffers from worn syncromesh, which costs £300-plus to fix; if the problem isn't caught in time, the bill will escalate to £1000-plus.

Check for whining from the rear axle, which is based on the Sherpa van's but has a crown wheel and pinion that is specific to the RV8. There's a Quaife LSD fitted, and once the crown wheel and pinion are damaged you will be looking at a £1000 bill to rebuild the unit.

MG RV8
SPECIFICATIONS

Engine
3946cc OHV all-alloy V8, Lucas fuel injection

Power
190bhp @ 4750rpm

Torque
234lb ft @ 3200rpm

Transmission
Five-speed manual

Suspension
Front: Double wishbones, telescopic dampers, anti-roll bar
Rear: Live axle, elliptic leaf springs, telescopic dampers, anti-roll bar

Brakes
Front: 270mm ventilated discs
Rear: 228mm drums
No ABS available

Weight
1101kg (2422lb)

Performance
0-60mph: 6.9sec
Top speed: 138mph

Value
Cost new: £26,030
Value now: £10,000-£20,000

»

Above
Disc front brakes, modern dash controls plus classic styling with a contemporary twist: the MG RV8 offered the lot.

Suspension, steering and brakes

The RV8's suspension is closely based on the B's, so don't expect the handling to be a revelation even if everything is in good condition. One of the B's failings is also common here; that of worn upper and lower inner wishbone bushes. They can be replaced easily and cheaply enough, and while you're at it, it's worth going for longer-lasting polyurethane items at £40 per side. Bumpstops also wear out, but new polyurethane ones are available at £25.85 apiece.

Front springs settle, leading to a nose-down stance – new units are £58.75 each. The Koni dampers aren't ideal as they're not bespoke. It's possible to get them revalved but one compromise is to stiffen them up by removing and compressing them and twisting them clockwise. Most owners don't realise they're adjustable, yet it's a quick and easy fix that sharpens up the handling usefully. Alternatively, Clive Wheatley does Koni replacements which are better suited to the car; the originals are no longer available.

Wheelbearings wear out, so listen for rumbling from each corner. At least you can now buy the bearings on their own (for £76 per side); until recently you had to buy a whole hub assembly at over £300.

Power-assisted steering was never available from new, but it can now be retrospectively fitted. The MG Owners' Club can perform the necessary surgery – but you'll need to find around £2500.

Lack of use is the RV8's biggest enemy, with the brakes being the most likely victim. The rear wheel-cylinder pistons tend to seize up after a while, but even fitting new ones won't break the bank as they're just £25 each. It's the same at the front, with the four-pot calipers sticking all too readily. The caliper halves are the same as were fitted to the Ambassador and Princess, but with a wider spacer in the middle so they're unique to the RV8. They're easy enough to source, but expensive at £190 each.

If you're keen to retain originality, make sure the wheels are undamaged; they were made especially for the RV8 and are no longer available. Clive Wheatley has put the three-piece units used on the RV8 prototype back into production, at £290 each. The originals were 15-inch items, but 17-inch units can be obtained at £350 apiece.

Bodywork, electrics and trim

If the bodywork is showing any signs of corrosion it's because the car has been pranged, then bodged to get it back on the road. Panels don't rust; bodyshells were electrophoretically dipped after the metal had already been zinc-coated to reduce corrosion as far as possible.

The one exception to this rule is the windscreen surround, which is made of steel box sections. Look out for the

From left: Classic style with modern-day reliability. Seats were too well padded when new; most have settled by now.

»Info

TIMELINE
» 1992: RV8 introduced, based on MGB bodyshell but with extensive mechanical and bodywork revisions.
» 1995: Final RV8 produced; it is number 1982 off the production line.

SPECIALISTS
» Brown and Gammons (parts). +44 (0)1462 490049, http://bg.mgcars.org.uk
» Clive Wheatley (MG V8 parts, maintenance). +44 (0)1746 710810, www.mgv8parts.com
» MGOC Spares (parts, maintenance). +44 (0)1954 234001, www.mgownersclub.co.uk
» Classic & Sportscar Consultants and Nicky Paul-Barron (sales). +44 (0)1296 622770, www.classic-sportscar.co.uk

CLUBS
» MG Car Club. +44 (0)1235 555552, www.mgcars.org.uk/carclub
» MG Owners' Club. +44 (0)1954 234001, www.mgownersclub.co.uk

BOOKS
» MG by McComb (F Wilson McComb), Osprey. ISBN 1-85532-831-3
» MG V8 (David Knowles), Windrow & Greene. ISBN 1-872004-89-X

rubbers lifting, indicating rot underneath. Sometimes repairs are possible; if not, you will need a new surround. Clive Wheatley does a carbonfibre and glassfibre equivalent at £935, or a steel unit from Brown and Gammons is £200 more.

The interior is beautifully trimmed, with lashings of wood and leather. The woodwork can suffer from the veneer separating from its backing. In the case of the door trims and glovebox it's not too tricky to effect repairs reasonably cheaply, but remedial work to the dashboard will be pricey as it has to be removed.

It's always better to restore than replace because the wood was matched during the build process; if the whole lot is refurbished now, it will be possible to get it done as a matching set again. Bank on £350 for the work. The leather soon gets baggy, and beyond 30,000 miles a good valet will be needed as all interiors were finished in cream leather.

Make sure that the hood is in good condition, as you'll have to pay £760 if it needs replacing. The frame and covering are basically from the MGB, albeit modified – if the whole lot has to be renewed the parts bill alone is over £1300. If the rear window is damaged it can be replaced independently of the rest of the roof.

Japanese-market cars were fitted with air-conditioning; in the UK it was an option that was rarely specified. The system is reliable but there is a small penalty to pay in that the passenger footwell is slightly smaller to accommodate everything. The air-con needs to be recharged every three years or so, but that's not a problem.

Conclusion
It's easy to listen to those who have never driven the RV8 but have nothing good to say about the car. Ignore them and speak instead to those who have owned (or at least driven) one of the few examples around. They'll regale you with tales of endless torque, surprisingly good build quality and head-turning rarity.

Although RV8s are hard to come by, you can still be choosy. Of the cars available at any one time, most are very low mileage and will have been cherished. Spend less than £10,000 and you'll be buying a money pit; far better to invest another £4-5000 to get a really nice example. Most models were finished in Woodcote Green, which is why cars painted in other colours carry a premium – although it's hard to say how much. Whatever you settle on, once you've bought your RV8 you can show it to the prophets of doom who warned you against purchasing it in the first place – and see how quickly they change their mind. △

'Owners will regale you with tales of endless torque, good build quality and rarity'

£231.45

1993 MG RV8
Value: £13,000
Quote: **£231.45** (£100x/s unlimited mpa)

MGA (1955-1962)

It's arguably the most beautiful MG ever – but does this classic sportscar have an ugly side, too?

Words: Richard Dredge Photography: www.magiccarpics.co.uk

Above
Lively and agile to drive – yet it can be a challenge to restore.

While some of MG's pre-war cars look more charming, none of the marque's models has ever been as beautiful as the A. But this isn't a machine that's all show and no go, because to match those flowing lines the A also offers lively performance and surprising agility. It may not be fast, but it's well balanced and handles superbly – something that's even more impressive when you consider the car came out more than 50 years ago.

Under the skin, the A had more in common with its predecessor, the TF, than MG would have liked. But with well-tested mechanicals such as the 1489cc B-Series engine, drum brakes all round and a four-speed manual gearbox, the A's specification is on a par with that of its rivals, and this makes restoring and owning the car that much easier.

Nearly half a century after the final MGA was built, the model is easier than ever to own, thanks to fabulous specialist and club support. However, there's a multitude of traps that can catch out the unwary, so you have to be very careful before committing to purchase. Be especially prudent if you're thinking about taking on a restoration project: these cars have a more complex

construction than you might think.

For this article, we spoke to the UK's foremost A specialist, Bob West. With more than 30 years of experience under his belt, there isn't much that he hasn't seen. Bob says: 'If you buy a project, expect to pay £3000-£4000 for a coupé or £4000-£6000 for a roadster. Usable open cars are £8000-£12,500, with equivalent coupés £5000-£10,000. The best roadsters are approaching £20,000, while a coupé in similar condition fetches about 25 per cent less.

'The problem is, restoring a coupé costs around 30 per cent more than a roadster because of the extra complexity – yet it's worth significantly less. As a result, you need to be especially careful when buying a fixed-head, although there are some good cars out there. Indeed, coupé values have risen recently, but 90 per cent of buyers still want an open-topped car.'

Bob continues: 'If it's a Twin Cam that you fancy, open cars top out somewhere around the £25,000 mark, with closed models still worth around 25 per cent less. Average examples are £16,000-£18,000 for a drophead or £12,000-£14,000 for a fixed-head. However

you need to be very careful with any average MGA; for example, you might pick up a genuinely okay 1500 roadster for £12,000, but it's more likely that you'll end up with a car that needs significant work even though it looks good. That's why I focus only on models that need restoration or ones that have already been rebuilt; there's often too much uncertainty with anything in between.'

Engine

There were two families of engine offered in the A; the familiar B-Series unit or a twin-cam that's rare, hence costly to rebuild. The B-Series doesn't throw up anything to be particularly worried about; all the bits are available to revive the most tired of units, although as long as it's looked after this powerplant will despatch a quarter of a million miles without murmur.

One of the most common problems with an MGA engine is its origins; this unit was fitted to all sorts of other BMC products and it's very easy to slot in a motor from something more mundane such as a Farina saloon, although MGB mills are common, too. It's also possible to swap between 1500 and

Safety fast!

THE **MG** SERIES **MGA**

'Nearly half a century after the final MGA was built, the model is easier than ever to own, thanks to fabulous specialist and club support'

MGA 1600 MkI roadster
SPECIFICATIONS

Engine
1588cc in-line four, eight overhead valves. Cast-iron head and block. Two SU carburettors

Power
79.5bhp @ 5600rpm

Torque
87lb ft @ 3800rpm

Transmission
Four-speed manual Rear-wheel drive

Suspension
Front: Independent with double wishbones, coil springs and lever-arm dampers
Rear: Live axle with semi-elliptic springs, lever-arm dampers

Brakes
Front: 279mm discs
Rear: 254mm drums

Weight
916kg (2015lb)

Performance
0-60mph: 15.6sec
Top speed: 98mph

Value
Cost new: £940 (1959)
Value now: £5000-£20,000

1600 editions, and while that isn't necessarily an issue, if you want something that's original (or at least to original spec), it's another thing that you need to check.

The signs of a tired B-Series engine are classic; blue oil smoke while accelerating through the gears belies worn piston rings and/or cylinder bores. There should be 50-60psi on the oil pressure gauge with the engine spinning at 3000rpm.

Leaks are also par for the course; the scroll oil-thrower on the back of the crankshaft is the culprit, allowing lubricant to seep from the bottom of the bellhousing. This wears, along with the block which it acts upon, eroding both. Once the wear has taken place it's a potentially costly process to put everything right, as to produce a lasting fix, a new block and crank could be needed – and neither is available. However, it's usually possible to install an oil seal conversion at around £200 – although this would be the cost only if the engine has already been dismantled.

The potential problems don't end there, because the cylinder heads are also prone to cracking, so look for evidence of water

loss around the top of the engine along with signs of the car having overheated. The classic symptom will be a blown head gasket, so check for any signs of a white emulsion on the underside of the oil-filler cap.

Meanwhile, the twin-cam engine is an altogether different beast – one that's very expensive to revive if it goes wrong. Not only is it fragile, but it also requires specialist restoration skills. Many who attempt to rebuild these units don't really know what they're doing, causing big problems in the process. The unit gained a reputation for burning pistons when it was new, and because the engine can end up destroying itself all too readily you could easily end up with a bill for £5000+ to put everything right.

Transmission

The A's gearbox is a proven weak point, now that most have been rebuilt. The problem is that used parts are often fitted to keep costs down: as a result, failures are common. Second-gear synchromesh usually goes first, so see if there's any baulking as you go up and down through the ratios. Also listen out for chattering in first and reverse, signalling

that the laygear is on its way out.

You can get an exchange box for around £450, as long as no fresh gears are required. If a transmission has damaged cogs replacements are available, but many owners prefer to fit a close-ratio set, which costs an extra £1000. This is an option that was available when the cars were new; models that were specified with it will have the letters 'DA' in the engine's commission number. However, just because the letters are there doesn't mean there's still a close-ratio gear set fitted; many of these cars will have had replacement boxes by now.

Clutches and propshafts are strong but can still suffer from slipping and imbalance respectively. The universal joints fitted to the propshaft will also wear eventually; you will feel if this has happened as the drive is taken up when moving off in first or reverse. More serious is a worn differential; they're very strong but that doesn't mean they last forever. Once a huge mileage has been covered, whining will be evident; expect to pay around £550 for an exchange unit.

More likely than a worn diff is damage to the axle casing, leading to a bill of £350 ▸▸

»Info

SPECIALISTS

» Bob West, Yorks. +44 (0)1977 703828, www.bobwestclassiccars.co.uk
» Brown & Gammons, Herts. +44 (0)1462 490049, www.ukmgparts.com
» David Manners, West Midlands. +44 (0)121 544 4444, www.davidmanners.co.uk
» Leacy MG, Birmingham. +44 (0)121 356 3003, www.leacymg.co.uk
» MG Owners' Club Spares, Cambs. +44 (0)1954 230928, www.mgocspares.co.uk
» Moss Europe, London. +44 (0)208 867 2000, www.moss-europe.co.uk
» For a full list of Heritage-approved MG specialists, please see www.bmh-ltd.com/directory.htm

CLUBS

» MG Car Club. +44 (0)1235 555 552, www.bmh-ltd.com/directory.htm
» MG Owners' Club, +44 (0)1954 231125, www.mgcars.org.uk

BOOKS

» MGA, MGB & MGC Collectors Guide by Graham Robson. ISBN 0-1-899870-43-1
» Original MGA by Anders Clausager. ISBN 0-7603-1450-0
» MGA, The Complete Story by David Styles. ISBN 0-1-86126-466-6
» MGA by John Price-Williams. ISBN 0-1-903706-56-4

to put things right. It's caused by the hub nuts being left loose; they should be tightened but the 1 61/64in hub nut is an odd size – and it's also got eight sides. However, you can buy the correct socket from specialists such as Bob West, for about £20. If the nuts aren't tightened up, the bearing spins against the axle casing, damaging both. The most obvious symptom of this having occurred is oil, from the diff, having leaked onto the brakes.

Suspension, steering and brakes

The most likely suspension issue is worn or tight trunnions. The former is a result of a lack of lubing; greasing should be done at least annually. The latter problem occurs when replacement trunnions are fitted but they're not lapped in to fit the kingpins properly. It may be that a matched trunnion and kingpin needs to be fitted; you'll pay £205 for each side for parts alone.

Lever arm dampers have a habit of leaking, especially as many aren't rebuilt particularly well. Look for evidence of hydraulic fluid seeping out; it's an MoT failure point and it won't do the car's ride or handling any favours, either.

Early MGAs featured drum brakes all round; the Twin Cam and De Luxe boasted an all-disc system, while the 1600 had a disc/drum set-up. Some owners feel the need to upgrade their 1500 to a front-disc system, but it's not necessary because the car's light weight ensures there's plenty of stopping power with the standard set-up. All parts are available new, and thanks to the simplicity of the system there's nothing to worry about; leaks and corrosion are the extent of your concerns, so checks are easy to make.

Although disc wheels were standard fare, many As now sport wires. Again, everything is available new, but be wary of rims that have lots of rusty or broken spokes, or worn splines; it's indicative of a generally neglected car and fitting new parts will soon get costly.

Bodywork, electrics and trim

Although many MGAs now resident in the UK were initially sold in the US – and especially in the sunshine states – that's no guarantee of a corrosion-free shell. These cars have been coming back to Blighty for over two decades, so a badly restored/rustproofed car that has been here for 20 years could well be rotten by now.

The sills and A-posts are the areas most commonly affected by tin worm; all panels are available to effect a decent repair, but the process is tricky so expect a specialist to charge at last £1750 per side. Wings are also usually corroded; replacements are available but because of the difficulty in attaining even panel gaps, you're better off repairing the lower portions of each rather than trying to replace wholesale.

In addition, the bottom of each door needs careful checking along with the boot floor; both are likely to be holed unless the car has been restored. The bonnet, boot-lid and doors all have aluminium panels over a steel frame, with a strip of wood thrown into the bonnet and boot-lid to prevent dents. Predictably, the wood rots and electrolytic corrosion between the metals is the norm, so things can get very messy and expensive.

It's not only corrosion that you need to look out for; accident damage is common. Because this can distort the body and chassis, and so wreck the handling, many MGAs out there don't drive as well as they should.

If a car has been crunched, chances are that the panel gaps will be all over the place. That's certainly the case if it hasn't been repaired using the correct jig; one seam that's just slightly out will invariably lead to another one being miles out. It's also worth looking at all the flanges and seams where the wings attach to the main bodyshell; any rippling here means the car has been shunted.

Although the chassis is impressively stiff, a hard knock will distort it. It's tricky (if not impossible) to put things right. The key areas to check are the front and rear chassis legs, the former running under the car from the engine bay.

The chassis on US imports may well be largely unaffected by corrosion, but genuine UK As may be completely rotten so you'll need to get underneath to have a good poke around. The key areas to check are the floorboard supports, as these are usually the first to corrode. The boards are wooden, so while you're under the car see if they're intact; rotten timber is common. Also take a look at the battery boxes, the crossmember behind the seats and the side rails below the A-post and inner sill.

If you're in any doubt as to where the car was originally sold, the first digit of the chassis number should tell all. A genuine RHD UK model will start with a 1, while export RHD markets begin with a 2. Completely knocked-down (CKD) RHD kits will have a 5 prefix. However, if it started out as left-hand drive, the first digit will be a 4 if it was initially supplied to the US. A 3 denotes another export LHD market, while a 6 says it was a CKD car.

Lucas electrics were fitted throughout, and all parts are available to revive even the most tired A; instruments, switchgear, lighting and looms can all be replaced. Not every A was sold with a heater, yet you can buy all the bits to fit one should you wish to, for around £400.

It's a similar story with the trim, both interior and exterior; you can replace any of it, but as with the electrics you need to make sure that this hasn't already been done with incorrect parts being fitted. It's quite common to find earlier or later seats, instruments or lights. Also bear in mind that although the repro parts are often very good, when it comes to brightwork the bits originally fitted to the car are usually more durable.

The bottom line is that it's almost always better trying to salvage original parts rather than simply replace with new, because the fit is often better. Hence retrimmed seats, rechromed bumpers and replated brightwork are often preferable to repop spares – although mazak components such as the windscreen grab handles and vents on the shroud are notoriously tricky to reclaim. You're usually better off buying these new.

Conclusion

Of the 101,082 MGAs built, fewer than 6000 were sold in the UK while over 80,000 were snapped up across the Atlantic. As a result, many of the cars now in the UK were originally bought in the US – but don't let their left-hand-drive nature stop you. Converting to right-hand drive is technically easy; all that's needed is a fresh dash, a new steering rack

and pedals; there's no need to hack the bodyshell or chassis about. The problem lies in sourcing the bits, as dashboards and right-hand-drive steering racks are very scarce; serviceable used racks are already changing hands for upwards of £700.

If originality is important to you there are all sorts of checks to make, because incorrect trim parts and non-original mechanical components are common. For example, MGB engines are often used as US specialists can source these more readily than the correct A units. MGB seats are also frequently installed, so if the car is supposedly complete check that all the parts are correct.

Be very wary about buying a restoration project; it'll cost a fortune to renovate professionally and will test your skills if you fancy doing it yourself. Key to remember, though, is that while originality can be hard to come by, good cars abound and all editions offer practical driving pleasure regardless of spec. Whether it's a 1500, 1600 or Twin Cam, all MGAs – if properly sorted – are agile, surprisingly perky and handle beautifully. You'll love it! △

» **Thanks to Bob West for his help with this article.**

£104.40

FOOTMAN JAMES
Insurance specialists. At your service.

1959 MGA 1600 Coupé
Value: £8000
Quote: **£104.40** (£50x/s unlimited mpa)

If only one model could be regarded as the epitome of the classic car, then surely the evergreen MGB would be amongst the front runners. With more than 500,000 examples built over a production run that lasted almost 20 years, the MGB is regarded by enthusiasts around the world as the definitive classic car.

Spawning a specialist supply, restoration and service industry the MGB has become an icon of the classic car boom years of the late Eighties. The clean lines of Syd Enever's design, mated to simple but effective vault-like mechanicals in a comfortable two-seater package have provided the MGB with an endearing quality which has not only stood the test of time, but also transcended the generations to attract admirers who appreciate MG's sports car for the common man.

Although a product of the Swinging Sixties, it was during the Thatcherite boom years that the B scaled new heights as a growing and increasingly affluent middle-aged and middle class market turned to the classic car scene to recapture their youth. And where better than the aspirational 'B roadster which was once unattainable, but now affordable in their bid for wind-in-the-hair motoring?

»

CHROME BUMPER MGBS

Driving the I, II and MkIII of MG's shining star. But which is best?

Words: Martyn Wise Photography: Paul Harmer

Encouraged by a growing band of wannabe owners, a whole industry appeared to spring up overnight to cater for the insatiable demand for a classic MGB. Rust-free examples were repatriated from the States in their droves, while rotten home-grown examples could be refettled with new bodyshells and panels made on the original presses. Suddenly immaculate MGBs restored to original as-new standards were changing hands at more than ten times the 1962 car's original £949 asking price.

The boom years couldn't last but, when the classic car bubble burst in the recession-hit early Nineties, the MGB fared better than most. If anything, the burgeoning prices had taken this humblest of roadsters once again beyond the reach of those to whom it had appealed and the enforced repositioning in the market place returned the sports car back to real devotees.

Today the MGB roadster continues to be the first choice for many looking to get on the classic car ladder. Restored examples abound and for all but the most committed DIY restorer, purchasing an original or renovated car is the most sensible and cost-effective route to ownership. Selection is also relatively easy. The shape and look of the MGB roadster remained almost unaltered during its 18-

'Few appreciate the subtle differences which separate the three (or some may argue four) variants spanning the chrome era'

year production run, save for the 'rubber bumper' model which was introduced in late 1974 in a nod towards US market safety requirements.

But while even the least informed buyer is aware of the simple choice between 'chrome' and 'rubber' MGBs, few appreciate the subtle differences which separate the three – or some may argue four – variants spanning the 'chrome' era from 1962-1974.

Introduced at the 1962 Earls Court Motor Show alongside the MG 1100 saloon, the MGB was well received by the motoring press of the day who appreciated the new, modern design afforded by the monocoque shell. Replacing the successful MGA was never going to be easy, but chief designer Syd Enever and his team proved successful in producing a combined package of looks, performance and handling which were right

for the space age Sixties just as its predecessor had been for the 'never-had-it-so-good' decade previously.

In an overall package which was shorter than the MGA, the B was far roomier inside the two-seater cockpit as well as offering greater luggage capacity. Construction was pretty well straightforward, with the Pressed Steel body/chassis structure giving the MGB its inherent strength. Following the conventional front-engine, rear-wheel-drive format, the flat floorpan rises over a central transmission tunnel which is joined to the front bulkhead with a box-section. A rear box-section runs across the car behind the seats, while side members run forwards to bear the engine and front suspension and rearwards over the rear axle to act as rear spring hangers. Front wings are then bolted on and rear wings welded, essentially leaving the outside bodywork unstressed.

Although the MGB carried over the live rear 'banjo' axle from the MGA which sits on semi-elliptic leaf springs, the front suspension was a direct descendent from the Y-type and TD with independent wishbones and coil springs mounted on a detachable subframe. With hydraulic lever arm dampers fitted both front and rear, the MGB afforded a softer suspension than the outgoing MGA.

'Few appreciate the subtle differences which separate the three spanning the chrome era'

Power came from the four-cylinder overhead-valve pushrod B-Series engine which had been gradually modified over the years and stretched to 1798cc. Producing 84bhp, this gave a 0-60mph time of around 12 seconds while the MGB went on to a top speed of more than 100mph.

Not scintillating figures by today's standards but more impressive if viewed over 40 years ago. On the road this translates into a pleasant driving experience with reasonable performance allied to predictable handling. Those looking to extract that bit more from their 'B are well catered for with a host of after-market products designed to improve both power and handling.

Today it is possible to completely change the heart of an MGB without affecting its aesthetic period look, but such changes are a matter of individual preference. And while enhanced performance may appeal to owners already familiar with the MGB package, first time buyers tend to be swayed more by originality.

For the earliest models – MkI MGBs manufactured

1962 to 1967 with chassis numbers beginning with GHN3 – that means the three-synchro gearbox and, with examples produced up to October 1964, the three-bearing engine. Other distinguishing features include, again on models up to October 1964, pull door handles and strap-on fuel tank. All MkI MGBs come with a wider gap between the front grille and sidelights when compared to later cars as well as a narrower transmission tunnel with a different shaped speaker housing.

The attractive fascia features the larger, three-spoke steering wheel with centre horn push, while externally MkI cars are not fitted with reversing lights and the rear tail lights feature 'curved' covers. Side quarter lights are also fully chromed as opposed to the stainless steel variants which followed.

MGBs manufactured between October 1967 and October 1969 which begin with a GHN4 prefix are regarded as MkII models. The major change is the introduction of the four-synchro gearbox and the

AUTOMATIC CHOICE?

At the time of our photo shoot we were fortunate that Nigel had acquired a 1969 model with the ultra-rare automatic option.

Many people would dismiss an automatic offhand as not being a proper sports car, but Nigel reckons this auto 'B is perhaps the finest driving example of any Roadster he's come across in almost 20 years trading.

After a brief test drive, it is easy to see why. The auto box was very smooth, just a slight tendency to snatch between first and second when attempting quick traffic light grand prix getaways. Once familiar, the auto makes for very smooth progress through the gears, hanging onto ratios to change up at optimum revs. For a nigh-on 40-year-old car the auto offered surprisingly good acceleration, pulling strongly and evenly in response to throttle input.

Ideal as a long distance tourer and perfect in urban driving, this particular example comes with originality that is hard to find thanks to its modest 27,616 recorded miles. The asking price of £9500 seemed reasonable for what is truly a unique car.

»

Below
MkI cars gained a five-bearing engine in October 1964, but never lost the three-synchro gearbox.

'It is possible to change the heart of an MGB without affecting its look, but such changes are a matter of individual preference'

Above and right
Wire wheels were always a popular option, but the auto gearbox was rarely selected.

SPOT THE DIFFERENCE

MGB MkI (GHN3)
Sept 1962 – Oct 1967
» 3-synchro gearbox
» 3-bearing engine (up to Oct 1964)
» Pull door handles (up to Oct 1964)
» Rear 'banjo' axle
» Narrow transmission tunnel
» Wider gap between front sidelights and grille
» No reversing lights
» Curved' rear tail-light lens covers
» Chrome quarter-lights
» Strap-on fuel tank (up to March 1965)

MGB MkII (GHN4)
Oct 1967 – Oct 1969
» 4-synchro gearbox
» Rear 'tubeless' Salisbury axle (NB – also available on some late production MkIs

» Pre-engaged starter motor
» Reversing lights fitted
» Reclining seats available on late cars

MGB MkIII (GHN5)
Oct 1969 – Sept 1974
» New recessed grille in black
» Smaller drilled, three-spoke steering wheel
» Revised dash/fascia air vents (from Oct 71)
» New vinyl reclining seats
» BL emblems on front wings
» Rubber inserts on chrome over-riders
» 'Straight' rear tail-light lens covers

Production changes from October 1972:
» New grille with chrome surround and centre bar together with black plastic 'Honeycomb' mesh
» Padded steering wheel (with three slatted spokes), centre console, door pulls and armrests

'The change must not have proved popular as the chrome grille reappeared, but with a black plastic insert'

tubeless Salisbury axle. An improved starter motor was also fitted and reversing lights added. Late MkII models also featured new black reclining seats, but without headrests.

MkIII models followed in October 1969 with GHN5 chassis numbers and changes to the cosmetics. A new, smaller, leather-bound drilled three-spoke steering wheel was introduced while leather seats were discontinued in favour of a vinyl pattern. Externally cars were offered with new 'Rostyle' wheels and the plastic rear tail light covers featured 'straight' edges. For 1971 model year cars, a new facia with face-level air vents and rocker switches was introduced, along with a new lift-up arm rest and brushed nylon

facings to the seat covering. The most striking changes though came with a revised grille. Up to late 1972, this featured a black recessed version which, it may have been felt, was complemented by the black rubber inserts on the front bumper overriders. However, the change must not have proved popular as the more traditional chrome grille re-appeared, although with a black plastic 'honeycomb' insert.

On the road there is little to choose between the three models although, as with any car which features non-synchromesh on first gear, the three-synchro examples need a little more care when changing down if the driver is to avoid the embarrassing 'crunch' at road junctions. Early

models also tend to feel they have a longer throw between gears which can sometimes delay quick changes until the gearbox is mastered.

Handling is in the true Safety Fast tradition, although sudden changes in direction and undulating roads which feature changes in camber are best taken at a more sedate speeds. The larger three-spoke steering wheel with its narrow rim is also not suited to an aggressive driving style and perhaps it should be remembered that whilst sporting cars in their day, these early examples of the MGB Roadster are best regarded as touring cars and 40-year-old models should be treated with a respect the marque's status has earned.

Below
British Racing Green remains one of the most popular colours (along with red) for chrome-bumper MGBs.

Above: Leather was standard on early cars, but piped covers are a popular mod for all models.

Above: Auto gearbox isn't the only rarity on this car: original leather seats are few and far between today.

Above: The MkIII saw a switch to vinyl seat facings with a knit-backed pattern in the centre panels.

Above: Upright rear lights conformed to BMC house style, and were shared with contemporary Midget.

Above: MkII kept the rounded style of lense, but gained a pair of reversing lights on the tail panel.

Above: Squarer tail light was introduced with the MkIII and lasted through rubber-bumper production.

Later MkII and MkIII models obviously benefit from the more familiar four-synchro gearbox which makes for less stressful changes, while mechanical modifications also make for less general maintenance. But which is the preferred choice for the would-be buyer? Top London dealer Nigel Guild of Former Glory has sold hundreds of MGB Roadsters during his 18 years in business, but he maintains there is no particular example that buyers gravitate to.

'Demand for chrome bumpers and tax exempt cars has always been high, but beyond that people do not really show much preference,' he said. 'People tend to come to us looking for a nice example not requiring any work other than general maintenance, not too interested whether it is a MkI, II or III model. Years ago everyone wanted Tartan Red or British Racing Green. These colours are still the best sellers, but they have been used on so many restorations that some buyers want something more individual.'

Having driven thousands of MGBs, what remains the dealer's choice when looking for a

'WHILE SPORTING CARS IN THEIR DAY, THE EARLIEST EXAMPLES OF THE MGB ROADSTER ARE NOW 40 YEARS OLD AND BEST REGARDED AS TOURING CARS'

classic MGB Roadster? 'I like the look of the very early MkI models but prefer the driveability from the early Seventies,' says Nigel.

It seems that if even one of the most experienced MGB devotees cannot make up his mind then, if you're in the market for a classic 'B Roadster, then the best advice is to consider all the options and enjoy your search for that perfect car.

» Our thanks to Nigel Guild at Former Glory for supplying the test cars featured. For further details Former Glory's stock MGB of Roadsters and GTs, contact 0208 991 1963 or visit www.former-glory.com.

BUYING TIPS

Inspect bodies, particularly sills, door bottoms and wing joints for rust, even on restored/Heritage shell cars. Replacement panels are reasonably priced, but the cost of professional fitting soon adds up. If originality is your thing, the British Motor Industry Heritage Trust at Gaydon can, for a modest fee, provide a build certificate detailing the car's chassis and engine numbers, colour, trim and any extras supplied at the time of purchase.

Cars being sold privately by club members are likely to have been looked after, especially if they have been owned for a number of years. But some private sellers overestimate the value of their cars, especially if they were expensive rebuilds of a few years ago. Many dealers have a better understanding of today's market value and give the benefit of a warranty and other statutory purchase rights. Expect to pay between £5000 and £10,000, or up to £13,000 in exceptional cases.

MGB (1962-1980)

The archetypcal classic sports car, and for very good reason

Words: Richard Dredge Photography: www.magiccarpics.co.uk

Above
Chrome-bumper is most elegant; rubber-bumper cheapest, and stands taller.

The A was such a success for MG that it had to be replaced with something that was a genuine step forward. Something that was easier to live with, easier to drive and cheaper to build. And that's just what happened, which means that when it comes to buying a practical and affordable classic, the MGB is right there at the top of the list. With unrivalled club and specialist support, masses of good examples to choose from and a choice of open or ultra-practical hatch, the B makes sense on many levels.

You don't have to spend a fortune to buy a good one. The cheapest B you'll buy is a rubber-bumpered GT. A runner will cost you less than £1000 but it will need work to keep it going. A running rubber-bumpered roadster will set you back around £2000 while an equivalent chrome-bumpered GT is £1000 more.

The most valuable – and desirable – B is a chrome-bumpered roadster. Top price for one of these that's just been built around a Heritage shell is £13,000. Factory V8s start at £4500 for usable examples, with little difference between chrome or rubber-bumper cars.

Engine

Apart from the V8-engined cars, all MGBs were fitted with the same 1798cc B-series engine, although there were some developments along the way such as the switch to five main bearings in October 1964. That means parts interchangeability is good and thanks to its bulletproof design and build, the B-series will happily cover 130,000 miles between rebuilds.

MGB engines aren't normally all that quiet, with some tappet noise evident

even when set up properly. With the engine warm at tickover there should be 15-25psi oil pressure and at 3000rpm this should rise to 50-65psi. Anything less means the crankshaft or its bearings or both are worn – which means an engine rebuild – or the oil pump is on its way out.

Although you probably won't get the chance to check oil consumption, if a lot is being consumed it may be because the crankcase breather pipes are blocked, causing oil to be sucked into the cylinders. Also bear in mind that the plastic oil filler cap is a consumable item that needs to be replaced every 12,000 miles as it contains the breather for the crankcase. Other reasons for high oil consumption include the valve guides and stem seals being worn. Check for a puff of smoke when you apply the

'When it comes to buying a practical and affordable classic, the MGB is right up there at the top of the list'

throttle after the over-run – if you see one it's time for a rebuilt cylinder head. If the engine isn't burning the lubricant, it's probably leaking it. First places to check are the front and rear crankshaft seals, and replacing the latter means removing the engine first. Also look at the tappet chest side covers which live behind the exhaust manifold.

If the engine misfires it could be because the heater valve, positioned directly over the distributor, is leaking. The only cure is to fit a new valve, but much worse, the misfiring could be because the cast iron cylinder head has cracked between the spark plugs, allowing coolant to leak out. But as points and timing settings go out of tune very easily it could be that these just need to be reset.

Just 2591 examples of the GT V8 were built (there were no factory roadsters), and because the engine is in a low state of tune (there's just 137bhp on tap) it should keep going forever. That's as long as the oil has been changed regularly, along with the coolant. The former is essential if the camshaft isn't to wear prematurely while the latter is needed to prevent the engine corroding internally, leading to blocked up coolant passages.

Transmission

There were three different transmissions fitted to the 1.8-litre B. Rarest of the lot is the three-speed automatic; just 1737 were made, and few survive. That leaves the manual transmissions, in either three-synchro or four-synchro flavours. Because these generally last around the same mileage as the engine, the two rebuilds are often done together.

Swapping from one manual 'box to another isn't possible without also swapping the flywheel, backplate and starter motor. As doing this in turn requires bodywork mods it's not something that can be done easily so don't let the vendor tell you it's an hour's work if you want to go from a three-syncro to an all-syncro gearbox.

Don't be surprised if a three-syncro gearbox is noisy in first and reverse, as they all are. It's something that most owners live with until the gearbox is rebuilt, which is usually done because the synchromesh has started to give up.

Clutch problems are common, usually centred around the carbon release bearing breaking up. If the clutch is ridden in traffic, 3000 miles is all a bearing might manage, but it's now possible to buy an uprated unit. So if

Above
Always twin SUs, whether 'four' or V8. Structure revived later for RV8.

»

'With thousands of MGBs still on the roads, the car for you is out there'

**MGB
Roadster**
SPECIFICATIONS

Engine
1798cc in-line four, 8
overhead valves. Cast-
iron head and block. Two
SU HS4 carburettors

Power
95bhp @ 5400rpm

Torque
100lb ft @ 3000rpm

Transmission
Four-speed manual

Suspension
Front: Independent with
coil springs, double
wishbones, lever arm
dampers
Rear: Live axle with half-
elliptic leaf springs, lever
arm dampers

Brakes
Front: 273mm discs
Rear: 254mm drums
Servo-assisted

Weight
965kg (2128lb)

Performance
0-60mph 12.9sec
Top speed 103mph

Value
Cost £847 new (1967)
Value now £3000-£13,000

there's vibration through the pedal and a screeching noise, start looking for £350 to fix it. Also make sure the pedal isn't spongy. If it is, the hydraulics are on their way out and you'll have to spend £85 on new master and slave cylinders – don't be tempted to just replace the seals as it's a false economy.

There are few chrome-bumpered Bs that don't have overdrive, and it was fitted as standard to the rubber-bumper cars. It doesn't usually give problems although the electrics can play up and the oil level can fall below the minimum, both of which will stop it working. Similarly, if the oil is allowed to become choked with swarf because the oil filter which lives inside the housing hasn't been cleaned out every 30,000 miles or so, the overdrive will stop engaging. If you're looking at a car without overdrive, don't let the vendor tell you that it's easy to just bolt an overdrive unit onto the back of the existing gearbox.

If there's any vibration coming from the driveline when you take the car for a test drive it's probably because one or both of the propshaft U/Js has worn. Replacement is easy, and you don't need to pay more than £60 for a reconditioned propshaft.

Suspension, steering and brakes

The MGB's simple suspension doesn't generally give problems, except for the kingpins wearing. Unless they're greased every 3000 miles they'll wear, so make sure they're in good order. Jack up the front of the car and try rocking the wheel at the top and bottom while somebody applies the footbrake. If there's any movement detectable, the kingpins will need replacing at £45 each plus fitting, which normally takes a couple of hours for each side.

The front wishbone bushes also perish and collapse, but a visual check is all that's needed to see what state they're in. Fit V8 items if new ones are due, at £1.50 each (£6 a set), and reckon on up to three hours per side to fit them.

You'll need to drive the car before buying, and if it seems that there's rear wheel steering it'll be because the U-bolts and rubber bushes which locate the rear axle have come loose or corroded. But it's cheap to fix with the kit of parts costing just £15.

Lever arm dampers were fitted front and rear, and they're are notorious for leaking. If you're not worried about originality it's

possible to swap to telescopics, but the ride will be harder. To really sharpen up the handling it's worth fitting uprated front and rear anti-roll bars, which will transform the car's dynamics for just £100 or so. Make sure all the rear tyre is visible – if it disappears under the wheelarch the springs need replacing at £35 per side plus a couple of hours each side to do the job.

Servo-assisted brakes were fitted from 1973. If you're inspecting an assisted car but it feels like there's no assistance, it's because the seals have gone, allowing the brake fluid to be sucked into the engine and burned. If the original master cylinder is fitted it'll need doing before long – check its external condition to gauge what state it's in internally or look at the brake pedal to see if there's fluid leaking down it. Getting the servo rebuilt isn't really worthwhile, so count on paying £150 for a new unit.

The original Rostyle or pressed steel wheels are often swapped for wire units and although there aren't generally clearance problems, spokes can break on wires. These wheels can go out of balance very quickly so if they're on the car you're inspecting, make sure that all the spokes are in good shape

and that the splines aren't worn by jacking up the car and trying to turn the wheel backwards and forwards. It helps if somebody can hold the footbrake on for you, which will make any wear in the splines obvious.

Bodywork, electrics and trim

The B's monocoque bodyshell can be seriously weakened by rust; there are plenty of places where you're likely to find rot, and the chances of bodged repairs having been carried out are high. But if the worst happens and the 'shell really is beyond economical repair you can buy a Heritage bodyshell into which you can transplant the car's major organs. But bear in mind that although a Heritage shell is only £5-6000, you'll also have to fork out for paint and if you're going to do the job properly you'll also buy new brakes, steering, suspension, electrics and trim for the interior and exterior. Before you know it that's another £6000+. But with decent metal and the chance to rustproof the car from new with modern chemicals at least you can put together a car which will in theory last indefinitely.

The Heritage shell is a mix of the different panels used throughout 18 years of MGB production – so it will always vary (if only in detail) from whichever car you're rebuilding. Also remember that early cars built around new Heritage shells weren't that accurately made – even now, panels have to be fettled to get the best results. So that leaves another option, which is the Californian import shell. Converting from left-hand drive isn't difficult and, although the shells won't be totally rust-free, they will be original.

The most common rot spots are the multi-panelled complex sill structures, which are prime fodder for bodge merchants. That's because for the best results the front and rear wings need to be cut off below the trim strip. The alternative is to unbolt the front wings, rather than cut the lower portion, but on a roadster you have to take off the windscreen surround too.

Because the sills can be tricky to repair properly, there are various bodges. The first is to fit a cover sill, which just hides the problem. The second is the stainless steel over-sill, which looks very pretty – but also masks potential big problems. These over-sills are often used legitimately as well, so don't assume the car's a bad one just because they're fitted. The final bodge is for the outer sill to be repaired with the metal underneath left to dissolve. To be certain you're not buying a pup take a look from underneath and see that everything lines up properly.

Next check the back of the front inner wheelarches, by first removing the front wheels. This will allow you to see if the box section that's positioned at the top is still there – it collects mud and rots away if it isn't cleaned regularly, and repairing it is very tricky. Also check the general condition of the wheelarches, especially the rear of both the front and rear panels, which are especially vulnerable. Be wary of plastic wheelarch liners, which may hide rot – but if the car looks cherished they're probably there for all the right reasons. If the car has had new front wings and it's got chrome bumpers, make sure the wings are of the same pattern – in November 1968 the sidelights were moved, and you could end up buying a car with odd wings, although it's not especially noticeable.

While you're checking the rear wheelarches take a »

»Info

TIMELINE

» 1962: MGB debuts at the British Motor Show in Tourer (roadster) form only, at £949. The suspension is based on the MGA's.
» 1964: A five-bearing engine replaces the three-bearing unit previously fitted.
» 1965: GT arrives; a stylish hatch that's a true mini Grand Tourer.
» 1967: MkII MGB arrives, with an all-synchro gearbox, negative earth electrics and an alternator. There's also an automatic gearbox option and the MGC is also launched.
» 1973: MGB GT V8 debuts, using the classic Buick-derived Rover V8. There's no drop-top option but the model is obsolete by August 1976.
» 1974: Rubber bumpers replace chrome; the new car is more usable and far more comfortable in everyday use with greater refinement, but the raised ride height doesn't help handling.
» 1980: The last MGB is put together on 22 October, the last 1000 cars being special edition LE models.

SPECIALISTS

» Brown & Gammons, Herts. 01462 490049, http://bg.mgcars.org.uk
» Frontline Costello, Bath, 01225 852777, www.frontlinedevelopments.com
» Fisher Services, London, 020 8776 7695, www.fisher-services.co.uk
» Moss Europe. 0800 281 182, www.moss-europe.co.uk
» MGOC workshop, Cambs. 01954 230928, www.mgownersclub.co.uk
» Moss Europe. 0800 281 182, www.moss-europe.co.uk
» The MG Centre, Worcs. 01886 853007, www.mgcentre.co.uk
» Former Glory, West London. 020 8991 1963, www.mgcars.org.uk/formerglory
» MGB Hive, Cambs. 01945 700500, www.mgbhive.co.uk
» Welsh MG Centre, Wrexham. 01978 263445, www.welshmg.co.uk
» MG Motorsport, Herts. 01442 832019, www.mgmotorsports.com
» Midland Sports & Classics, 01905 621331, www.mgpartsuk.co.uk
» SC Parts, several branches, UK and Europe, 01293 847200 www.scparts.co.uk

Above and below
GT arrived in 1965; early interiors looked antique but progressively modernised.

look at the spring hangers, which might be rotten. Next to the offside hanger is the battery tray (chrome-bumper cars have one each side), which is easily overlooked. Make sure it's intact by checking from underneath and also make sure the floorpans are in good order – the original underseal doesn't do a very good job due to cracking and peeling off.

The top of the fuel tank is corrugated for strength, so water collects between the top of the tank and the underside of the boot floor, where it's attached. So if you can smell fuel assume the tank has perforated and needs replacing, at around £50 plus fitting. Roadster and GT fuel tanks are interchangeable.

If you're looking at a GT, make sure that the double-skinned tailgate isn't rotten and, whether drop-top or fixed head, check the scuttle where it meets the base of the windscreen. If it's rusty here it'll mean taking the windscreen surround off (on a roadster) to fix properly. The final bodywork part to check is the bottom of each door. Although door skins are available cheaply for £20 it's normally more cost-effective to buy a whole new door at £160 because getting the new skin to fit properly is so involved.

All the trim is available, but if it all needs replacing the cost adds up quickly. A new hood plus fitting will set you back £120 upwards depending on material. A set of new seat covers costs £200 for leather or £120 for vinyl, and carpet sets costs anywhere between £50 and £150. Similarly the exterior trim is all available, although new windscreen surrounds aren't – but it is possible to buy reconditioned units on an exchange basis at £260.

Up to 1974 a pair of six-volt batteries was fitted – after this date a 12-volt unit was installed. There can be earthing glitches because of poor connections between the earthing strap and the body. The battery tray is located behind the front seats so you'll have to take the cover(s) off to check. Twin-6v cars suffer from duff batteries if the car isn't used regularly, as they drain each other.

Conclusion

With thousands of MGBs still on the roads, the car for you is out there. Early cars aren't that easy to live with on a daily basis, but running costs are low, parts are easily available and specialists are easy to come by. Not only that, but you'll also have access to one of the best car clubs going.

Even though the B has been out of production for over two decades, the network of specialists that look after them has continued to grow. So where the B previously had a few downsides, such as handling that wasn't too sharp, just about everything has been solved now thanks to a raft of affordable upgrades that have been developed.

£86.55

FOOTMAN JAMES
Insurance specialists. At your service.

1970 MGB/C Roadster
Value: £5000
Quote: **£86.55** (£50x/s unlimited mpa)

»Info

CLUBS
» MG Car Club. 01235 555552, www.bmh-ltd.com/directory.htm
» MG Owners' Club, 01954 231125, www.mgcars.org.uk

BOOKS
» MGB, Jonathan Wood & Lionel Burrell. Haynes: ISBN 0-85429-948-3
» Original MGB, MGC and GT V8, Anders Clausager. Bay View: ISBN 1-87097-948-6
» MGB & MGC, Jonathan Edwards. Crowood, ISBN 000-1-86126-469-0
» MGA, MGB & MGC Collectors Guide, Graham Robson. MRP, ISBN 000-1-899870-43-1
» MGB, MGC & V8 Gold Portfolio 1962-1980, Brooklands Books. ISBN 000-1-85520-071-6
» MGB, MGC & MGB V8, David Knowles. (Haynes), ISBN 000-1-85960-958-9
» How To Improve MGB, MGC & MGB V8, Roger Williams. Veloce, ISBN 000-1-901295-76-1

MGC (1967-1969)

An MGB with extra power? Sounds perfect but the C wasn't a sales success – but it makes a great classic sports car!

Words: Richard Dredge Photography: www.magiccarpics.co.uk

A six-cylinder development of the MGB, the MGC was built for a mere two years, with all of 9002 examples being produced. Last year marked the 40th anniversary of the model reaching the marketplace, but it's one of the most frequently forgotten – and under-rated – classics around. If you like your Bs rare and faster than usual, and with the smoothness of six cylinders, this could be the derivative for you, especially as you can buy it in GT or roadster forms.

Substituting the MGB's B-series engine for the 2912cc straight-six of the C meant much more than merely removing one and fitting the other. The unit was taller than ideal, so a revised bonnet line was needed. The floorpans forward of the car's centre also had to be redesigned, because the B's beefy crossmember had to be swapped for a smaller, less sturdy item, to provide clearance. As a result, the front suspension also had to be changed, so the loads could be fed into the car's structure in a different area; the development team settled on longitudinal torsion bars, running back to a central crossmember.

As the floorpans were being redesigned, the opportunity was taken to widen them so an automatic transmission could be accommodated. At the same time, the radiator was moved forward eight inches, as well as being increased in size. Because of the extra weight over the front wheels, a less direct steering rack was fitted, offering 3.5 turns between locks instead of the B's 2.9. To finish things off dynamically, the wheels grew an inch in diameter to become 15 inches across and half an inch wider.

The C was launched in both roadster and GT forms in October 1967, but it was greeted with little in the way of enthusiasm by the motoring press. It was dynamically disappointing, with stodgy handling, lifeless steering and strong understeer, largely down to an error in tyre choice and tyre pressures. Despite the roadster's competitive price of £1102 in 1967, buyers stayed away. They preferred to spend an extra £24 on an Austin-Healey 3000, so it was no surprise that after two years of trying to find buyers, MG gave up with the C; the final cars were produced in August 1969. With large stocks of unsold cars to shift, it made more sense to admit defeat – some cars hung around in showrooms until early 1971.

Predictably, the roadster is worth

'If you like your Bs rare and faster than usual, and with the smoothness of six cylinders, this could be the derivative for you'

significantly more than a GT, and it carries a hefty premium. While a project GT that's complete can be bought for £1000 or so, an equivalent roadster is more like £1500. Similarly, a decent GT is £3750 while a roadster is closer to £5500. Valuing the best cars is tricky; superb open-topped Cs are officially worth around £7000 with open-topped editions £9500. However, truly superb roadsters with sympathetic upgrades have been known to change hands for over £15,000 – which just proves that the C is appreciated in some quarters.

Because the C is so closely related to the B, most of the B's weak spots also relate to the C. So, unless mentioned here, assume you need to make all the same checks with a C as you would for a B (pages 122-126); the key differences are in the engine and transmission.

Engine and transmission

Although the C's engine is based on the Austin 3-Litre unit, they're not the same as the valves, springs and sump are unique to the C. However, the main structure of the engine is identical and it's generally a long-lived unit; even once it's started to wear the powerplant will keep on going, getting ever noisier and smoking increasingly.

The biggest weak spot is the piston rings, which can wear quickly. It's easy enough to spot though, as oil being burned is the symptom; just look for blue smoke from the exhaust when you accelerate through the gears. Once this occurs you're going to have to undertake a bottom-end rebuild, but parts are available and it's nothing to be frightened of. It's a similar story where the top end is concerned, as rocker

shafts also have a habit of wearing badly. That's why you need to listen out for a really clattery top end; don't assume it's just a question of the valves needing adjustment. If a new rocker shaft is needed, a replacements is just £35 and it's easy to do the work yourself.

It's the gearbox that's the C's weakest spot, thanks to the engine's torque. The first thing to go is usually the layshaft bearings, resulting in the shaft dropping and putting pressure on the cogs. If things have started to go awry, it'll be obvious from the whining on the test drive; worn gears will be noisy even if the bearings and alignment is corrected. Instead of getting the box rebuilt, it makes more sense to fit a five-speed conversion, offering lower transmission losses (so economy is improved), better ratios, quieter operation and the ability

»

Above
Looks like an MGB? Only the bonnet bulge gives it away to the average onlooker but performance is very different...

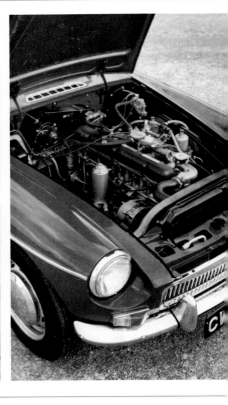

MGC Roadster
SPECIFICATIONS

Engine
2912cc in-line six, 12 overhead valves. Cast-iron head and block. Two SU HS6 carburettors

Power
150bhp @ 5250rpm

Torque
174lb ft @ 3500rpm

Transmission
Four-speed manual

Suspension
Front: Independent with torsion bars, telescopic dampers, anti-roll bar
Rear: Live axle with half-elliptic leaf springs, lever arm dampers

Brakes
Front: 279mm discs
Rear: 229mm drums
Servo-assisted

Weight
1109kg (2445lb)

Performance
0-60mph 10.0sec
Top speed 120mph

Value
Cost £1101 new (1967)
Value now £5000-£11,000

to perform a faster clutch change.

Gearbox ratios varied during production, with early non-overdrive cars having the same spec as the B. Cars with overdrive featured a close-ratio gearbox, but part-way through production all cars were fitted with this unit. The change was introduced for the 1969 model year at chassis number 4266 for Roadster and 4236 for GT in November 1968.

Differential ratios also varied, and while the back axle looks the same as the B's, the internals are different. Non-overdrive cars featured a 3.07:1 ratio, with overdrive and automatic examples having a 3.3:1 unit. However, during production (from the same chassis number as the gearbox change above), this was changed so autos and non-overdrive cars got the 3.3 unit while C's with overdrive got a 3.7:1 unit.

Vibration from the driveline signifies one or both of the propshaft universal joints has worn; considerable gearstick movement suggests worn or broken gearbox and/or engine mountings. Replacing propshaft joints is easy, and you don't need to pay more than £60 for a reconditioned propshaft. Engine and gearbox mountings are fiddly but straightforward.

Bodywork and running gear

The C's monocoque is just as susceptible to corrosion as the B's, but whereas Heritage supplies replacement bodyshells for the latter, there are none available for the C. However, all exterior panels except the bonnet are shared with the MGB, as are the sill and floor structures. The fuel tank is also rot-prone for the same reason as the B's; once again, Roadster and GT fuel

tanks are interchangeable and are the same as chrome-bumper MGB units.

If you're looking at a GT, make sure the double-skinned tailgate isn't rotten and analyse the scuttle where it meets the base of the windscreen. If it's rusty here it'll mean taking the windscreen surround off (on a roadster) to fix it properly. The final bodywork part to check is the bottom of each door. Although door skins are available for £20, it's normally more cost-effective to buy a whole new door at £160 because getting the new skin to fit properly is so involved. MGC doors are the same as post-1968 MGB items.

All MGCs had a servo, two on some North American models with dual-circuit brakes. If it feels like there's no brake assistance, it's because there will be damage to the main diaphragm in the servo, not allowing the intended pressure variations that gives the assistance. This is often accompanied by a 'hiss' air leak and often the engine is less smooth because the air leak upsets mixture. There's also the same potential problem as the B's servos; that of the seals going. Once again, a rebuild isn't worthwhile so bank of spending around £250 for a new unit.

MGC buyers had the choice of pressed steel or wire wheels when the cars were new. You need to make all the same checks as if you were buying an MGC, but assume that if the wheels are in poor condition, reconditioning is usually uneconomic as new wheels are cheaper. However, bear in mind that there are no supplies of pressed steel wheels, so if the original steel wheels are beyond reconditioning, the only viable option is conversion to alloys or wires.

Above
GT or Roadster, the MGC offers better performance and cruising ability over an MGB.

From the publishers of Octane magazine

SIGN UP FREE TO
iGIZMO

NEW!

Turned on to technology

iGIZMO

MODERN CLASSIC...
NINTENDO 64

TESTED...
NIKON D60

EXCLUSIVE REVIEW
HTC Shift
Part mobile, part laptop
But does it live up to the hype?

HDTV • Mobile • Gaming • Sat-Nav • Movies • Gadgets

iGIZMO is the **WORLD'S FIRST fully interactive digital magazine,** dedicated to bringing you the very latest and best in consumer technology, straight to your inbox - **FREE every fortnight**

WIN ALL THIS WORTH £4,500!

52IN
LCD TV

TOSHIBA
Leading Innovation ›

PLUS YOUR CHANCE TO **WIN** A FANTASTIC TECHNOLOGY PRIZE BUNDLE **WORTH £4,500!**

WATCH
PRODUCT REVIEWS
Straight-talking video reviews of the products that matter.

SEE
PRODUCTS IN ACTION
The latest in consumer tech is brought to life in this great interactive format.

DISCOVER
THE NEXT BIG THING
Find out about the next must-have products long before they hit the shops.

PLAY
360º PHOTOGRAPHY
Stunning 360º shots allows you to virtually touch the latest in consumer tech.

IT'S FREE FOREVER, SIGN UP AT
WWW.iGIZMO.CO.UK

(1954-2004)
MORGAN 4/4, PLUS 4 AND PLUS 8

No other sportscar has such a distinctive character as a Morgan, whether it's the four-cylinder Plus 4 or the V8-powered Plus 8. They're fun, fast and reliable, and a good one will hold its value like few other vehicles

Words: Richard Dredge Photography: www.magiccarpics.co.uk

Who could have foreseen that when the cowled-radiator Morgan 4/4 was first seen more than half a century ago, it would still be in production now? Yet while it looks as though there has been no evolution along the way, there are masses of differences between the first and the latest cars. What hasn't changed is the handbuilt nature of the car, along with the charm – and, of course, the great driving experience. Strap yourself into any Morgan and you're instantly transported to a bygone era, where traffic calming and speed cameras were just a distant nightmare.

The original Morgan 4/4 was launched in 1936, complete with a flat radiator, but it's the classic shape that we'll deal with here, which was first

seen in 1955. Retrospectively named the Series II, this was the first of the classically shaped Morgans, with a cowled front end. While things remained the same on the outside, there were no fewer than five different Series of 4/4 between 1955 and 1968 – with another five variants on offer over the following quarter of a century. These all featured different powerplants and transmissions and there were numerous detail developments along the way. But the basic construction has never changed – and it's the same for the Plus 4 and Plus 8.

As well as the two-seater cars, there were four-seater versions of the four-cylinder models also available. Although these account for only around 10 per

cent of production, they're not that rare that you can't track them down. So there's no need to hog the fun when you buy a Morgan – the whole family can enjoy it, too.

If you want a Plus 8, however, you'll have to settle for a two-seater only – but that's not much of a sacrifice to make for this hot rod. If you were asked to name the fastest-accelerating cars ever built, it's unlikely you'd think of this ancient-looking roadster from Malvern. Yet there was a time when the Plus 8 could slaughter far more expensive, sleek and glamorous machinery on the drag strip. Capable of sprinting from a standing start to 60mph in just 6.7 seconds (later cut to 6.1), the Plus 8 offers exhilaration like few other cars. It's a great model to

'Although there are very few early cowled-radiator Morgans around, they're still worth less than their newer counterparts because the more recent cars are so much more usable'

own too; like its four-cylinder siblings, parts availability is generally good and it's pretty much impossible to lose money on a Morgan, as long as it's looked after.

However, while the cars are great to own, buying can be fraught with problems. Fail to spot structural rot, or assume that corrosion is a mere cosmetic affectation, and you could end up paying over the odds for an example that needs a complete rebuild.

CVH-engined 4/4s are the most valuable as they're the newest and most usable. Most pre-CVH cars have been exported, and restoration projects of any type are rare. For a tatty complete project you'll pay £5000, with a good car worth double that or even slightly more. The nicest examples are closer to £18,000, with a fuel-injected CVH 4/4 fetching up to £20,000.

After 31 years with the marque, Melvyn Rutter has a pretty good insight into all things Morgan. He comments: "The market is currently exceptionally strong for all Morgans, although I'm not sure why. The cars are always in demand, of course, but right now there are some models that are in really short supply. The chief one is the early Plus 8 with the Moss gearbox; those get snapped up as soon as they come onto the market, usually by people who want to take part in historic motorsport. You'd be lucky to

find one for less than £25,000, which is a lot of cash when you think that a decent example of the later 3.5-litre Plus 8 can be worth as little as £16,000. However, newer Plus 8s with 3.9 or 4.6-litre engines can be rather more valuable, with such cars changing hands at up to £35,000.

"Popularity isn't skewed one way or the other in terms of four and eight-cylinder models, but unsurprisingly, the Plus 4 is worth rather less than an equivalent Plus 8. The classic Plus 4s, with TR engines, are typically worth £12-£16,000 for a decent example, but Rover-engined cars are more like £15-23,000. That's entirely predictable, because the latter cars are so much newer, but it raises an interesting aspect.

"Although there are very few early cowled-radiator Morgans around, they're still worth less than their newer counterparts because the more recent cars are so much more usable. Buyers perceive the earlier Morgans as unreliable and impractical – so they'll pay good money for a newer example in which they can take occasional long trips to really enjoy the car."

Engine
Series II 4/4s were equipped with an 1172cc Ford 100E engine, which typically lasts no more than 50,000 miles between

rebuilds. Because it's fitted with whitemetal bearings, rebuild costs are high, and while it's possible to convert to shell-type bearings to reduce renovation costs, the distance between those rebuilds won't be altered. Rings are prone to wear (and even breakage) because of the engine's long stroke, so you should look out for oil smoke and listen for 'tinkling' as you accelerate up through the gears.

The Ford 105E Anglia engine was fitted to Series III 4/4s. This 997cc unit is very simple, with no inherent faults as such. But you'll still need to check for the usual sign of wear – blue smoke from the exhaust under acceleration. It was Ford's Classic 109E that donated its three-bearing 1340cc powerplant to the Series IV, and it's a weak unit that suffers from various maladies such as worn bearings, piston slap and broken piston rings. So listen for rumbling or knocking from the bottom end, along with, yes, tinkling under acceleration.

All these early cars are very scarce in the UK now, so it's Kent and CVH-engined examples you're likely to find. The Kent motor will be familiar to many classic enthusiasts, and it was this unit that powered the 4/4 1600. The most likely ailment here is worn camshaft and followers, given away by a clacking sound from the top of the engine.

Above
In 2004, Plus 4 was revived after a four-year break, using Ford 2-litre Duratec engine offering 145bhp.

'Many
Morgans
have wire
wheels
fitted, so
check for
worn
splines and
broken
spokes'

Once supplies of the Ford engine had dried up in 1981, Morgan turned to Fiat to power the 4/4, with a 1600 unit. Only 93 such cars were produced and they're very rare in the UK. After these, the XR3 donated its CVH motor to the 4/4 1600, the most common malady being worn valve guides. Oil being burned is the result, so look for blue smoke under acceleration as you go through the gears. The CVH unit survived until 1993 (with fuel injection from 1991), when the 1.8-litre Zetec engine superseded it.

The first-generation Plus 4 (1954-1968) featured Standard/Triumph powerplants, spares for which are readily obtainable. There are no inherent weaknesses to watch out for, with the units being notoriously strong; just make the usual checks for overheating and general wear such as rumbling bottom ends, noisy valve gear or heavy oil consumption.

The second-generation Plus 4 (1985-2000) featured Rover engines, which don't generally give problems. However, it's worth swapping the cam belt straight away, unless you know it's been done recently.

As long as anti-freeze concentrations have been maintained and the oil has been changed every 5000 miles, the Plus 8's Rover V8 is reliable. The unit is so

unstressed that 250,000 miles can be despatched with ease; just check it's been maintained properly. However, if the motor has been neglected, or it's covered an inter-galactic mileage, it will have worn – and that's bad news if you're keen to retain originality. While slotting a different powerplant in is easy enough, parts to keep some Plus 8s standard are getting hard to find – especially those built up to 1976.

Transmission

Thanks to Morgans being so light, their transmissions are reliable as long as the cars aren't thrashed. The problem is that these cars are frequently driven very hard, and once wear does occur, repairs can be costly. The difficulty sometimes is poor parts supply; it's four-speed Plus 8s that are affected the worst, but the Plus 4 isn't immune. Where parts are available, they can be extremely pricey – especially in the case of the Moss box.

As you'd expect with a car fitted with a Ford engine, the 4/4's transmission also hails from the Blue Oval. That's apart from the few Fiat-engined cars built, which featured the Italian company's five-speed manual. The Series II featured a three-ratio box, while the Series III and IV had an extra ratio. None

of these gearboxes had synchromesh on first gear – that had to wait until the Series V appeared in 1963.

The Ford boxes are incredibly tough, with replacements never being needed – they literally seem to go on forever. Propshafts are equally long-lived, but you have to make sure the differential isn't on its last legs. A Salisbury differential was fitted to Series II to V cars, and parts for this are now unobtainable. If it's whining horrifically it'll need to be replaced with a new unit from BTR, as fitted to the current 4/4.

Such a swap costs over £2000 because other bits (such as the propshaft) need to be replaced in the process. Although the rear axles are strong, they tend to leak oil. Unless the level is topped up regularly, the unit will run dry and wreck the crown wheel and pinion in the process. The diff's lifespan will have been increased if its oil has been renewed every 10,000 miles.

On a Plus 8, do all the obvious checks such as listening for rumbling from the gearbox, ensuring it doesn't jump out of gear and making sure the synchromesh hasn't gone – although there isn't any first-gear synchro on the Plus 8 Moss box. It's the same with the rear axle; make sure it's not whining or leaking oil.

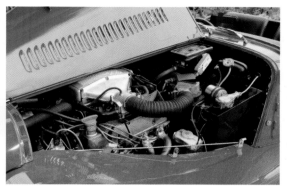

'Buy a corker and for exhilaration per pound it's hard to beat the Malvern wonder'

»Info

SPECIALISTS
» Allon White, Beds. +44 (0)870 112 0872, www.allonwhite.co.uk
» Berrybrook, Devon. +44 (0)1392 833 301, www.berrybrookmorgan.co.uk
» Brands Hatch Morgans, Kent. +44 (0)1732 882 017, www.morgan-cars.com
» Harper's, Herts. +44 (0)1923 260 299, www.harpers-morgan.com
» Heart of England Morgans, Worcs. +44 (0)1299 250 141, www.heartofenglandmorgans.co.uk
» Melvyn Rutter, Herts. +44 (0)1279 725 725, www.melvyn-rutter.co.uk
» Richard Thorne, Berks. +44 (0)118 983 1200, www.rtcc.co.uk
» Steve Simmonds (trimming), Worcs. +44 (0)1684 541 888, www.simmonds.uk.com
» Thomson & Potter, Perthshire. +44 (0)1828 670 247, www.morgansinscotland.co.uk
» Vintage Sheetmetal, Worcs. +44 (0)1684 540 677, www.morganspecialist.com

CLUBS
» Morgan Sports Car Club, www.mscc.uk.com
» For a full list of Morgan clubs worldwide, click on the links section of the MSCC's website

BOOKS
» Original Morgan 4/4, Plus 4 and Plus 8 by John Worrall. MBI: ISBN 0-7603-1644-9
» Morgans to 1997 by Roger Bell. MRP: ISBN 000-1-899870-78-4
» Morgan – The Cars And The Factory by John Tipler. Crowood: ISBN 1-85223-750-3 (out of print)
» Morgan Four-Wheelers From 1968 by Ken Hill. Veloce: ISBN 1-874105-34-0 (out of print)

All these cars featured a Salisbury back axle, with limited slip in the case of the Plus 8. Parts are hard to find, but specialists can rebuild your existing unit for you – at a price. However, only seals, bearings and gaskets are available; if a new crown wheel and pinion or any gears are needed, you'll need to convert to a BTR axle, at around £2500.

Suspension, steering and brakes
Expect play in the steering, but more than a couple of inches at the steering wheel means it's time to get the wallet out. Until 1984, all Morgans featured a Burman-made worm-and-peg steering box, using old-fashioned technology, so it's somewhat imprecise. Tyres getting progressively wider put increasing strain on the steering gear, causing it to wear ever quicker.

Post-1984 Plus 4s featured a Gemmer steering box, which can be fitted as a direct replacement for the earlier box – budget on £620 to buy one. This is lighter in use and also has better self-centring – it's also got a longer lifespan. From 1984 the Plus 8 featured rack-and-pinion steering, which is usually trouble-free, aside from the gaiters splitting – but they're an easy and cheap fix.

Really heavy steering points to worn track rod ends, with new items £55 apiece. Open the bonnet and try to move the steering column; if there's significant play, it's time for a new universal joint at a cost of £100. You also need to check for vertical movement of the steering wheel, indicating that the collapsible steering column top and bottom bush has worn. Your best bet is to get a replacement column from Melvyn Rutter for £350, (exchange) which is machined and improved to eliminate this weak spot.

The sliding pillar suspension works well but the kingpins last no more than 20-25,000 miles, while the rear leaf springs sag and replacements cost £70 each. More significant are leaks from the lever arm dampers, so check for signs of fluid. If these need replacing you'll pay £100 (exchange) per unit – but many owners will have swapped them for telescopic units by now anyway. The sign of a caring owner is one who has fitted a remote greasing point for the front suspension, which makes lubricating the kingpins much easier. At just £35 per side, it allows the front suspension to be lubricated from under the bonnet.

Many Morgans have wire wheels fitted, so look for worn splines and broken or damaged spokes. To check for »

Above
Plus 8s always came with the Rover V8 engine, but later models had fuel injection.

»Info

TIMELINE

» **1954:** Cowled-rad Plus 4 arrives, replacing flat-rad Series I and fitted with a 68bhp 2088cc Standard Vanguard engine or 90bhp 1991cc TR2 powerplant.

» **1955:** Series II 4/4 model arrives, five years after demise of flat-rad Series I. Now with 36bhp Ford 100E 1172cc engine and three-speed gearbox. 386 made.

» **1956:** The 100bhp TR3 engine is now optional for the Plus 4.

» **1960:** Series III 4/4 is launched with Ford Anglia 105E power and four speeds. 58 built.

» **1961:** Plus 4 Super Sports appears, with a tuned TR3 engine offering 116bhp. Series IV 4/4 also goes on sale, with Ford Classic 1340cc engine and disc brakes at the front. 114 produced.

» **1962:** From this point, a 2138cc TR4 engine is standard on Plus 4; it's been optionally available since 1961 though.

» **1963:** Series V 4/4 gets the Cortina GT's powerplant and a gearbox with synchromesh on all forward gears. 639 made. Unloved Plus 4 Plus debuts; it's a glassfibre-bodied coupé with TR4 power, but just 26 are built.

» **1965:** Until the end of production, the Plus 4 now has a TR4a engine.

» **1968:** The 4/4 1600 arrives, using Ford's 1599cc Kent engine. Four seats available for the first time. 3513 produced. The Plus 8 goes on sale with a Moss four-speed gearbox, while four seats are available for the first time for the Plus 4. Also, the Plus 4 is discontinued.

» **1972:** The Plus 8 gets a Rover four-speed manual gearbox.

» **1976:** There's now a Sports Lightweight edition of the Plus 8 available; just 19 are made though.

» **1977:** The Rover SD1 engine and gearbox are now fitted to the Plus 8 and the car's width is increased to accommodate wider wheels and tyres. Alloy panels optional from this point.

» **1981:** Fiat 1584cc twin-cam engine available for the 4/4, alongside Ford Kent unit. Offers 98bhp but just 96 are made before model's demise in 1983.

Plus 8 3.9 (1989-2004)
SPECIFICATIONS

Engine
3946cc V8, pushrod, 16 valves. Alloy head and block. Lucas electronic fuel injection

Power
190bhp @ 4750rpm

Torque
235lb ft @ 2600rpm

Transmission
Five-speed manual, rear-wheel drive

Suspension
Front: Independent with sliding pillars, coil springs, telescopic dampers
Rear: Live axle with semi-elliptic leaf springs and telescopic dampers

Brakes
Front: 279mm ventilated discs
Rear: 228mm drums
Servo-assisted

Weight
935kg (2057lb)

Performance
0-60mph: 6.1sec
Top speed: 122mph

Value
Cost new: £25,229
Value now:
£25,000-£35,000

worn splines, jack up the car and get someone to sit in it, pressing on the footbrake. Try to turn the wheels backwards and forwards – if there's any movement it's because the splines need to be renewed at a typical cost of £135 per side at the front and £275 each side at the rear.

Bodywork, electrics and trim

The Morgan's construction is based on pre-war technology, with a steel chassis and an ash frame, over which are stretched steel or alloy panels. Even if the outer panels are fine, the chassis and/or ash frame could be rotten. Post-1986 cars survive best, as their treated wood and wings were painted before being fitted, rather than after. Earlier cars are more likely to have a rotten frame, speeded by moisture getting into the seams between the outer panels due to cracked paint. The key thing is how well the car has been stored.

Major dismantling is costly, and new front wings are nearly £900 apiece; rear items are almost £400 each. Also, major panels are supplied for an approximate fit – getting them to line up properly often requires plenty of labour, but at

least there's no welding anywhere, apart from on the chassis.

Start by checking for play in the door-hinge post, by holding the door along its trailing edge and seeing how much vertical movement there is. Ensure the play is in the hinge pins and not the post; the former are easily replaced but the latter is a significant problem that costs £1500+ per side to fix, plus painting. While the door is open, push on the B-post (or elbow rail in Morgan parlance); if the wood behind the bodywork is rotten there'll be plenty of movement.

New body tubs are available, which come as an ash frame that's panelled and includes doors. The cost is around £3500, which may be cheaper than paying for lots of localised repairs.

Wing edges need careful checking for corrosion; for strength, each edge is rolled around a steel wire which causes electrolytic corrosion with alloy panels. Things are little better with steel panels, so inspect the inside edge of each outer panel and make sure the wire isn't hanging out, weakening everything.

The chassis is simple but durable and strong enough if in good condition. Until 1986 the chassis was just painted – galvanising was optional after this

Technology, Tradition, Craftsmanship, Performance - a unique blend that only Morgan can deliver. After nearly 100 years of bespoke manufacture, Morgan customers the world over understand what it is to own and cherish the finest and most individual motor car money can buy. To find out more or arrange a test drive contact your nearest dealer, delivery available 2008.

Melvyn Rutter Ltd
Hertfordshire
01279 725 725
www.melvyn-rutter.co.uk

Newtown Motors
Wales
01633 485 251
info@newtown-motors.co.uk

Richard Thorne Classic Cars
Berkshire
0118 9831200
www.rtcc.co.uk

John Gill Ltd
Yorkshire
01677 423134
carolgill@johngill.co.uk

Berrybrook Motors Ltd
Devon
01392 833 301
www.berrybrook.co.uk

Lifes Motors Ltd
Lancashire
01704 531 375
sales@lifesmotors.com

Thomson & Potter Ltd
Scotland
01828 670 247
david@tandp.net

Perranwell Garage
Cornwall
01872 863 037
alan@perranwell.co.uk

Mike Duncan
Worcestershire
01299 250 025
www.morgans4sale.co.uk

Williams Morgan
Bristol
0800 0582983
www.williamsautomobiles.com

Wykehams Ltd
London
0207 385 3377
morgans@wykehams.com

I & J Macdonald Ltd
Durham
01207 520 916
info@macdonald-racing.com

Brands Hatch Morgan Ltd
Kent
01732 882 017
sales@morgan-cars.com

Mole Valley
Surrey
01306 710088
www.mole-valley.co.uk

Allon White Sports Cars
Bedfordshire
0845 3457666
www.allonwhite.co.uk

Russell Paterson Morgan
Scotland
01738 44 4004
russell@rpm-morgan.co.uk

SGT
Berkshire
01628 605 353
www.sgt.co.uk

London Morgan
London
0207 837 2000
www.londonmorgan.com

Stratton Motor Company
Norfolk
01508 530 491
www.strattonmotorcompany.com

San Lorenzo Garages
Guernsey
07781 107 084
ianbowtle@cwgsy.net

Parkgate Garages Ltd
Northern Ireland
028 9065 5149
philip.kennedy@
parkgategarages.co.uk

Ledgerwood Morgan
Lincolnshire
01724 733228
phil@philledgerwood
wanadoo.co.uk

Car show AeroMax from £110,950 - Limited Edition run of 100 all pre-sold
Morgan range from £25,210 ex factory on the road
Official Fuel consumption in mpg (litres/100km) for the Morgan range
Urban 28.7 (9.8) - 17.05 (16.5) Extra Urban 53.1 (5.3) - 34.3 (8.2)
Combined 40.5 (6.9) - 25.11 (11.2) CO2 emissions 164 - 269 g/km

»Info

TIMELINE

» **1982:** Ford 1597cc CVH engine replaces Kent unit in 4/4. Gives 96bhp and 2222 are built.

» **1983:** Fuel injection now optional on Plus 8.

» **1985:** Lowline option now available on 4/4, offering wider wings (by an inch) and 6in Cobra wheels. Meanwhile, the Plus 4 is reintroduced, with 2-litre Fiat twin-cam power.

» **1986:** Fuel injection is now standard on the Plus 8.

» **1988:** Rover's 2-litre M16 engine supersedes the Fiat unit in the Plus 4

» **1989:** The Plus 8 now features a 3.9-litre engine.

» **1991:** The 4/4's CVH engine now has electronic fuel injection to give 100bhp. 195 built.

» **1992:** The Plus 4 adopts the Plus 8's wider chassis, while the latter now has telescopic rear dampers in place of the previous lever arm units. Rover's T16 engine supersedes the M16 unit previously fitted to the Plus 4.

» **1993:** Ford Zeta engine now used, in 121bhp 1796cc form.

» **1997:** A 220bhp 4.6-litre engine is now optional for the Plus 8 (and offered for just two years), while all cars have longer doors and a redesigned fascia.

» **2000:** The Plus 4 ceases production, although it's revived in 2004 with 2-litre Ford Duratec power.

» **2002:** Le Mans '62 commemorative edition of the Plus 8 is offered; 40 are made.

» **2003:** Anniversary edition of the Plus 8 celebrates 35 years of production; 200 are built.

» **2004:** Plus 8 production ends after 6233 are made; it's replaced by the Roadster with Ford 3.0-litre V6 power.

date and standard from 1997. The crossmembers are the most rust-prone areas, especially the one at the back; replacement means the rear of the car has to be dismantled. Also check the chassis around the engine mountings as cracks can appear here, which spread if left unrepaired and can mean a new chassis is required.

At the front of the chassis is the crossframe, which carries the suspension. A hefty whack from the front will distort this, so make sure the car pulls up straight and get underneath to look for signs of an impact. New crossframes cost £460 (with replacement needing a jig), but if the chassis has distorted it's £700 for a new one – and 500+ hours to rebuild the car around it. The key area to check is forward of the toe board, which is where the most distortion is likely to be after a big shunt.

Starting problems can be caused by the battery's earthing strap corroding; it's a particular problem with two-seaters, where the battery is located at the back of the car and gets bombarded by road spray. Lights, switches and instrumentation are cheaply available, but the rocker switches in post-1976 cars can be temperamental. These

incorporate warning lights, and their contacts tend to fall apart with age.

Conclusion

Few marques enjoy the loyalty that Morgan does, and for a multitude of reasons. With few direct competitors, it's no surprise that many people buy a Morgan then stick with the marque for decades to come. However, you have to have your wits about you – particularly buying any example built before 1986.

Back then, little thought was given to durability. Something that may appear insignificant may require the car to be dismembered then rebuilt around a new bodyshell. Buy a corker though, and it's hard to beat the Malvern wonder; there are few safer places to put your cash. ⚠

» **Thanks to Matthew Parkin at Morgan, along with Melvyn Rutter.**

'Inspect a car thoroughly; something that may seem minor may require rebuilding it around a new bodyshell'

(1950-1964)

PORSCHE 356

A good 356 can be a joy forever, but prices have risen dramatically
of late so make sure you invest your money wisely

Words: Richard Dredge Photography: www.magiccarpics.co.uk

'If any major work is required, you can get any parts you need to give the engine a complete overhaul, although a total rebuild costs between £5000 and £8500'

You may not realise it, but you want a 356 – you really do. Get behind the wheel of a decent example and you'll want one so bad that it'll hurt; buy a bad 'un and it'll be an even more painful experience. Ever since its launch in 1950, the 356 has been accused of being no more than a poshed-up Volkswagen. Yet while early 356s featured some Beetle parts and the same basic layout, the Porsche was an all-new model with a significantly different construction – plus superior aerodynamics and a far better power-to-weight ratio.

That is why although early 356s have relatively little power or torque, they accelerate quicker and top out higher than you'd think. It's not just about speed, though; while the 356 has a reputation for being tricky to drive in a hurry, the reality is that the rear-mounted engine and torsion bar suspension allow you to hustle the car along much faster than most contemporaries. Such agility and frugality are why the 356 has always been so highly sought after – although they have always been an expensive car; when new in 1953 you'd have paid a 50 per cent premium over the price of a Jaguar XK120.

If you're tempted to take the plunge, there are plenty of pitfalls, however. Fred Hampton, 356 registrar for the Porsche Club GB, offers several words of warning: "Beware of cheap cars; they're invariably heartbreakers rather than bargains. These models are also extremely costly to restore properly and there are few genuine 356 experts – and these machines demand expert restoration. However, with values having almost doubled in recent years, many people are now giving their 356s the attention they deserve. Bargains are rare, but any decently priced right-hand-drive car is likely to increase in value as there are probably fewer than 200 genuine UK examples left."

All 356s are now expensive, but factory-built right-hand-drive cars are especially so. What's more, in open-topped form they are astonishingly pricey. The most affordable 356 is a B coupé, with usable examples costing £15,000 – but these cars need specialist »

Above
Porsche 356's 'bathtub' shape (this is how it looked in 1953) is classically aerodynamic.

'While fixing the mechanicals can be costly, the value of any 356 is in its bodyshell'

Porsche 356B 1600 Super
SPECIFICATIONS

Engine
1582cc flat-four, two overhead valves per cylinder. Alloy heads and block. Two Zenith 32NDIX carburettors

Power
60bhp @ 4500rpm

Torque
81lb ft @ 2800rpm

Transmission
Four-speed manual

Suspension
Front: Transverse torsion bars, trailing parallel links, telescopic dampers, anti-roll bar
Rear: Transverse torsion bars, two trailing arms, telescopic dampers

Brakes
Front: 280x40mm drums
Rear: 280x40mm drums

Weight
870kg (1914lb)

Performance
0-62mph: 16.5sec
Top speed: 96mph

Value
Cost new: DM13,200 (1960)
Value now:
£15,000-£40,000

attention, so buying one is just the start of the expense. Values have risen noticeably in recent years, and at the top end things have gone crazy with mint Carreras and very early 356s selling for well over £100,000; a basket-case right-hand-drive Speedster sold not long ago for £75,000. That's dragged up the values of more ordinary examples, with a decent 356A, B or C coupé now fetching £27,000-£30,000; cabriolets are double.

Any 356 with the steering wheel on the right is very rare, so in the long term you're unlikely to lose out financially – but you're going to have to look hard to find a good one. However, mint left-hand-drivers in the US are much easier to track down – if still not exactly chicken-feed to buy. Still, you can't take it with you...

Engine
All 356s feature a relatively straight-forward flat-four – aside from the hyper-rare quad-cam Carrera models. None of these engines is quiet, but they should idle smoothly and rev cleanly with no misfiring or spluttering. There shouldn't be any oil leaks evident, although the clip-on valve covers sometimes weep slightly, so interiors usually smell of oil;

major puddles under the car means an expensive rebuild is imminent.

If any major work is needed, you can get any parts you need to give the engine a complete overhaul; although a total rebuild including ancillaries costs any-where between £5000 and £8500. With genuine parts prices being very high, some pattern spares are now being used; they're not necessarily inferior either, just more affordable.

The first sign of engine work being needed is blue smoke from the exhaust, which reveals that oil is being burned through worn valve guides. Fumes leaking into the cabin is an indication of the exhaust leaking, the best solution being a new factory system for around £650.

Transmission
A four-speed gearbox was fitted to every 356, with synchromesh on all ratios from 1952. Until this point none of the gears featured synchromesh, but whichever unit is fitted it should soldier on for huge mileages. The first thing to go is normally the bearings, which will start rumbling while the car is cruising; the next stage in the box's destruction will be first and second-ratio synchromesh giving up;

you'll pay £750 to fix this, while having a rebuilt gearbox fitted costs £3500. If you're struggling to get the gears it's merely because the linkages need fresh bushes; an easy and cheap fix at £75.

Suspension, steering and brakes
The torsion bar suspension used at each end of the 356 is simple and reliable, although at the front you need to make sure there's no play in the bushes that support the four arms. There's a pair on each side and they link the arms to each kingpin and stub axle assembly; a bit of play is inevitable but it's easy to fix.

To test the front suspension properly you'll need to put the car on axle stands. Grab the top and bottom of each wheel and try rocking them; if you can feel or hear any movement the king pins need replacing; doing the whole job can easily cost the thick end of £1000.

Until 1957 there was worm-and-peg steering; after this it was a worm-and-gear system. Whichever set-up is fitted, the steering should be light and direct with no tight spots. As long as the box is kept lubricated it'll keep going with no problems. However, if it runs low on oil

TIMELINE

There were dozens of 356 variants over the years; these are the key developments.

» 1950: 356 arrives in 1086cc form only, with 40bhp.
» 1951: 1300 derivative offered, with 44bhp; there's also now a 60bhp 1488cc 356. From the following year there are also 55bhp and 70bhp versions of this engine.
» 1952: All-synchro four-speed gearbox replaces previous crash unit.
» 1955: 356A on sale with 1290cc, 1498cc or 1582cc powerplants. A curved windscreen replaces the previous split item. The first Carreras go on sale in September.
» 1959: 356B appears, with more modern bodyshell featuring higher bumper and headlamps, opening quarterlights and a larger rear window. There are 1582cc or 1966cc flat-fours on offer.
» 1960: The ultra-rare 1600GS GTL Abarth-Carrera appears for this year only, with alloy bodywork.
» 1963: The 356C brings with it all-round disc brakes and a choice of 1582cc or 1966cc engines.

SPECIALISTS

» Forest Fine (trim), East Sussex. +44 (0)1273 891660, www.forestfine.com
» Gantspeed, Lincs. +44 (0)1507 568474, www.gantspeed.co.uk
» Karmann Konnection, Essex. +44 (0)1702 601155, www.karmannkonnection.com
» Maxted, Page and Prill, Essex. +44 (0)1787 476338, www.maxted-pageandprill.com
» PR Services, Essex. +44 (0)7000 356911, www.prs356.com
» Retro Motor Company, Hants. +44 (0)1425 483 841, www.retromotorcompany.co.uk
» Roger Bray Restorations, Devon. +44 (0)1404 822 005, www.rogerbrayrestoration.com
» Sportwagen, Southend. +44 (0)1702 53 53 50, www.sportwagen.co.uk
» Klasse 356, Pennsylvania. www.klasse356.com
» NLA, Nevada. www.nlaparts.com
» Pelican Parts www.pelicanparts.com
» Restoration Design, Michigan. www.restoration-design.com
» Stoddard, Ohio. www.stoddard.com

and starts to wear, some owners then tighten things up – and that's a recipe for disaster because the whole system will quickly deteriorate.

Drum brakes were standard fare until the all-disc 356C of 1963. However, these weren't the usual cast-iron drums seen elsewhere; they were huge, finned, aluminium-alloy castings with a steel liner. In good condition they work well because the 356 is so light, but any car left standing for ages will have suffered from electrolytic corrosion. The game will be given away by violent pedal judder under braking, due to the liners being pushed out of shape; new drums cost £730 each, although 356A items aren't available.

Bodywork, electrics and trim

They all look much the same, but there were masses of panel changes throughout the 356's 15-year life. Crucially, there are two key factors you shouldn't under-estimate; the complexity of the bodyshell and its tendency to rot. Major corrosion needs expert attention, and many examples have been crashed at some point so bodyshells can be twisted. That's why you must ensure the car sits square on the road, the panel gaps are tight and even and none of the metal is rippled. While fixing the mechanicals can be costly, the value of any 356 is in its bodyshell – and rebuilding one costs anywhere between £18,000 and £30,000, which is why annual body inspections are essential. Cheap restos invariably entail the car losing its contours, which is why recognised specialists have to be used.

If you're happy that the body is straight, you need to ensure it's not riddled with rot. Although the 356 can corrode any-where, it's the front wings, wheelarch lips and headlamp bowls that are usually the first to go. These are usually quickly followed by the nose panel, leading edges of the rear wings, the door bottoms and the upper rear corners of the front wings where they meet the scuttle. These latter areas are a particular pain to fix, and accordingly are one of the most common bodge areas.

You need to check every square inch of metal, but other key rot spots include the spare wheel well in the nose, all panel edges and the seam where the floorpans meet the sills. Lifting the carpet to inspect these latter areas is essential; at least it is easy to check the sills as they »

Above
Speedster is ultimate open 356 – and thus a popular 'replicar' subject; B roadster is the most affordable soft-top.

'Before you commit to any purchase you must drive the car for at least 50 miles over a variety of terrains'

are of very simple construction with a box section located behind a cosmetic outer panel. While you're on your knees, take a look at the jacking points, the support panels for the front axle beam and the locating panels for the rear suspension torsion bar tube.

Most 356s featured six-volt electrics, although from 1958 some 1600GS models and all Carreras had 12-volt systems. By now most owners have converted their cars to run on the higher voltage, which is seen as a sensible modification.

Apart from the earliest pre-A cars, it's possible to buy most interior and exterior trim. The repro stuff is generally well made, with original parts now very hard to track down. Things like original steering wheels are notoriously tricky to source, and whether you're buying new, used or repro, some bits are very costly. It can also be difficult establishing exactly what's right for any car; many 356s have been restored with little regard to originality, so you'll need to find an expert who can tell you which way to proceed.

Conclusion

While the coupé offers the purest drive, it's the drophead that most buyers want because of its added glamour – you'll typically pay at least twice as much for a cabrio. And the chances are you will end up with a left-hand-drive car.

While there are myriad 356 derivatives to choose from, the general rule says that the newer the car, the more usable it is; B and C types have much nicer gearboxes, for example. They got progressively more powerful, better built and more thoroughly engineered. But before you commit to any purchase you must drive the car for at least 50 miles over a variety of terrains. Everything needs to be given a thorough work-out. ⚠

Above
Tuneable 356 is a great choice for classic events – though prepping it will never be cheap

£314.40

1963 Porsche 356C 1600
Value: **£30,000**
Quote: **£314.40** (£250x/s unlimited mpa)

»Info

CLUBS
» Porsche Club GB, +44 (0)1608 652 911, www.porscheclubgb.com
» Independent Porsche Enthusiasts Club, +44 (0)1246 279358, www.tipec.org.uk
» For 356-only clubs, see www.356registry.org or www.speedsters.com

BOOKS
» Original Porsche 356 by Laurence Meredith. Bay View, ISBN 1-870979-58-3
» Driving in its purest form by Dirk Michael Conradt. Beeman Jorgensen, ISBN 0-929758-09-9
» The 356 Porsche – A Guide To Authenticity by Brett Johnson. Beeman Jorgensen, ISBN 0-929758-08-0
» The 356 Defined – A Pictorial Guide by Brett Johnson. Beeman Jorgensen, ISBN 0-929758-14-S
» The 356 Registry magazine (subscribe through www.356registry.org)

THERE IS NO
SUBSTITUTE

Some argue that the air-cooled 911s are the best Porsches
of all – which means they are some of the best cars ever.
Robert Coucher introduces our guide to the 'classic' 911

Photographs: John Colley, Porsche archives, Paul Harmer

Love or loathe...

It is true to say that drivers either love or loathe this Porsche. The supporters agree that the 911 offers one of the purest and most thrilling experiences available behind the wheel. The detractors shout that it is dangerous and feels strange, with its six-cylinder engine slung out over the back tyres. And those who have not actually driven a 911 often dismiss the car as 'leaving them cold'.

A lot of this opinion has to do with social values. When the first 2-litre 911 was announced at the Frankfurt Motor Show in September 1963, there were some pretty spectacular sports cars on the market: the Jaguar E-type, Aston Martin DB6, Corvette Sting Ray and Ferrari 275GTB. Against this backdrop, the comparatively expensive 130bhp 911 was never going to be snapped up by the mainstream; instead, it was bought by drivers who wanted a quick and unobtrusive car.

Today, driving an historic automobile is a statement, and a 911 is a very strong statement. But it depends where you are. In the USA, a 911 is a small sportscar owned by single-minded enthusiasts. When you see a classic 911 pounding along a wide-open highway from the comfort of a large American sedan, you know that the guy behind the wheel is enduring rather severe conditions to indulge in his driving enjoyment.

On the Continent, 911s are used as fast and efficient tools, flat-out down the fast lane to get to the next meeting 100 miles away. Come the weekend, the European 911 is enjoyed up and down the twisting mountain passes, with skis strapped to the rear grille. A sharp and effective instrument.

But then we come to Britain. Ah, the eternal British diseases of envy and class. Initially in Britain 911s were appreciated by focused types, and through the years the cars' amazing performance and practicality made them the choice of every young man in a hurry. The urban myth of the time was that there were more 911s in central London than anywhere else. And when the financial markets really took off in the 1980s, it seemed that every barrow boy who had made a few quid in the City bought a bright red 911 to match his braces. But the bewinged and spoilered 'retail red' 911s were crashed early and sold quickly once the Filofax brigade realised that a 911 was not a status symbol, but a hard and uncompromising driving machine.

Within the Porsche world, 911s are now loosely divided into four categories. The early cars are the short-wheelbase 2-litre models built from 1965 to 1969, which are the race-eligible models in great demand among the hardcore historic race and rally competitors. Then there are the pre-impact bumper 911s built from 1970 until 1973. These are probably the most desirable road-going classic 911s, with engines ranging from 2.2 to 2.4 litres. In 1974 the impact-bumper 911s were introduced; these are some of the least desirable models, but the later (post-1978) 911SC and 3.2 Carreras make excellent usable classic drivers.

The 'modern' classics, if you like, begin with the 964, first launched in 1989. This is a very different machine to past 911s, with coil-spring suspension and dual-mass flywheels, and it was generally not well received by Porsche purists. The 964 marked the arrival of the tamer 911, aimed at the broader motoring market. The last air-cooled Porsche, the 993, was launched in 1994 and is an eminently usable daily classic with real character. That's why it commands higher secondhand prices than the later, water-cooled 996.

Over the following pages, we analyse and appraise each iteration of the air-cooled 911. »

Left
Purists love the original 911 for its ultra-clean shape, though SWB cars can be a handful.

The hardcore

1965-1969

911S model introduced in 1967, producing 160bhp (later 170bhp with fuel injection). In 1968, softer T (Touring) and base L models introduced, and the E (*Einspritzung*, or Injection) in 1969. 911 Targa available 1967-69. Weight: from 1080kg

Choice model: 1967 911S, 160bhp
Prices: £25,000+
Watch out for bodged restos and hidden rust. Cars need to be very carefully set up.

'Early 911s are the more fragile cars and not as user-friendly as later models. You need to rev the nuts off them and they are noisy, twitchy and hard'

Early 911s are the cars chosen by competitive historic racers because they are light – in racing trim the weight usually has to be kept *up* to the homologation level of around 1000kg – and they are fast. The standard 2-litre produces 130bhp and the hotter S 160bhp, with plenty more available to a skilled engine builder.

Just a few years ago, these small-displacement, peaky and difficult-to-tune, generally worn out and rusty old dogs were the runt of the litter. Thanks to the resurgence of historic racing and rallying, and the veritable army of specialists who now really understand these cars, early 911s can be made to run obediently and are regarded by the hardcore as the cream.

But early 911s are the more fragile machines and not as user friendly as later models. You need to rev the nuts off them and they are noisy, twitchy and hard. When the 911 was first released, experienced drivers were perturbed by its way-ward handling. Its six-cylinder engine weighed about 200lb more than the outgoing flat-four, hung out over the rear wheels, and the cars still wore 356-sized 4¹⁄₂-inch rims. All this conspired to induce immediate and severe oversteer when lifting off through a corner. Porsche tried to rectify this by adding 22kg of weight to the front

bumpers, which was hardly the ideal solution.

In 1969 the wheelbase was lengthened by two-and-a-half inches and the wheel rims widened to six inches, which helped the weight distribution and the previously hedge-busting handling.

Yet drivers such as 'Quick' Vic Elford had soon got to grips with early 911s and Monte Carlo Rallies and circuit races were vanquished. Many historic racers actually prefer the pre-'69 short-wheelbase cars, now that the chassis can be properly sorted by swapping tyres, dampers, roll bars, torsion bars, suspension pick-up points and so on.

An early 911 is an adrenalin pump to drive. The car feels small and light, and the joy of the flat-six is that it gets smoother and more eager as the revs rise. From the driver's seat you feel the car swivelling from your hips. You need to allow the lightly laden front tyres to squirm about and keep a loose grip on the steering wheel.

Once you accept that the sensation of driving a 911 is different from conventional cars, you will be hooked. The Porsche is so responsive, clean and quick-witted you will soon find yourself covering ground at serious speed and exiting bends ahead of the pack. Just never, ever lift off while going into a corner!

Road-going rockets

With sales taking off in the late-'60s (particularly in the USA), Porsche knew it had to widen the 911's appeal. A bigger engine and a spread of models were called for. In 1970 engine capacity was enlarged to 2195cc and T, E and S states of tune were made available, along with the semi-auto Sportomatic gearbox and Targa top.

These 911s remained lightweight, driver-focused sports cars, with a slimline look, minimal trim and vocal engines. Of the 2.2-litre motors, the S is again regarded as the one to have, because of its rev-happy nature and full quotient of 180bhp.

In 1972 the capacity was further enlarged to 2341cc, and fuel injection was used across the range. The 2.4S of '73 pumped out 190bhp, which meant a 0-60mph time of 6.6 seconds and a top speed of 145mph. In the real world, the less-cammy 2.4E is probably the most usable road car of this group while still having real driver appeal.

But in 1973 arguably the greatest 911 of them all was launched: the 911 2.7 Carrera RS. Just 1580 examples of this magnificent car were made in Touring, Sport and Race trim. With its distinctive

1970-1973
2.2-2.4-litre engines plus the 2.7RS in 1973
Power: 125-190bhp (210bhp RS)
Weight: 1100kg (940kg for RS Lightweight)

Choice model: 2.4E for road use, 2.4S for a bit more.
Prices: £30,000+; £40K for 2.4S; £150K+ for RS.
Beware of fakes; provenance is all, so check all numbers. Watch out for rust and crash damage.

and effective ducktail spoiler, front air dam, lurid Carrera script down each side and wider rear tyres, the 210bhp RS quickly became a sensation. Its engine was enlarged to 2.7 litres, which gave it a lovely dose of torque as well as free-revving power. Allied to a low weight of just 940kg in Lightweight trim, the Carrera proved a fast and flexible race winner.

An RS feels just as light and pointy as an early 2-litre car but it has the added full-fat wham of 188lb ft of torque, 18% more than the 2.4S. Yet a 2.7RS will happily spin to its 7300rpm maximum with unabated enthusiasm. These 150mph machines are extremely quick on the road, as well as on historic race or rally events. With mechanical fuel injection, the RS copes well with modern traffic, too.

But now that the Lightweight version of the 2.7RS commands over £150,000, the lesser 2.4S at around £40K begins to look like good value. As mentioned, for driving enjoyment on the road, the smoother and torquier 2.4E provides almost all the sensation, if not quite the out-and-out speed. A 0-60mph time of 6.8 seconds and top speed of 143mph are not too shabby.

'If you want an excellent, tough, reliable, rustproofed 911 to leave outside and drive on a daily basis, the 911SC from 1978 is for you'

From fright pig to daily driver

In order to meet American safety standards, Porsche fitted its 1974 models with large, impact-absorbing bumpers. These mid-'70s 911s are the least loved because they have all the problems of the 1970s cars – engines prone to breaking head studs, body rot etc – without the light weight of earlier models. The 911s of this period are cheap and have usually suffered years of neglect and abuse. European 2.7 and 3.0-litre models are rare and the post-'78 cars are simply a much better

1974-1989
2.7-3.2-litre engines
Power: 150-231bhp
Weight: from 1130kg

Choice model: SC for solid simplicity; 3.2 Carrera is easier to drive.
Prices: from £6000 for unloved 2.7; £12,000 for clean SC and £18,000 for best 3.2-litre Carrera. Ensure SC has had camchain tensioners modified to hydraulic type.

bet when it comes to using them regularly.

The first glimmer of hope that Porsche was sorting itself out was the mad, bad and dangerous-to-know 911 Turbo, launched on an unsuspecting world in 1975. We won't go into early Turbos here because they are monstrously expensive to maintain (they have 917 front brakes) and don't offer any real benefits over the normally-aspirated cars for regular use.

If you want an excellent, tough, reliable, rustproofed 911 to leave parked outside and drive on a daily basis, the 911SC from 1978 is for you. These models were fully galvanised (a feature first introduced in 1976), so they have modern levels of protection against the ravages of rust. From 1981 power was up to 204bhp, and in this form an SC will dash from 0-60mph in 5.9 seconds, carry on to 150mph and nothing will drop off along the way!

The SC is also the last of the 911 range you can fix with a socket set, screwdriver and hammer, and every time you shut the vault safe-style door with a solid thunk, you will smile, knowing this is one of the most carefully-constructed cars ever.

Classics for the modern era

The very different Porsche 964 was launched in 1989, initially in four-wheel-drive guise. It replaced the previous 3.2 Carrera and was claimed by Porsche to be 87% new. The suspension was totally different, with MacPherson struts and lower wishbones up front and semi-trailing arms with coils at the rear. Engine power was up to a strong 250bhp, so performance was excellent (0-60mph in 5.5 seconds, 161mph top speed).

When initially road tested, the 4WD 964 was felt to be a bit numb and unexciting, as it was prone to understeer. Sure, the hard over-centre clutch of the past had been replaced and the gearshift action was more conventional, while there was also unobtrusive power-steering. But the response was lukewarm. The two-wheel-drive 964, launched in 1990, was so safe and predictable it almost made the 4WD car redundant. Lift-off oversteer had finally been tamed, but the result was, er, dull. Not a word normally associated with a 911.

We have not gone into limited-edition offshoots here but the 964RS is worth a special mention. The car is just stonking, to use track-day parlance. First seen in 1991, the RS was criticised for its harsh ride. But what a machine! Stripped down to 1229kg and producing 260bhp, the 964RS combines a 2.7RS's deftness with modern levels of grip and braking.

Porsche tried hard with this car to make it a focused driving machine. Weight was shed by ditching the air-con, power-steering, electric seats (for heaven's sake...), central locking and rear seats. Glass was thinned and an ally bonnet fitted, along with Recaro composite buckets, Turbo-spec front brakes and 17-inch magnesium alloys. And the body was seam welded. This is one special Porsche, so it's no surprise that prices are rising fast. Expect to pay over £35,000 for one of only 2364 RSs manufactured.

In the meantime, 964 sales plummeted, in part due to the economic problems of the time. Japanese consultants were brought in – Mein Gott! But it worked. In 1993 the firm built just 8292 964s. By the end of 1994, it had turned out 16,643 examples of the new 993.

The 993 was again 80% changed. It ushered in fresh organic styling as well as cutting-edge multi-link rear suspension. It had a superb 272bhp air-cooled flat-six, and in 1995 Varioram induction was added (upping the power to 285bhp) to coincide with the launch of the very sexy, wide-bodied Carrera S. Available first with 4WD, then with more desirable 2WD a year later, the Carrera S (0-60mph in 5.3 seconds with a 168mph top speed) is a joy to drive. It's probably one of the most exciting and best-rounded 911s of the lot.

1989-1998
3.6-litre engines
Power: 250-285bhp
Weight: 1380-1400kg

Choice models: 964RS; pretty much any post-'95 Varioram 993 depending upon how you want to drive.
Prices: 964 from £14,000 to over £35,000 for RS; 993 from £20,000 to Carrera S at £35,000; RS over £40,000. Important to go for a desirable colour and ensure RSs have the correct magnesium wheels and other lightweight fittings.

> 'The two-wheel-drive 964 was so safe and predictable it almost made the 4WD car redundant. Lift-off oversteer had finally been tamed'

Left
Modern classics: from far left, 1990 964 Turbo, 1993 Carrera 2 and Turbo 3.6, 1995 993 Turbo.

PORSCHE 911 (1963-1989)

Air-cooled 911s are still amazing value and truely iconic

Words: Richard Dredge   Photography: www.magiccarpics.co.uk

Above & right
Impact bumper SCs
are most practical of
the classic 911s.

Porsche 911 Carrera (1983)
SPECIFICATIONS

Engine
3164cc air-cooled flat-six, twin overhead camshafts. 12 valves. Alloy heads and block. Bosch DME electronic fuel injection

Power
231bhp @ 5900rpm

Torque
210lb ft @ 4800rpm

Transmission
Five-speed manual

Suspension
Front: Independent with struts, torsion bars, telescopic dampers and anti-roll bar.
Rear: Independent with semi-trailing arms, torsion bars, telescopic dampers, anti-roll bar.

Brakes
Front: 282mm discs
Rear: 290mm discs
Servo-assisted
Weight: 1165kg (2569lb)

Performance
0-60mph 5.4sec
Top speed 150mph

Value
Cost £21,464 new (1983)
Value now £7,000-£20,000

The name hasn't changed for almost half a century, but the Porsche 911 has evolved massively, from a peaky race car for the road that was likely to bite you, to a docile, usable supercar that's as easy to drive as a Toyota – only far more exciting. When it comes to motoring greats, no car is more iconic than the mighty 911.

If you do decide to take the plunge, it's essential that you inspect lots of examples first and you buy from a reputable source. Asking prices are all over the place, while specification, history and condition make a huge difference to values. As a rule of thumb, the impact-bumper cars are worth the least, and of the earlier models, it's the T that's the least valuable. The most valuable is the S, which leaves the E in the middle. A Sportomatic gearbox chips 20 per cent off the value while Targas are also worth around 10 per cent less than an equivalent coupé. Cabriolets are worth 10-15 per cent more than an equivalent coupé.

You'll need at least £7000 to buy a project 911SC or neglected early car, but you'll need a lot of time, patience and expertise to revive it. You're better off finding at least £13,000 for a reasonable T or SC, but if you want something tasty you'll be doing well to spend less than £25,000 on a good Carrera 2.7 – which is the price of a really superb Turbo. If money really isn't an issue, you could try finding an RS 2.7, but depending on which model you want, a running car will cost upwards of £50,000 – and possibly three times that for an exceptional Lightweight.

Engine

All 911s have a flat-six engine, although a flat-four has also been available in the same bodyshell; these cars are known as 912s, and they're rare. Whichever generation of 911 you're looking at, it'll have an alloy cylinder block as well as alloy heads. Until 1969 there was an aluminium alloy block fitted; this was then changed for a magnesium unit until the 3-litre cars came along in 1974 (Turbo) and 1975 (Carrera).

The early aluminium casings are weak and will probably have been replaced by now with an improved design. It's the same story for the magnesium units, especially where the 2.7-litre engines are concerned, as distortion is common, leading to oil leaks. Even when new there were reliability issues, usually from the cylinder head studs pulling out because of differential expansion of the aluminium cylinders. Porsche later moved to a steel alloy called Dilavar, but this has proved brittle over the years, with SCs and 3.2-litre cars affected by the studs breaking. If the studs have been replaced things should be fine, but if the originals are still fitted, expect problems when the engine comes to be rebuilt. To guard against future problems, Autofarm offers a dowelling service; see www.autofarm.co.uk/engines/air_cooled/shuffle_pinning for more.

Within the period we're covering, in theory it's possible to fit any engine to any car because the mounting points didn't change across the various generations. It's also possible to tune the powerplants in various ways, so it's worth establishing exactly what's nestling in the car's rear end. Most US cars featured less powerful engines than equivalent UK models, so expect an import to serve up a little less fun.

The 911's flat-six is generally durable if maintained. The first sign of impending expenditure is (blue) oil smoke when the car is started up and on the over-run, signalling that the valve guides have worn out. By the time the guides have worn the timing chain will also have seen better days, so listen for rattling when the engine is revved. There's a better tensioning mechanism fitted to post-'81 cars, while the post-1984 design is even better – which is why it's often fitted to earlier 911s.

Low oil pressure isn't necessarily a concern; the dash-mounted level gauge is only accurate at tickover once the engine is up to temperature, which is why it's best to rely on the dipstick instead. Expect to see 45psi at 2500rpm and ask for evidence of the lubricant having been changed regularly,

using high-quality oil. Also, because the sump holds 10-11 litres of oil, engine life is much extended by getting the engine up to temperature before revving it hard.

What's of more concern than an apparently low oil pressure is any sign that the remote oil tank has rusted, as it could spell disaster. Once this steel tank has started to corrode, the debris finds its way into the engine, wrecking it by first destroying the main bearings. That's why the tank must be replaced with a stainless steel item as soon as there's any sign of rust.

Transmission
There were three types of manual transmission fitted across these various 911s, the first type being fitted to 2.0 and 2.2-litre cars. It's generally tough, but it will wear out eventually, which is why you need to listen for bearings that are on their way out. It's the intermediate gears that are affected, so listen for any whining, which will disappear when fourth is selected. Between 1972 and 1985 there was a stronger gearbox fitted, known as the 915 unit. However, like any gearbox it has a finite lifespan, so listen out for bearing wear and feel for baulking as you swap ratios. Whichever gearbox is fitted, rebuilding it will cost anywhere between £800 and £3500, depending on what needs replacing. Reputable specialists such as Autofarm will overhaul your own gearbox, replacing only what's necessary.

The gearbox fitted to post-1986 911s is the strongest of the lot. Called the G50, it's very durable but the linkages might be past their best, making gear selection difficult or at least unpleasant; a fresh set of bushes will usually work wonders.

Clutches also got better engineered as time progressed; the post-1970 item was a big improvement over what had gone before. However, once again it's the G50 clutch that's the best of the lot – but whatever is fitted, make sure it isn't slipping because they all have a finite lifespan, which can be severely shortened with abuse.

Suspension, steering and brakes
There have been all sorts of detail changes to the suspension specification over the years, with poverty-spec cars not usually getting an anti-roll bar while poshers editions did. Fiting an anti-roll bar to any 911 is worthwhile, particularly as modern tyres can't give their best when the car is really leaning over.

As long as decent dampers are fitted, any 911 should handle pretty well; many owners take the Koni route but Bilsteins are favoured by most people who really know these cars. Obviously the dampers need to be in fine fettle, and so do the bushes so look for any evidence of perishing because the handling will be adversely affected without a doubt. If the bushes have perished it's worth getting a fresh set fitted; costs vary depending on which generation of 911 you're looking at, but in general you should expect to pay around £1000 to have the work done – and on top of this you'll need to pay for a geometry check, which could add another £500 to the bill.

Any car that's been converted from left to right-hand drive should be avoided, even if it's temptingly priced. There aren't many such cars about, but there are some – and because the conversion is rarely done well you're

»Info

TIMELINE
» 1963: The 901 is launched, but complaints from Peugeot lead to a swift renaming; the 911 is born. With 130bhp from 1991cc, 130mph is on offer. These early cars have a short wheelbase, so handling is especially tricky.
» 1965: The first right-hand drive cars are built, and the 912 goes on sale, powered by a 90bhp 1582cc flat-four and a four-speed gearbox.
» 1966: Weights behind the front bumper help to tame the handling, but only by a bit. The 911S also arrives, with 160bhp, Fuchs alloys, vented discs and a rear anti-roll bar. The Targa also debuts, with a zip-down plastic rear window; a glass screen is optional from 1968 and standard from 1971.
» 1967: The 911T is a budget edition with 110bhp and four-speed gearbox. Standard car is renamed the 911L, with five-speed gearbox and dual-circuit brakes. The unloved Sportomatic also appears, with a four-speed semi-automatic transmission.
» 1968: The wheelbase is lengthened by 2.2 inches, the wheelarches are flared and there's now a lighter engine block. There are also now twin batteries ahead of the front wheels for better weight distribution. The L is renamed the E, which gets Bosch mechanical fuel injection, along with the S, to give 140bhp and 170bhp respectively.
» 1969: The 912 dies while the various 911s get a 2195cc engine and a raft of suspension changes.
» 1970: Some of the underbody panels are now zinc-plated.
» 1971: The flat-six is stroked to take the capacity up to 2341cc.
» 1972: The first right-hand drive Targas are available, but the big news is the RS 2.7 homologation special with Nikasil liners, big-bore engine, magnesium crankcase, lighter panels, wider wheels and optional duck-tail spoiler.
» 1973: The 3.0 RS and RSR editions debut; just 109 are made, of which 50 were RSR racers. The regular 911 gets impact bumpers (continued overleaf)

»Info

to meet US regulations, and the engine now displaces 2687cc. A 'whale-tail' rear spoiler option replaces the previous 'duck-tail' item.

» 1974: The most powerful 911 yet appears; the Turbo. The boosted 3.0-litre flat-six gives 260bhp and 153mph, but right-hand drive cars don't appear until 1975. There's also a whale-tail spoiler, deeper front spoiler, flared wheelarches and revised suspension. Other 911 changes include a move to galvanised bodyshells while the 2.7 Carrera can now be ordered with a duck-tail spoiler.

» 1975: The 912E marks a brief return for the four-cylinder 911, with a fuel-injected 90bhp 1971cc VW engine; just 2089 are sold. The Carrera also gets a 200bhp 3.0-litre engine. There's also better ventilation and engine cooling plus a lighter clutch.

» 1977: The 3.0 SC arrives, with 180bhp (188bhp from August 1979 and 204bhp from August 1980). 1978: Turbo gets a 300bhp 3299cc powerplant.

» 1982: The Cabriolet is introduced.

» 1983: The Carrera gets a capacity hike to 3164cc, giving 231bhp.

» 1985: The Turbo gets Motronic engine management and there's a Turbo-look body available for the Carrera.

» 1986: There's now a flat-nose Turbo option while the Cabriolet gets a power roof as standard.

» 1987: Carrera Club Sport coupé offered.

» 1988: The Turbo gets a five-speed gearbox.

» 1989: Speedster appears; 2065 are built.

SPECIALISTS

» Autofarm, Oxon. 01865 331 234, www.autofarm.co.uk

» Roger Bray Restorations, Devon. 01404 822 005, www.rogerbrayrestoration.com

» Edmond Harris, Oxon. 01993 778 423, www.edmondharris.com

» Francis Tuthill, Oxon. 01295 750 514, www.francistuthill.co.uk

(continued overleaf)

better off simply steering clear. As it were.

Although brake specifications evolved, there aren't any weak spots as long as the car is used regularly and properly serviced. Cars that haven't had enough use will probably be suffering from calipers that have seized up, while the rubber pipes and seals can disintegrate with age too. At least everything is available, but if the whole system needs a complete overhaul it's going to be an expensive job...

There are all sorts of aftermarket wheels available for the 911, and if you're not into originality, as long as what's on there has the correct clearances there's probably not much to worry about. However, you must ensure the tyres have a decent speed rating (VR or ZR). If you want original wheels you'll need to look closely at what's on the car because there's a good chance some refurbishment will be needed. Fuchs alloys, seen as the most desirable 911 wheels, are strong but can crack around the spokes if the car has been driven hard. If an overhaul of each wheel is required, Fuchs charges £300 to put each one right.

Bodywork, electrics and trim

The 911 has always been a very costly car, but that didn't stop the early ones from rusting badly; it wasn't until August 1975 that the bodyshells were galvanised. Even then, many early cars still corroded; the plating initially merely slowed the rate of rusting. However, Porsche's production methods got much better with the passing years, as the 1970s became the '80s, the cars are much better protected from the elements.

Many early 1970s cars suffered from undersealing

lifting to allow the moisture in, with the metalwork then quietly dissolving, out of sight. Poorly repaired accident damage is also a very real possibility; panel damage is common after off-road excursions, and repairs aren't always what they should be. The result of these bodged repairs is often extensive corrosion – which isn't always obvious.

Whatever the age of car, start by looking at the bulkheads at each end of the car, as rust can spread from the base of the front and rear screens. If there's any corrosion in these areas, you're better off finding another car because the necessary repairs will be involved and very costly.

Early galvanised cars tend to corrode where stone chips haven't been attended to quickly enough; cracks also develop in the paint around areas such as the A-posts and anywhere that the car has been jacked up. If you're lucky the corrosion will be no more than cosmetic, but there's a good chance that some structural rust will be present – that's why you must inspect the front fuel tank support, inner wings, sills plus the A- and B-posts.

Early 911s could corrode pretty much anywhere, and even relatively new cars, such as many from the 1980s, will have rusted unless they've been well looked after. You need to make sure that you take a look at the inner and outer wings, sills, battery boxes, floorpans and door bottoms – be on your guard for any evidence of plating or filling. Also scrutinise the front crossmember, battery boxes, heater tubes and the windscreen surround – as well as the metal around the sunroof if there's one fitted.

On this latter point, you're generally better off

Clockwise from left
Desirable Club Sport; SC model with spoiler; air-cooled engine; SC without spoiler.

»**Info**

» Gantspeed Engineering, Lincs. 01507 568474, www.gantspeed.co.uk
» Hendon Way Motors, London. 0208 202 8011, www.hendonwaymotors.com
» Charles Ivey, London. 0207 731 3612, www.charlesivey.com
» Karmann Konnection, Essex. 01702 601155, www.karmannkonnection.com
» Porsch-apart, Lancs. 01706 824053, www.porsch-apart.co.uk
» Porscheshop, Birmingham. 0121 585 6088, www.porscheshop.co.uk

CLUBS
» Porsche Club GB, www.porscheclubgb.com
» The Independent Porsche Enthusiasts Club, www.tipec.net

BOOKS
» The Used 911 Story (8th Edition) by Patrick Zimmerman. ISBN 0-9631726-6-2
» Porsche 911 Story (8th Edition) by Paul Frere. ISBN 000-1-84425-301-5
» Porsche 911 Identification Guide by Phil Raby. ISBN 0-9541063-8-5
» 101 Projects For Your Porsche 911 1964-1989 by Wayne Dempsey. ISBN 0-7603-0853-5
» Porsche 911 Illustrated Buyers Guide by Randy Leffingwell. ISBN 0-7603-0947-7
» Porsche 911 Red Book 1965-2005 2nd Edition by Patrick Paternie. ISBN 0-7603-1960-X
» 911 & 912 Porsche; restorer's guide to authenticity by B Johnson. ISBN 0-929758-00-5
» Classic 911s 1965-1989 Ultimate Buyer's Guide by Peter Morgan. ISBN 978-0-9549990-9-4
» Porsche 911 (Great Cars series) by Michael Scarlett. ISBN 000-1-84425-124-1
» Original Porsche 911 (1963-98) by Peter Morgan. ISBN 000-1-901432-16-5

without a sunroof as they add weight and don't really work very well because they're often unreliable and tend to add wind noise when open – they also remove valuable head room. If there is one fitted, open it and look for evidence of corrosion around the edges; the drain tubes also tend to block up, leading to the screen pillars rusting from the inside out.

If it's an impact-bumper 911 you're looking at, it's worth ascertaining whether there are hydraulic rams behind the bumper, or crushable steel structures. The former tend to shrug off any minor knock, while the latter squash, with the metal then corroding. Only some UK cars featured the rams, while US cars all had them; your best bet is to open the boot and see if the inner wings have started to rust, signalling that the steel has been crushed. While you've got the lid open, check the state of the boot floor; a hefty crunch will have led to rippled panelwork. Finish off in this spot by looking at the fuel tank, which tends to rot underneath, leading to fuel leaks – a strong smell of petrol will soon give the game away.

There have been huge numbers of trim changes over the years, with some bits now proving hard to find. However, in general there shouldn't be any issues with finding replacement parts as good used components are often available. Also, the trim is generally hardwearing so often survives well, but check that the seat bolsters haven't frayed and worn through. Also make sure the door trims and carpets haven't rotted – if they have, it suggests there are wider problems that need sorting.

Also make sure that the heating works, as the heat exchangers can prove problematic. They're prone to corrosion, but it can smell oily inside, even when everything is in good condition. The heater controls can also seize up, while the semi-automatic system fitted to the SC onwards (but not cabrios) can be temperamental.

When it comes to exterior trim there's not much to worry about. Early (steel) rear-quarter bumpers can corrode, as can the aluminium impact bumpers, although at least in the latter case it's only cosmetic. At least everything is available, with the exception of the horn grilles of the earliest cars – but just because it's available it doesn't mean it's affordable...

Conclusion

With such a wide array of models over the years, you've got a lot of choices to make if you want a classic 911. What you buy is usually dictated by your budget, but regardless of what you can afford there are certain gems worth seeking out. You'd be surprised how easy it is to work on the 911 yourself; even an engine rebuild isn't difficult although you'll need to trust certain items, such as the fuel injection system, to the experts. Buy well and the costs, unlike the enjoyment, will be kept to a minimum.

£196.80

1972 Porsche 911 T
Value: £15,000
Quote: **£196.80** (£250x/s unlimited mpa)

PORSCHE 914 (1969-1975)

The mid-engined 914 is an acquired taste, but will certainly stand out on the road   Words: Richard Dredge Photography: www.magiccarpics.co.uk

Below
Good to drive, if slightly unusual looking, 914 makes a much cheaper alternative to its 911 brother

If you've always hankered after a Porsche but don't want to follow the crowd, this could be the car for you. Thanks to the 914 being built with left-hand drive only (apart from just a dozen Crayford conversions), many potential buyers are put off the idea of tracking one down. There also aren't many around; this may have supposedly been a sportscar for the masses, but it was still expensive. When new in 1969, it was £1000 more than an MGB.

However, this is one of Porsche's rare attempts at a production car with the engine in the middle, and as a result the 914 is endowed with fabulous handling. While the 1.7-litre cars aren't at all quick, at least the bigger-engined versions are. What all 914s do offer though, is reliability in spades, but perhaps the clincher is the fact that when you take one out, nobody will know what it is.

In the mid-1960s, Porsche and Volkswagen had opposing problems. While the former wanted to expand but was constrained by the exclusive nature of products, the latter needed to inject a bit of glamour into its line-up – and hence its image. A marriage was the

perfect solution, and at the September 1969 Frankfurt motor show two versions of the Karmann-built 914 appeared.

Compared with the contemporary 911, the 914 is a doddle to drive quickly. While the iconic rear-engined monster can easily be provoked into exiting corners backwards at high speed, the 914 has much more grip than the chassis needs – especially if there's just a 1.7-litre engine fitted. This air-cooled four-pot could take the 914 to 107mph with its modest 80bhp, so if you're a speed demon you won't get your kicks here.

However, the 1.8 and 2.0-litre cars feel much more lively and are even better to pilot; with beautifully fluid handling and excellent stopping power thanks to disc brakes all round, you can really exploit their power. The 914 tips the scales at under a ton, so not only is it quicker than you'd think but it's fabulously agile too. The only fly in the ointment is the gearchange; while the 914 has the same box as the 911, the smaller car's tortuous linkage doesn't make swapping cogs an experience to savour. However, upgrades are possible and you can adapt to it, so all is not lost.

What to look for

Rust is the major problem, with the battery tray usually the first place to go. Once corrosion takes a hold here, the whole engine bay can corrode quickly. If left, the rear suspension mountings will rot through and the car will collapse around its wheels. Also check the sill steps, door bottoms plus front and rear boot floors, as rot is common here. The same is true of the boot floor, as the rear light seals can leak; the floorpans behind the seats also need checking. The key thing is to remove the targa top and try to open and close the doors; if the bodyshell has been weakened you may not be able to do so, or refit the roof panel.

The engines are generally reliable, although valves can drop. Potentially more serious is perished rubber fuel pipes; if these split the car can quickly become toast. Check to see how flexible they are; there's a good chance they'll be hard and brittle, and there will probably be signs of the rubber cracking.

Considering its lowly status relative to its bigger brother the 911, the 914 was more technically advanced in some ways. The 914 featured Bosch fuel injection while some 911s

'What all 914s do offer is reliability in spades, but perhaps the clincher is the fact that when you take one out, nobody will know what it is'

still had carburettors, and although some owners aren't comfortable maintaining this, preventative maintenance is possible up to a point. When major engine work is required it's easy enough to drop the unit and work on it outside the car, but general maintenance is easy, with no special tools required.

The fuel-injection system is reliable, but it can go wrong and when it does it's usually costly to fix. That's why some owners convert to carbs; various set-ups have been tried, but none of them work as well as a decently set-up fuel-injection system, which is why you're better off keeping things standard and getting an expert to sort it out properly.

Slotting a six-pot engine into a four-pot car spices things up, but it is rarely cost-effective. That's why you're better off looking for a 914/6 – although they're not easy to track down, which is the reason why most such conversions have taken place.

Try to roll the car on the flat and see if it quickly grinds to a halt; seized rear brake calipers are common, with replacement costing £150 apiece. Pre-1973 cars were fitted with a tortuous linkage that rather spoils the driving experience – especially once it's worn. A common trick is to upgrade the linkage, at a cost of £300.

Porsche 914 2.0 (1973-1976)
SPECIFICATIONS

Engine
1971cc flat-four, eight overhead valves. Alloy heads and block. Bosch D-Jetronic fuel injection

Power
100bhp @ 5000rpm

Torque
115lb ft @ 3500rpm

Transmission
Five-speed manual

Suspension
Front: Independent with Macpherson struts, longitudinal torsion bars, lower wishbones
Rear: Independent with oblique semi-trailing arms, coil springs, telescopic dampers

Brakes
Front: 281mm discs
Rear: 282mm discs
Servo-assisted

Weight
950kg (2090lb)

Performance
0-60mph: 10.5sec
Top speed: 118mph

Value
Cost new: £3689 (1973)
Value now: £8000-£16,000

Conclusion

Just 100 examples of the 914 were officially imported into the UK. Some of those haven't survived, but lots more have been brought in from Europe and the US, and there are now reckoned to be 350 examples here. You can pick up a 914 for as little as £3000, but you're better off avoiding any 1.7-litre model priced much under £5500.

An equivalent 1.8-litre car is £7000 and it's another £1000 for a 2.0 example. Add £2000 for anything nice; the best examples can fetch over £15,000, while you won't buy a decent 914/6 for less than £17,000, with a really nice one more like £25,000.

» Thanks to Bruce Manning of Porsche Club GB.

£127.50

1972 Porsche 914 1700
Value: £6000
Quote: **£127.50** (£250x/s unlimited mpa)

»Info

TIMELINE
» 1969: The 914 goes on sale in Europe; cheapest is the 914/4, powered by a fuel-injected 1.7-litre VW 411 engine; available alongside is the 914/6, with a 2-litre flat-six Porsche engine.
» 1970: The 914 becomes available in the UK, but at £2261 for the 914/4 and £3475 for the 914/6, there aren't many takers.
» 1971: A right-hand-drive conversion is now available from Crayford; at £550, it's too costly for most.
» 1972: The 914/6 is replaced by the 914S/SC/2.0, fitted with an enlarged and strengthened Volkswagen 411/412 2-litre engine.
» 1973: The 1.7-litre powerplant in the 914/4 is taken up to 1.8 litres; power remains unchanged at 80bhp while the B-pillar (or sail panel in Porsche parlance) is now trimmed in vinyl.
» 1975: The final 914 is built in September, when the model is replaced by Porsche's new collaboration with VW/Audi, the 924.

SPECIALISTS
» RSK, Cheshire. +44 (0)1829 752 597
» Carrera Performance, West Sussex. +44 (0)1403 891 911, www.carreraperformance.com
» 914 Conversions, www.914conversions.com
» Automobile Atlanta, Georgia. www.autoatlanta.com
» Mittel Motor, Germany. www.mittelmotor.com

CLUBS
» Porsche Club GB, +44 (0)1608 652 911, www.porscheclubgb.com
» http://autos.groups.yahoo.com/ group/uk914

BOOKS
» 914 and 914-6 Porsche, A Restorers Guide To Authenticity by B Johnson. ISBN 0-929758-21-8
» How To Restore & Modify Your Porsche 914 & 914/6 by Patrick Paternie. ISBN 0-7603-0584-6
» Porsche 914 & 914-6 by Brian Long. ISBN 0-1-84584-030-5

Below

While the SS1 will never be worth as much as many more familiar sporting classics, decent cars are now sought after.

With the Spitfire, MGB, TR7 and Midget consigned to history, and the X1/9 breathing its last, it's hard to see how Reliant could have failed with the Scimitar SS1 when it was unveiled at the 1984 NEC motor show. The SS1 tag was an abbreviation of Small Sports 1, and with its low purchase price, simple mechanicals and sharp chassis, the SS1 was bound to be a roaring success. The company planned to make 2000 examples every year, which surely wouldn't be difficult, even with those awkward lines. Yet in a production run that lasted from 1984 until 1995, just 1507 SS1 models rolled off the production lines.

The Scimitar SS1 was designed by Giovanni Michelotti; it was to be the last car he styled before his death. While open-topped two-seaters had been all the rage in the 1970s, by the 1980s it was the hot hatch that was king, and it seemed that Reliant had missed the affordable convertible bandwagon.

Perhaps it was the three-wheeler connotations that put people off – whatever, a redesign in 1988 (when the car became the SS2) and another hefty restyle in 1990 didn't do anything to halt the decline in sales. This latter version was called the SST (the T being for Towns, as in the designer William Towns), and it provided a far neater solution. Not only

was it much simpler to build, which meant lower production costs, but it also looked better as the lines were far smoother. Gone were the bug-eye headlamps, replaced by conventional pop-up units, and in came the Ford 1.4-litre CVH engine. There was still the option of a Nissan 1.8Ti powerplant, too – but still buyers stayed away.

In 1992 there was another restyle, with the car now known as the Sabre, and subsequently the Scimitar Sabre. Now there was the choice of Ford 1.4 CVH or Nissan 1.8 Turbo engines along with the 1.4-litre Rover K-series unit. A couple of 1.8 turbo versions exist, but while a 2.0-litre Rover variant was listed, none was built. Despite the chunkier flared wheelarches, 15-inch alloy wheels and more sporty looks of this latest derivative, the writing was on the wall.

By 1995 it was all over, with Reliant calling in the receivers. With so few SS1s having been built, the car was bound to become a classic – especially with its affordable two-seater formula. It's well made, great fun to drive and cheap to run, while most parts are still available.

With so many positives and no significant negatives, it's no surprise that values are starting to climb, albeit fairly slowly at the moment. That's almost certain to change though, with demand easily outstripping supply – especially for

the high-performance derivatives. At the moment, £300-600 buys an early 1300-1600 for restoration, while £1300 will get you a usable everyday car; £2000 upwards nets a really good example, but you need to add around 50% more to each of these values if it's a turbocharged car you're after.

Engine

Considering how few SS1s were built, it's amazing that there were five different engines available during its lifetime. The 1300, 1400 and 1600 Ford CVH units are familiar powerplants that are easy to source. The Nissan Silvia 1800 Turbo is harder to find, but the 1.4 K-series motors are plentiful. It's easy to swap between the various CVH powerplants, while the chassis mounts on galvanised cars will take either CVH or Nissan units – although there are small differences between the Silvia engine and the Reliant one. The coolant pipes are made of mild steel, which (predictably) corrode. They don't need to be renewed too often, but if new ones are required you can fit replacements for around £13 a throw or buy stainless steel items from Queensbury Road Garage (QRG). Check for signs of overheating, such as a mayonnaise-like substance on the underside of the oil-filler cap. This gives

It may have failed to save Reliant, but the SS1's rarity, low cost and fulfilling drive make it a decent classic to own today
Words: Richard Dredge Photography: www.magiccarpics.co.uk

RELIANT SCIMITAR SS1 (1984-1995)

_1600_

**Reliant
Scimitar SS1
1800Ti**
SPECIFICATIONS

Engine
1809cc in-line four, SOHC,
eight valves. Alloy head,
cast-iron block. Nissan
electronic fuel injection,
Garrett T2 turbocharger

Power
135bhp @ 6000rpm

Torque
141lb ft @ 4000rpm

Transmission
Five-speed manual,
rear-wheel drive

Suspension
Front: Independent with
coil springs, double
wishbones, telescopic
dampers, anti-roll bar
Rear: Independent with
semi-trailing arms, coil
springs, inclined telescopic
dampers, anti-roll bar

Brakes
Front: 226mm
ventilated discs
Rear: 203mm drums
Servo-assisted

Weight
930kg (2048lb)

Performance
0-60mph: 7.0sec
Top speed: 129mph

Value
Cost new: £13,500 (1990)
Value now £1000-£4000

'With so few having been built, the SS1 was bound to become a classic. It's well made and fun to drive, while most parts are still available'

away the fact that the head gasket has gone; if things are really bad, the cylinder head itself may have warped too, as all SS1 powerplants featured an alloy unit.

Because the radiator sits significantly lower than the top of the CVH engine, there can be problems with air locks in the cooling system. A genuine Reliant CVH motor will have a 17mm bolt by number one exhaust port, so the cooling system can be bled. If the engine has been swapped for a Ford unit, its thermostat housing also needs to be fitted, or it won't be possible to bleed the system properly, resulting in air locks. This will be evident by a tendency to run hot, along with a lack of decent cabin heating.

The CVH engine should have had its oil changed every 6000 miles and a new cambelt within the last 30,000 miles or five years. As long as it's looked after (with preferable 3000-mile oil changes being the key), it shouldn't be hard to coax 200,000 miles out of a CVH powerplant. CVH camshafts lose their sparkle after around 50,000 miles, but will soldier on for at least double this mileage as long as – again – the oil is changed regularly.

The Nissan unit is also long-lived, but its turbocharger will fail long before the engine does unless it's treated with kid gloves. That means renewing the oil every 3000 miles, as well as getting the motor up to temperature before using the revs. If the engine isn't left to tick over for a couple of minutes before switching off, the turbo's lifespan will also be reduced. A sure sign that an owner hasn't followed these rules is white smoke being emitted from the exhaust at idle. However, beware of an unscrupulous owner who may have increased the idle speed to hide a worn turbo – the white smoke is only emitted when the engine is ticking over at its correct idle speed of 800-850rpm. By the way, an exchange turbo is nearly £500.

Listen for blowing from the exhaust manifold of any Nissan-engined car. It could just be the manifold-to-turbo gasket has failed, or something more sinister such as a cracked manifold; These units aren't a Nissan item, but a Reliant mirror-image copy and they're no longer available. They have a weak spot due to a casting flaw which can be easily fixed if removed – a

piece of flashing can break off and take the turbo with it. A tubular version is currently being sourced via a group of owners.

Transmission

SS1s with Ford or Rover engines are equipped with the same four or five-speed gearbox that was fitted to the Sierra. Notchy changes and difficulty in selecting the first and second ratios when cold give away the fact that the transmission hasn't been filled with the correct Castrol SMX mineral oil, which can be bought at Ford dealers. If conventional gearbox oil has been used, the unit will be unpleasant to work with but its lifespan shouldn't be compromised. Other than this, the gearboxes are very tough, partly due the SS1's light weight which doesn't put much strain on the transmission.

All SS1s used a Sierra 3.92:1 differential, which is bulletproof as long as oil levels are maintained. This, as with the gearbox, has no drain plug so – unless you want to suck the lubricant out with a tube – you can only top it up rather than renew the oil completely. It should be filled with SAE 90.

Above
Cloth upholstery should still be fine even at 100,000 miles: leather is costly to revive, while Alcantara suffers the most.

»

»Info

Unless the car has been to the moon and back, it's unlikely that there'll be any problems with the rest of the transmission. Clutches are very durable and so are universal joints and driveshafts; you need to check the gaiters on the latter. If anything does need replacing, it's all available cheaply.

Suspension, steering and brakes

One of the key selling points of the SS1 is its sharp handling, which can be easily upset by wear, damage or changes to the standard specification. If the car feels floaty, it's because the shock absorbers have worn out. If you insist on originality you can spend £25 per corner on standard replacements – but they don't help the dynamics. A far better bet is to invest two or three times this on Spax or AVO adjustables, which give a far better ride/handling balance. Polyurethane bushes are also available, from QRG.

It won't help if any of the wishbones have cracked in the front suspension, something that they're prone to; used ones are available for £40 or so. You'll need to remove the front wheels to get a proper look, and while you're at it, take a peek at the state of the anti-roll bar links because they are prone to breaking – replacements cost £14 apiece.

The SS1 was originally fitted with 5Jx13 steel wheels or 6Jx14 alloys, but many owners are tempted to beef things up. While this doesn't necessarily cause problems as such, it doesn't do the car's dynamics any favours. It's far preferable to keep things as they were when the model left the factory. However, it is true that fitting 6x15

wheels helps stability a little, but anything larger causes tramlining.

The brakes are marginal at best, thanks to the standard MG Metro-derived system. To get the best out of this, ensure the discs are at full thickness (10mm) and that the pads are in good condition. Fitting uprated pads such as EBC Greenstuff is a worthwhile move, especially as a set costs just £33. Alternatively, you can upgrade the whole set-up; Graham Walker does a bolt-on ventilated disc kit for £320 – or you could put together your own system; see www.ss1turbo.com for more on this.

Bodywork, electrics and trim

Thanks to bodywork that's entirely plastic, there's no need to worry about corrosion of any of the panels. Despite these vehicles being built by hand, the shut lines were inconsistent even when the cars were new, so don't expect really tight panel gaps. However, that doesn't mean that there are no issues with the panelwork, because problems can arise.

The nosecone is susceptible to cracks, as it's made of moulded rubber which perishes over time. Once the paint has cracked, moisture gets in and makes things worse. It's possible to fill and repaint the nosecone, but if it's badly damaged you'll be better off finding a used replacement for about £100; a new one is £350.

The plastic panels are a disadvantage as well as a benefit, as painting them can cause problems. Because the SS1's outer skin is of

varying materials, it can be tricky to achieve a consistent finish and colour across all of them. The doors, rear deck, headlamp surrounds and floorpan all used traditional hand-laid glass-reinforced plastic. But the bootlid and bonnet were made from vacuum-moulded glassfibre (as used by Lotus), while the nosecone and bumper, as well as all four wings, were rubber mouldings by Dunlop. They were all sprayed as a complete unit by Reliant, but over the years the panels can discolour at varying rates.

What you really need to concern yourself with is rot in the chassis – especially with cars that don't have a galvanised frame. These were officially fitted from chassis 900, but some appeared as soon as 700 because Reliant wasn't fussy which order it built the cars in. These earlier cars didn't have a galvanised frame, and it's unlikely you'll find one that doesn't need at least minor chassis repairs. Even the later cars, fitted with a zinc-plated unit, can suffer from major corrosion. It only takes a minor scrape to remove the coating and the corrosion will start – and unless it's nipped in the bud things will just go from bad to worse. Repair sections are available from QRG.

The key areas to analyse chassis-wise are the crossmember below the radiator, along with the main rail that runs behind the boot; it's the one to which the bumper is mounted. Also take a look at the backbone and differential housing – and, in the case of the latter, there can be problems with cracks as well as rot. There was a factory recall for a reinforcement to be added to the front diff

Clockwise from left
Pop-up headlamps replaced original styling in 1990 revise. Wedge design epitomises era.

»Info

SPECIALISTS
» Graham Walker, +44 (0)1244 381777, www.grahamwalker.co.uk
» Queensberry Road Garage, +44 (0)1536 513351, www.qrgservices.co.uk

CLUBS
» Reliant Owners' Club, www.reliantownersclub.co.uk
» Reliant Sabre and Scimitar Owners' Club. +44 (0)20 8977 6625, www.scimitarweb.com
» Scimitar Drivers' Club. +44 (0)117 951 8741, www.scimitardriver.co.uk

BOOKS
» Reliant Sportscars by Don Pither. Sutton, ISBN 0-7509-2388-1
» Rebel Without Applause by Daniel Lockton. Bookmarque, ISBN 1-870519-64-7

mount; this only affects cars built in the first year of production. There's a chance some models were missed, but they'll almost certainly have had the work done by now anyway; if so, there should be no further problems. The worst rot occurs in the sills plus the A and B-posts, along with the jacking points on the front and rear tubular outriggers. The fuel tank, located at the back of the car, can also corrode. Smell for leaks; if you can see there is a problem, you can buy a stainless steel replacement from QRG for £265. The 1800Ti was fitted with a different tank from the rest of the range, and it isn't interchangeable.

If there's any significant corrosion in the chassis, it's easy enough – if time-consuming – to remove all the body panels. Except for the five wing nuts that hold the nosecone in place, all outer panels are secured with either pop rivets or T25 Torx screws. Once everything has been taken off you'll probably find some rot in the sills, but it's not a tricky job to put everything right. You'll also need to remove the front wings and doors for access to the A-posts, which have a tendency to rot through. This will be given away by the doors sagging; once it's been weakened by corrosion, the whole A-post bows under the strain.

As well as the chassis, there are a few other potential rot spots that you need to check very closely. The quarterlight frames aren't very durable, and once they've gone the windows will start moving about. This in turn will lead to rainwater getting into the cabin, so make sure the frames haven't rotted or cracked. Replacements

are about £150 apiece – plus fitting and painting.

The interior trim is very simple, with cloth fitted as standard to the 1300, 1400 and 1600 cars; this should still be in fine condition even at 100,000 miles. However, if you're looking at a vehicle with leather upholstery make sure there's no damage, because the cost of repairing hide-covered seats and panels is high. Worst to suffer is the standard Alcantara trim on the 1800Ti – even low-mileage cars can have worn-out seat covers, which is why leather is a better option.

Door panels go home on all cars, with seatbelt dents normal on the trailing edge; good second-hand items are sometimes available. At least the carpets are virtually indestructible, even after years of water ingress if the hood isn't up to scratch. The vinyl roof (mohair on Sabres) is durable enough, and not expensive to replace at £200 plus fitting, but still check for splits and holes. Even better if the car has a hard-top fitted; they're a desirable extra and a decent one will fetch £200-300.

If you're looking at an 1800Ti, make sure the heat shield is fitted between the turbocharger and the wiring loom. If it's missing, there's a good chance the cables will have been cooked, causing them to go brittle and potentially to short out. On the 1800Ti you also need to check for water leaks; both the ECU and air-flow meter can suffer badly from water ingress.

Ensure that the headlights go up and down exactly as they should; they often fail for a multitude of reasons. While it's occasionally because the linkages have seized, it's more likely

to be an electrical fault such as a burnt-out motor, failed relay or poor connection. Replacement motors are about £40, although the usual problem is down to corroded parking contacts inside the motor terminal box. A few minutes with a soldering iron plus two 20p diodes will fix it (see www.scimitarss1.co.uk).

Most SS1s were also equipped with electric windows, mirrors and aerial, so check these all work because they often don't. It's usually down to poor connections though, so any fixes shouldn't be costly.

Conclusion

While the SS1 will never be worth as much as many more familiar sporting classics, thanks to the quirky looks, its value hit rock bottom quite a while ago. This means if you don't find a good car soon you're going to have to pay significantly more when you eventually do.

Pick of the bunch is definitely anything with a Nissan 1.8T engine, but just 208 of these were built, so you'll have to look hard. Luckily most have survived.

£150.60

FOOTMAN JAMES
Insurance specialists. At your service.

1990 Reliant Scimitar SS1
Value: £2000
Quote: £150.60 (£100x/s unlimited mpa)

SUNBEAM ALPINE & TIGER

Offering five incarnations, great affordability and a fun drive, Sunbeam's roadster is definitely worth a look – and we defy you to ignore its awesome V8-powered Tiger sibling Words: Richard Dredge Photography: www.magiccarpics.co.uk

'The Sunbeam Alpine offers a superb alternative to the more predictable British sportsters available'

Try to think of an affordable two-seater roadster from the 1960s and you'll invariably end up with images of an octagon-badged drop-top in your mind. But look beyond the obvious and there's an even more affordable mass-market convertible that for some reason has always been overlooked – Sunbeam's Alpine. With lines that are discreet yet stylish, plus heaps of affordability and easy maintenance on its side, the Alpine offers a superb alternative to the more predictable British sportsters available.

All Alpine derivatives are worth a look, but it's the later models everyone wants, as the car was developed significantly throughout production. There were five key variations offered on the Alpine theme, yet there's little difference in values between them even though the later ones are more sought after. You can expect to buy a shed that has an MoT but needs work for £2000. A usable car that needs nothing but is cosmetically tatty will set you back £4000, while a really nice example can be up to £7000. Something that's close to concours will command an asking price of £10,000.

Engine

The powerplants fitted to Rootes cars are generally famed for their durability thanks to straightforward engineering, although none of them turns the Alpine into a fast car. As tweaked versions of engines found in Rootes' contemporary saloons, those fitted to the Alpine should not give many problems, the most likely being overheating due to previous neglect. The alloy cylinder heads are prone to warping if they've not been torqued down properly after replacement, and if the anti-freeze level has been allowed to drop in the coolant there's probably some corrosion within the system.

One of the common bodges is that of fitting an engine from a Minx or Sceptre and passing it off as a genuine Alpine unit. Outwardly there's little difference, but put your foot down and you can feel that it's less powerful.

Another potential problem is that of a cracked block, due to a fault line that is given way along the water jacket – although this is only really an issue if the coolant within the engine has been allowed to freeze. Spotting whether or not the block has cracked isn't necessarily that easy (water seepage is the most likely symptom), but repairing such damage isn't too difficult anyway.

Oil leaks are also common, as the engines use a scroll-type oil seal. That also means the crank pulleys will wear, and eventually you'll need a new one, at £80 plus fitting.

Although Alpine engines are inherently durable, they're sometimes thrashed to get the most out of them. Any of the units fitted from the factory should take 130,000 miles quite happily, but they don't like neglect very much. The most likely cause of problems with the 1725cc motor fitted to the Series V is using an incorrect procedure for changing the oil and filter. It's a convoluted process, which if not adhered to will lead to seized big-end bearings thanks to oil starvation.

When you test drive the car take a look at the oil pressure when the engine is up to temperature. At least 15psi should be showing at idle on a three-bearing unit (pre-Series V cars), with 50-55psi

showing over 2000rpm. The 1725 engine will give 25psi at idle quite happily, with 45psi or more showing at 2000rpm.

Transmission

From the outset overdrive was available on the Alpine, but it wasn't always fitted. That's a shame because cars without it aren't nearly as nice to use, and locating a unit to retro fit isn't that easy as overdrive set-ups are getting increasingly scarce. In fact, they're so hard to find that you can now expect to pay up to £500 for a reconditioned overdrive box, and you can't beat the system by trying to use a Hunter unit as it won't fit.

The four-speed manual gearbox fitted to all Alpines is nice enough to use, but it wasn't until the Series IV that syncromesh was available on all ratios. Earlier cars did without first-gear syncro, but if you don't like swapping gears at all you could always buy an auto Alpine – as long as you're happy with a Series IV. Not fitted to any of the other derivatives, the Borg Warner type 35 auto box is a reliable unit that was used in all sorts of

vehicles throughout the sixties.

Autos are traditionally frowned upon by 'those who know', but the self-shifting box in the Alpine isn't a bad one at all. The problem is that only 87 of these cars were made and some of those have been converted to manual transmission. If you wanted to reverse the procedure you can do it, as long as you can track down the relevant parts from a suitable Rootes Group car (such as a Sceptre or Minx).

Suspension, steering and brakes

All Alpines were fitted with the same basic semi-trailing wishbone suspension layout, but there were detail changes along the way. Series I-III cars got a front suspension that used a lower trunnion and kingpin set-up which needs regular greasing to stay sharp. Many cars don't get the regular TLC they need, leading to sloppy handling through worn or seized kingpins – and finding new bits for the suspension of a Series I-III car isn't easy. Series IV and V cars used Metalastik bushes instead, to reduce maintenance

and give a more comfortable ride. And although you don't have to grease kingpins frequently, the chances are that the bushes will need replacing by now, especially as they've probably been soaked in engine oil. Polyurethane items are available, at £10 each for the lower units and £7 for the upper ones.

At the rear, lever arm dampers were replaced by telescopic items from the introduction of the Series III. But apart from checking for the usual leaks, there are no inherent problems with either type of suspension.

The steering boxes fitted throughout production have a habit of leaking, while the idler assembly also likes to wear or seize. But everything is available to keep the steering sharp, although replacing a box isn't the easiest task to perform unless you know what you're doing.

Wire wheels are very popular with Alpine owners – especially if the vehicle doesn't get used very much. As a result, you have to check the rims carefully, as broken spokes and worn splines are almost a given if the car has seen much

'Just about all trim is available either new or reconditioned, although many of the cabin parts have been remade rather than being new-old stock'

»

Above
Rot is the Alpine's main enemy: the tinwork will not stand up to the rigours of hard use as well as the mechanicals.

use. There aren't any problems associated with the braking system on the Alpine, although the self-adjusting rear brakes that were initially fitted to the Series V didn't last long – by November 1967 they reverted to the manually-adjustable system fitted to Series I-IV cars.

Bodywork, electrics and trim

Until a decade or so ago there was a surprisingly large number of Alpines being used every day. But despite the car's practicality, such use will take its toll on the bodyshell, which doesn't soldier on like the mechanicals can. That means repairs on a shoestring are commonplace, so you've got to have your wits about you if you're not to be done up like a kipper. It's also worth getting an expert to look over the car before you buy – it's easy not to notice the signs of a bodged restoration, and sometimes even a trained eye can miss things.

A lack of factory-applied rust protection takes its toll, although the monocoque is very strong as long as the tin worm hasn't got to it. The most important place to check, and the first place that's likely to rot, is along the length of the sills. These are essential to the car's strength, so

make sure that all three layers of the sill are present. Without taking the car to pieces that's not possible, so if work has been done make sure you look at photographic evidence.

Unrestored cars in good condition are pretty much extinct – if the vendor claims the example you're looking at is original a possible giveaway is to check that the sills are curved to match the convex profile of the door. Cheap replacement panels are straight and don't look quite right, and once water has got into the leading edge of the sills it works its way to the back, wreaking havoc along the way.

The problem starts when the caulk seal that should bridge the gap between the front wing and the inner wheelarch drops out, allowing the water in. Another thing to check is that there's a step in the splash panel at the back of the front inner wheelarch. If the panel is smooth, it's just a cover panel that's almost certainly masking something nasty.

Unless the car has been properly restored you can bank on having the sills rebuilt on pretty much anything you look at – expect to pay £800 to get each side fixed, including blending the paint in. If possible, to check the integrity of the sills, jack the car up both front and rear to see

if the back door gap closes up – if you can no longer open the door you know the structure of the car has been weakened. But you can expect to see 1-2mm movement of the door in its aperture and you have to make sure that the jacking points themselves aren't just a memory.

You'll probably find rust around the headlamps, along the base of the windscreen and at the back of the engine bay under the master cylinders, so lift the bonnet (which rarely rots) and inspect closely. The doors aren't especially rust-prone, but the hinges wear allowing them to drop. The front edge and underside are the most likely places where rot will be lurking, and if the door's been reskinned ensure the rubber seal is there and that the profile of the whole panel is correct.

Check the back of the car, particularly the base of the wings which should have a drain hole visible. If it's not there, some poor repairs have been made at some point. And while you're sniffing around this area, analyse the inner rear wheelarches. Open the boot to inspect the back corners of the boot floor and also ensure that the trailing edge of the bootlid isn't riddled with rot.

Floorpans can corrode badly, so make sure you lift the mats or carpets in the

TIMELINE
» 1959: Series I Alpine arrives with 78bhp 1494cc engine, four-branch manifold and alloy head. Based on Hillman Husky floorpan. 11,904 are made.
» 1960: 80bhp 1592cc Series II on sale, still with fins and detachable aluminium hard-top of its predecessor but more comfortable seating. 19,956 are built.
» 1963: Series III on sale, with GT option: no folding hood, to keep weight and cost down, plus wooden trim and steering wheel. Sought-after now only if converted to have a folding roof. Detachable hard-top steel instead of aluminium and twin fuel tanks replaced earlier cars' single item. Just 5863 Series IIIs are made, making it rarest Alpine (except for the Harrington fixed-roofs). The most refined of the big-finned models.
» 1964: Series IV arrives with the tailfins almost gone. Grille is a single chrome bar. 12,406 Series IVs were built.
» 1965: Series V appears. Five-bearing engine for first time. It's a 1724cc unit with two Stromberg carbs and 92bhp – still only enough to push it to 100mph.
» 1968: Final Alpine is built, after 19,122 Series Vs have been produced.

SPECIALISTS
» Sunbeam Spares Co. +44 (0)121 313 1668, www.thesunbeamsparescompany.co.uk
» Sunbeam Supreme, Leics. +44 (0)1162 742 525, www.sunbeamsupreme.co.uk
» Sunbeam Classic Spares, Derbys. +44 (0)1332 850 856
» Alpine West Midlands. +44 (0)1564 783 222, www.sunbeam-alpine.co.uk
» Sunbeam Alpine Centre, Berks. +44 (0)1488 686 773

CLUBS
» Alpine Owners' Club
» Tiger Owners' Club

BOOKS
» Sunbeam Alpine and Tiger, The Complete Story by Graham Robson. Crowood: ISBN 1-85223-941-7
» Tiger, Alpine, Rapier by Richard Langworth. Osprey: ISBN 0-85045-443-3 (out of print)

front footwells to see what state the leading edges are in. The area around the accelerator is especially rot-prone. Try rocking the seats, too – they may be attached to crumbling metal, just like the handbrake, which is mounted to the right of the driver's seat.

While you're inside the car, take a look at the mountings for the rear spring hangers. These are located behind the front seats on an angled panel, and signs of rust may be only the start of the story – the spring hangers are a real pain to repair properly and you won't want to buy a car on which they're rotten. However, just because the floor above them has rusted it doesn't mean the hangers themselves need work. Make sure you check them from underneath anyway, and while you're there also inspect the jacking points closely, as they may have dissolved.

The final rot-spot is the rear corners of the hard-top, if it's one of the steel items fitted to Series III cars onwards. The earlier aluminium roofs don't give problems, but the steel ones invariably corrode and the perspex windows craze.

From September 1965 an alternator was fitted in place of a dynamo, and these fed a regulator and warning lamp

relay on the inner wing. If the unit is overcharging these ancilliaries will get fried (and cost you £50 to replace), so it's worth checking the alternator's output to ensure it's working correctly.

Just about all trim is available either new or reconditioned, although many of the cabin parts have been remade rather than being new-old stock. Rubber mats are no longer available but most people want carpet sets anyway, and even the exterior trim is available (except for bumpers), as it's all been reproduced.

Conclusion

If you're searching for a motor to drive regularly you're better off with a Series V, as due to its larger five-bearing engine the car is more usable. But if you want an Alpine with fins your best bet is to look for a Series III car as it has a much larger boot and more comfortable seats.

Probably the nicest Alpine is one that wasn't officially made: the GT (complete with wood trim) but boasting a soft-top plus Series V engine and suspension.

None of the cars is very quick, but if you want some serious power in an Alpine shell you could always look at buying a Tiger. If there isn't enough power there, you're probably beyond help... △

Sunbeam Alpine Series V
SPECIFICATIONS

Engine
1725cc in-line four, eight overhead valves. Alloy head, cast-iron block. Two Zenith-Stromberg 150 CD carburettors

Power
92.5bhp @ 5500rpm

Torque
110lb ft @ 3700rpm

Transmission
Four-speed manual

Suspension
Front: Independent with coil springs, double wishbones, telescopic dampers, anti-roll bar
Rear: Live axle with half-elliptic leaf springs, telescopic dampers bar

Brakes
Front: 250mm discs
Rear: 229mm drums
Servo-assisted

Weight
1020kg (2246lb)

Performance
0-60mph: 13.6sec
Top speed: 98mph

Value
Cost new: £877 (1966)
Value now: £3000-£10,000

BUYING A TIGER

'Take one Alpine
Series IV, a car styled as
innocuously as an MGB, then
shoehorn in a 260cu-in V8 – and,
voila; a cut-price Cobra'

Above
All-American
power for a very
British car: Tiger
was a roaring
success – until
Chrysler said no..

Take one Sunbeam Alpine Series IV, a car styled as innocuously as an MGB, then shoehorn a snarling 260cu-in (4.2-litre) V8 into its nose. Change the steering box for a rack to improve precision, add a tougher Salisbury axle along with a Panhard rod to the rear suspension to help keep the thing on the tarmac – and, *voila*; a cut-price Cobra alternative.

The Tiger came about after Ian Garrad, Rootes' US West Coast manager, saw a sportscar race in which Shelby Cobras trounced its rivals. He reckoned there was a market for a hot Alpine, so he approached Carroll Shelby to discuss feasibility. Within a month Shelby had readied a prototype and, thanks to the relatively small amount of re-engineering involved, the real thing was developed in just nine months. It was sold in the US in 1964 – the car wouldn't reach Britain until the next year. The Tiger was developed for export only (and specifically the American market), as the contracted builder Jensen didn't have the capacity to meet early demand.

Although the Tiger proved an immediate success, the writing was already on the wall. Chrysler had taken a controlling stake in Rootes Group and it didn't want a rival maker's engine under the bonnet. A MkII version was marketed briefly in 1967, again for export only; just 10 right-hand drive cars were officially built. This second derivative featured a 289cu-in (4727cc) engine pushing out 200bhp; top speed rose to

125mph but the plug was pulled in June 1967 with just 6551 MkIs and 534 MkIIs being built.

Ever since then, demand's exceeded supply. In the past few years prices have spiralled and there is no such thing as a cheap Tiger any more. Unrestored examples can still be found for around £10,000, but good show-condition MkIs are now £17,000-£20,000, with reimported MkIIs converted to RHD starting at £25,000.

Although the US market is buoyant, cars are frequently brought back into the UK. Meanwhile, in the US speculators are pushing up prices for the ultra-rare MkII, and the model's been tagged the Shelby Sunbeam Tiger. While a Tiger will never be worth as much as an equivalent Cobra, prices are moving in only one direction. So don't sit there waiting for values to drop!

Engine
Ford supplied the small-block V8 in its lowest state of tune, so all it takes to keep trouble-free is an oil change every 3000 miles. The awkward-to-reach rear spark plugs are sometimes left in for too long (one has to be changed from within the car, via a bulkhead panel). The V8 was prone to overheating but most cars have been uprated.

It's the same with the carburation; the original Ford Autolite wasn't up to the job of feeding such a big powerplant, which is why most owners replace it with a Carter or Holley on an

alloy manifold. Because parts for the 4.2-litre are getting hard to find, some owners fit a 4.7 (289cu-in) or even 5.0 (302cu-in); they're a straight swap and parts for these bigger powerplants are much easier to track down.

Transmission
Despite the Tiger's sporty nature, its four-speed gearbox is more or less bomb-proof – although the rest of the transmission doesn't last forever. If the car has been driven hard, the universal joints will be ready for replacement. Listen out for clonks as the drive is taken up.

If reverse is difficult to select, it's because the linkage has worn (around £250 to repair). Also make sure the clutch isn't slipping; a new one costs from £650. Fitting a modern Ford five-speed box is popular; it raises the gearing from 24mph/1000rpm in top to 37mph/1000rpm – but it's a pricey job at close to £6500 all-in.

Suspension, steering and brakes
The Tiger's primitive suspension struggles to contain the car under full power. There's a chance the Panhard rod will have been torn from its mountings, so check its condition; it's an easy £250 repair, though.

While the Alpine has a steering box, the Tiger's rack-and-pinion set-up gives greater precision. Although there's a lot of weight over

a roaring success...

SUNBEAM *TIGER* V8

The supreme
sports car
for rallying
motorway or
town traffic

test it and be thrilled...

the front wheels, the rack doesn't wear rapidly unless it's neglected.

With front discs and rear drums, the servo-assisted brakes are up to the job. Shared with the Alpine, the set-up is completely conventional, and aside from the usual checks for leaks and seizures, there's nothing to be wary of. The Tiger looks great on wire wheels, but the original 13x4 1/2J design was too fragile to cope with the torque – which is why alloys are a popular revision.

Bodywork, electrics and trim

Everything we've said about the Alpine, in terms of inspecting the bodywork, applies equally to the Tiger. Although there are difference between the two bodyshells, the weak spots are the same. It's a similar story for the electrics, which are straightforward, but age and heat takes its toll on connections and some of the components. A new loom is just £120 and fitting it is simple, so if the original wiring has suffered any damage it's worth just taking out the whole lot and starting again.

The original trim isn't especially durable, but good quality repro items are available – and they're not expensive. It helps that the MkI Tiger's interior is the same as the Series IV Alpine's, while the MkII Tiger's matches that of the Series V. Consequently, it's easy

enough retrimming a car from scratch, including fitting a new hood. Hard-tops are also available – at a price. Because the rear corners are rust-prone, decent original ones are scarce, which is why you'll have to pay £850 for a restored example.

Conclusion

The Tiger has never been more sought after than it is now, with values reflecting this. The result is that dogs are few and far between, but it also means Tigers are rarely bought for the fun they can provide – they're getting too valuable. While it has a well-deserved reputation for being a real handful thanks to its short wheelbase, primitive suspension and torquey V8, it also makes a surprisingly civilised long-distance tourer. Buy yours now before prices go stratospheric.

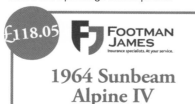
Sunbeam Tiger MkI
SPECIFICATIONS

Engine
4261cc V8, OHV with single camshaft, 16 valves. Cast-iron head and block. Single Ford twin-choke carb

Power
164bhp @ 4200rpm

Torque
258lb ft @ 2200rpm

Transmission
Ford four-speed manual

Suspension
Front: Independent with coil springs, wishbones, telescopic dampers, anti-roll bar
Rear: Live (beam) axle, half-elliptic springs, Panhard rod, telescopic dampers

Brakes
Front: 250mm discs
Rear: 228mm drums

Weight
1163kg (2565lb)

Performance
0-60mph: 9.5sec
Top speed: 117mph

Value
Cost new: £1446
Value now:
£10,000-£40,000

SUZUKI CAPPUCCINO (1991-1997)

Suzuki's sports car created a real buzz when it arrived – and it's just as popular now more than a decade after production stopped

Words: Richard Dredge
Photography:
www.magiccarpics.co.uk

Above
Light weight, trusty mechanicals and a brilliantly set up chassis means that the Cappuccino handles beautifully.

If you want economy motoring but don't want to cut back on the fun factor, this is the car for you – as long as you're not built like an over-sized rugby player! However, despite the Cappuccino's stunted exterior dimensions, it'll accommodate surprisingly big people – although there is a limit.

These Suzukis also offer plenty of fun per pound – until a few years ago, they held their value amazingly well, but things have calmed down a bit now to the point where you don't need more than four grand to snap up something worthwhile. You'll enjoy the buzz of using one every day and they're dirt cheap to run – 45mpg is no problem.

The Cappuccino is also brilliantly adaptable, because it converts between fully open and fully closed with the minimum of fuss. You can also go for the halfway option, by leaving the sliding rear window in place and travelling targa-style – although if you've got any luggage to carry that might be all you can manage because the boot is tiny and carrying the roof panels more or less fills it right up. Then there's always the other halfway option, the T-roof...

The Cappuccino came about due to Japan's Kei-Jidosha (K-class, or small car)

rules, which restrict size, power, engine capacity and top speed. As a result, the micro sportster weighed in with a 657cc engine that gave 85mph from its 63bhp. But don't let those numbers sway you!

'Punchy' sums this car up, as although the three cylinders have to be used hard to maintain progress, the light weight gives great agility. But the engine thrives on revs (it redlines at 8500rpm and the limiter doesn't cut in until 9300rpm!) and it'll probably take more abuse than you feel comfortable giving it.

The motor is mounted up front, but it's the rear wheels that are driven – and the Cappuccino weighs just 1599lb (725kg) so acceleration isn't bad with the dash to 60mph taking around eight seconds. When cruising the noise can get very tiring – remove the speed restrictor and your eardrums would need major surgery when sitting at the newly available ton. Doing so will also almost certainly lead to reliability problems.

But the Cappuccino isn't about ultimate speed – it's on the twisties that the fun starts. With a 50:50 weight distribution and a brilliantly set up chassis, it handles beautifully. Strong brakes and plenty of grip from the 165/65x14 tyres also mean you don't have to worry about losing it if you get carried away into a bend.

The steering is weighted perfectly, and the five-speed gearbox changes ratios smoothly and sharply. Even the ride is good, especially when the car's low weight is taken into account.

What to look for

As Japan doesn't use salt on its roads, these cars weren't particularly well rust-proofed – so you need to be very wary with those originally sold in that country. Even UK type-approved cars that were sold officially by Suzuki new in the UK didn't get much rot prevention – the floorpans were pretty much left untreated despite a six-year anti-corrosion bodywork warranty. As a result, the floorpans, sills and arches can all rust, although many of the lower exterior panels are plastic anyway – but the panels behind them aren't.

The area around the rear number plate is another area prone to corrosion, as is the engine bay. If you can find a car that's been Waxoyled from new, you're in luck – even better if it's been retreated every few years.

The roof panels, boot lid and bonnet are all made of aluminium, which is great for keeping the weight down but not so good when it comes to dent resistance. Bearing in mind the high

»Info

TIMELINE

» 1987: Suzuki starts work on a new two-seater sportscar.
» 1989: An initial concept is shown at the Tokyo Motor Show.
» 1990: K-car rules change, allowing slightly longer cars and engines of 660cc instead of 550cc.
» 1991: Cappuccino sales begin; talks start with UK importer about adapting the car for the British market.
» 1992: The Cappuccino makes its UK debut at the British Motor Show.
» 1993: First cars are sold in the UK.
» 1995: Final UK cars sold, as revised car goes into production in Japan. This has a different engine, an optional three-speed auto, power-steering, ABS, driver airbag and limited-slip differential.
» 1997: The final Cappuccinos are made.
» 1998: Last cars are sold, in Japan.

CLUBS

» Suzuki Cappuccino Owners' Register for Enthusiasts (SCORE), www.suzuki-cappuccino.com

SPECIFICATION

» **Engine**
657cc in-line three, DOHC, 12 valves, alloy head, fuel injection, turbocharger
» **Power**
63bhp @ 6500rpm
» **Torque**
63lb ft @ 4000rpm
» **Transmission**
Five-speed manual, rear-wheel drive
» **Suspension**
Front: Independent with coil springs, double wishbones, telescopic dampers, anti-roll bar
Rear: Independent with upper wishbones, multi-link, coil springs, telescopic dampers, anti-roll bar
» **Brakes**
Front: 231mm ventilated discs
Rear: 232mm solid discs. Servo-assisted
» **Weight**
679kg (1494lb)
» **Performance**
0-60mph: 11.3sec
Top speed: 83mph (restricted)
» **Value**
Cost new: £11,995
Value now: £1500-£4000

replacement cost, check these carefully. The seals that go round all these panels crack and let water into the cabin – a complete set will add up to over £150 but the biggest problem is a damp interior. Joining SCORE, the club for Cappuccino owners, will net you a set of mats which will protect the ones already fitted.

Buying a car with history is desirable because the engine needs its oil changing every 3000 miles to protect the turbocharger. This is usually very reliable but if it fails you're looking at over £2000 to fix it. Check for white smoke and, while you should be able to hear the turbo, it shouldn't be particularly loud.

If the car has had its restrictor removed, or its brain remapped (chipped), the chances are that it'll have seen some hard use. You can't tell if either of these things have been done just by looking at the motor, but an owner is likely to own up as they often see these things as a selling point. Cambelts need changing every 60,000 miles – on any high-mileage car it's worth replacing this as a matter of course.

Second-gear synchro can wear out, so try to beat it on the test drive. If all doesn't seem well, haggle hard on price as although the part needed is only £50, the labour rates to fit it will soon push up the cost.

It might be a spiritual successor to the Spridget, but the Cappuccino is a lot more complex. Along with a turbo and intercooler there's multi-point fuel injection and a pair of overhead camshafts acting on a quartet of valves for each cylinder. There are also plenty of toys as standard such as air-conditioning and electric windows, but they don't usually give problems.

Servicing costs are low but once you need replacement parts things tend to get pricey – so make sure everything is intact. A new exhaust is over £400, as is a headlight unit. A starter motor is more than £200, and if you need to replace the centre and side panels for the roof you're looking at £750. Ouch!

Conclusion

You don't need any special tools to service the Cappuccino, but because the engine's Electronic Control Unit (ECU) is best quizzed by a Suzuki dealer, your best bet is to join the Suzuki Cappuccino Owners' Register for Enthusiasts (SCORE). This club has a deal with various Suzuki dealers around the country, allowing you to get discounted Cappuccino servicing.

A tatty Cappuccino costs £1500, with the best ones going for up to double that. Low-mileage cars carry a premium, especially at the top end, where the difference in value can be up to £2000. But your best bet is to find a usable example for around £3000 and just enjoy it – you'll probably get most of your money back when you come to sell anyway.

£157.95

FOOTMAN JAMES
Insurance specialists. At your service.

1993 Suzuki Cappuccino
Value: £2000
Quote: **£150.60**
(£100x/s unlimited mpa)

TOYOTA MR2 MK1

Fun, reliable and cheap. Is there anything more you could as for from a sports car? Words: Richard Dredge Photography: www.magiccarpics.co.uk

MR2 is shorthand for Midship Runabout 2-seater, on account of its rev-hap py 1587cc fuel-injected engine mounted behind the two seats and driving the rear wheels.

As soon as it was launched the MR2 received rave reviews. *Car* magazine tested the MR2 on its April 1985 UK launch and struggled to find anything to criticise – the packaging, build quality, equipment levels, handling, braking, performance, economy and practicality were all worth writing home about. And at just £9295 it was a bargain. The steering getting light above 100mph was all they could come up with, but of course back in the real world you can learn to live with such things...

Such capable performance was down to the MR2's twin-cam four-pot engine with a quartet of valves for each cylinder and a 7600rpm red line. The key was a two-stage throttle set-up which took advantage of the engine's efficient top-end breathing without compromising its running at low revs. 122bhp was on offer and along with 104lb ft the car served up a top speed of 119mph and was capable of despatching the 0-60mph sprint in just 7.7 seconds. As long as the car's been looked after it should still be able to deliver that – yet you can pick one up for just £1000.

For the Japanese market there was a 1452cc version available, with a measly 83bhp on tap. A single overhead camshaft and a single carburettor conspired to keep the power output down, but performance still wasn't bad at 109mph all out, although it's definitely the poor relation alongside its bigger brother.

All UK cars came with a removable 'moon roof', which can be carried under the front bonnet when not in place. From October 1985 there was also the option of a T-bar roof, with a removable glass panel above each occupant, and a few early cars were painted in two-tone colours. Between the car's introduction and its demise there were few changes and the last Mk1 was sold in April 1990, which is when the Mk2 MR2 arrived. In those five years around 14,000 examples were sold in the UK, although many more have been imported from Japan since then.

A donor car can be yours for as little as £100, while a restoration project which runs reliably with an MOT can be picked up between £500 to £800. An average car can be obtained for £1000 to £1500 depending on its age. Pristine examples with 60,000 miles are still obtainable, for anything between £2000 and £4000. Prices of supercharged cars fluctuate around the £3500 mark.

Engine

The MR2's engine is as reliable as you'd expect from a Japanese unit. That means it'll clock up 150,000 miles with ease – and much more if well serviced and not thrashed too mercilessly. It's worth asking when the injectors were last cleaned, as it's good practice to do it every 12,000 miles. The oil should have been changed every 6000 miles with an intermediate service every 12,000 miles and a full service every 18,000 miles.

The cambelt should have been changed at 60,000 miles, and even if the car you're looking at has done well under this mileage but it's still on its original, it should be replaced anyway. Genuine dealerships attach a small silver sticker to the top of the cambelt cover detailing the date and mileage at which it was last changed. The belt will have hardened with age and despite claims and experience that the engine is 'free running' it's pretty daft to wait for the inevitable as you could be facing a hefty engine rebuild. A cambelt will cost you under £30, while a franchised dealer would typically charge a set fee of £150 to £200 to perform the routine change for you.

The main engine problems occur from blown head gaskets as a result of using the

'The engine will clock up 150,000 miles with ease, and much more if well serviced and not thrashed too mercilessly'

incorrect coolant strength. Toyota supplies specialist pre-mixed coolant to avoid such problems, which is a deep red colour, although other coolants are suitable. The key thing is to ensure that the coolant you use is of a good quality for use with aluminium heads and is not over-diluted. The level can be checked by looking into the white plastic expansion tank towards the rear of the engine bay.

Whilst here, check the tank's cap as early ones become brittle and crack which could result in air entering the system. Because of the mid-engined layout the coolant system involves long pipe runs from the back to the front of the car. The system should be bled correctly to avoid air locks, which can fool the various temperature sensors causing the revs to fluctuate between 600rpm to 2000rpm, when at idle.

If the engine is experiencing a high idle after initial warm up this suggests there's a worn idle-up valve. This is a simple electrically operated air solenoid, mounted onto the input air piping, that effectively connects an air pipe to bypass the throttle body and permits a small amount of extra air into the engine when cold. The oil pressure gauge should be reading in the top 1/3rd of the scale with the engine running above 2000rpm.

Make sure the exhaust system isn't going to need replacing soon, because the cost of new

systems is high at around £300. The standard unit can last up to 60,000 miles, but there are now several high quality stainless steel systems available which can be cheaper.

Transmission

The five-speed transmission fitted to all UK-market MR2s is pretty reliable, the only likely problem being worn synchromesh on second gear. Some Japanese cars were fitted with an automatic gearbox, and even then it was available only with the smaller engine and also as an option on supercharged cars, so if you look at a car with an auto make sure you can trace its history before parting with your cash.

It's fairly common for the manual gearbox to develop fifth-gear problems at around the 100,000-mile mark – it'll jump out of gear when you either press or lift off the throttle. The problem occurs over time due to increasing slack in the selector mechanism causing the hub engaging teeth on the fifth gear wheel and the hub sleeve to run with only partial engagement. As the slack increases with age, the wear on the gear components increases until finally the teeth take on a helical pattern causing the hub ring to slide off the gear wheel under load. The first signs of this occurring are with excessive movement of the gearstick when in top gear, so

watch out for this on a test drive. Caught early enough the life of the fifth gear components can be extended by shimming or tightening the selector fork, but badly worn components will need replacing. Before embarking on gearbox rebuilds remember that fifth gear can be accessed without removing the box, but replacement parts costs, brand new, are generally more than that of an exchange gearbox, so weigh up the options prior to any work.

The clutch is controlled hydraulically, and if it seems to be juddering when you're changing gear, it's worth checking and bleeding the system before embarking on fitting a new clutch plate.

Suspension, steering and brakes

Shock absorbers typically last around 70,000 miles before replacements are needed – if you're doing the work it's worth evaluating uprated units, as either adjustable or non-adjustable dampers can be purchased for equivalent prices to original equipment – around the £80 mark. Early cars used oil, later cars used gas, so when purchasing you need to confirm your model year to account for differences.

If there's a knocking noise coming from the front of the car when it's driven over uneven surfaces, it's probably due to worn roll bar drop

1 Das Cockpit.

2 Die Instrumentierung.   3 Das Lenkrad.   4 Die Mittelkonsole.   5 Die Spiegelverstellung.   6 Die Fensterheber.   7 Der Fahrer.

links or possibly worn steering rack bushes. Both are relatively easy replacements for the home mechanic – original equipment parts will cost £40 to £50 a side. But the droplinks are effectively only ball joints, so the imaginative home mechanic can easily make their own adjustable units from standard catalogue parts.

All MR2s were fitted with alloy wheels, the design of which was changed in October 1985. By now the lacquer will probably have seen better days whatever the design, but it's easily fixed for around £50 per wheel.

Cars supplied within the first six months of UK sales suffered from warped brake discs because they were too small to take the hard use they invariably got. Most undersized discs were replaced under warranty and from October 1985 larger units were fitted that were better able to cope with harsh treatment. Check for juddering under braking which will show the car needs new discs – the most you can expect from a standard pair is 30,000 miles, unless the car is driven gingerly. Many brake component manufacturers have now produced improved discs that give better performance and life.

The MR2 has disc brakes all round, and while they work very well, it also means the system is a more complex than the average classic's. Rear calipers can seize because of worn handbrake cables and/or worn seals, but a home mechanic can rebuild both calipers with the official repair kit for under £70. Alternatively, exchange units can be purchased for around £90 each, while handbrake cables weigh in at around £50 a set.

Bodywork, electrics and trim

Because panels for the MR2 are very expensive, it's just as well that any example that's been well cared for shouldn't need any. Poorly repaired accident damage is more likely than rotten metal. Inspect the panel fit and shut lines closely, especially around the front of the car.

But there are areas where MR2s tend to rust, and the rear wheelarches are the most common. These are followed by the quarter valances as the rot spreads, so check the whole of each rear wing very carefully – thankfully the Drivers' Club now manufactures replacement/repair panels.

There's a seam that runs across the bulkhead behind the spare wheel in the front luggage compartment. On pre-1987 cars this area is prone to rot, as is the front valance, which is vulnerable to stone chips. Later models used a plastic valance to alleviate this problem. There's another luggage bay at the back, behind the engine. Water can collect in the rearmost corners, where it makes a bid for freedom by munching its way through the metal. There are rubber bungs here which should remain unblocked, but if removed, can let the water escape.

Ask if the car has had a new windscreen, because replacing the bonded-in unit can lead to all sorts of problems. A fitter who doesn't know what they're doing will dig all the sealant out and take the paint with it. Once the new 'screen is in the surround will be rusting away out of sight.

The base of the A-post can corrode quite badly as well as the bottom of the B-post. If the car is a T-bar with leaking seals it'll be even worse, so lift

the carpets and make sure there aren't any holes where there should be metal. The inner front wheelarch liners – and on later versions the side skirts – will fill up with leaves and act as a moisture trap leading to rot on the A-posts. Check these areas, as they need regular cleaning and if the doors are creaking it's down to worn door stay pins, which is easily cured by rotating the pin through 90 degrees.

Check that all the bungs are in the various holes on the underside of the chassis, in particular the areas under the footwells and seats, as water can enter here through damaged underseal and go undetected beneath the carpets.

The front bumper reinforcement bar corrodes heavily, and you can test for this by squeezing the bumper moulding where the indicators are mounted – listen for the sound of crumbling rusty metal. A new bumper iron costs around £120.

The underside of the car uses various plastic trays to shield components such as the fuel tank, cooling pipes, cables and engine sump from road dirt and debris. For many service jobs these require removing and there is a tendency for bolts to rust or shear off. Some older cars may be missing these protective trays if lazy mechanics haven't bothered to drill out rusty bolts to provide new fixings.

Compared with most classics the MR2 has a complex electrical system, but that doesn't mean it's unreliable. The nylon cogs for the electric windows can strip, necessitating the replacement of the motor. These can be obtained secondhand but their life expectancy may be limited – new motors will be upwards of £100 each. The driver's

TOYOTA

MODEL RANGE
INTERNATIONAL MOTOR SHOW 1986

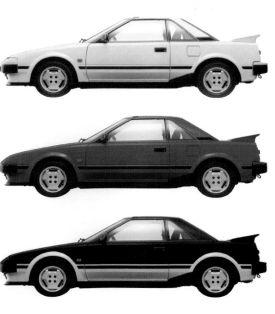

window switch is prone to failure, which may leave the window stuck down.

Pop-up light motors are reliable, with failures a rare occurrence, although the headlight units can become tired as the reflective coating ages.

The engine electronic control unit can also pack up, and genuine ones are becoming harder to source. Generally these are best obtained from donor cars or second-hand parts suppliers – expect to pay from £50.

Sometimes the alternator gets too hot because of its location in the engine bay. Once it overheats its life expectancy is reduced significantly so make sure it's charging or you'll be looking at having to fork out around £100 for an exchange rebuilt unit.

T-bar MR2s can suffer from compressed sealing rubbers, which will lead to water leaks into the cabin. Although new seals are available they can be tricky to fit and are fairly expensive, so most owners rebuild worn seals with one of the many silicone seal rebuild products available from most motoring shops for under £10. Once water starts to get in it'll lead to dampness in the seats, carpets and dash. Because there's no escape for the water, predictable damage will occur if damp carpets are not lifted and dried out.

Late T-Bar models came with perforated leather upholstery, which is prone to cracking if it's been neglected. Older cars may suffer from lazy seat belt return mechanisms and cracked internal door lock lever surrounds.

The triangular plastic trim that covers the wing mirror mountings on the inside front corner of each door can work loose, which will cause an increase in cabin wind noise whilst driving. The gear gaiter can be worn down by the linkage and the ashtray on post-1986 cars has a lid prone to snapping off. Universal aftermarket windscreen wipers are not as good as the originals, which are handed to match the curve of the screen.

Conclusion

Be cautious of low-mileage cars, as whilst the bodywork may be sound, the most common and expensive mechanical problems happen between 100,000 and 120,000 miles.

Imports are generally isolated to just the Supercharged or G-Ltd versions originally built for the Japanese and American markets. General things to watch for on imports are the conversion from KPH to MPH on the speedo, the quality of the underseal and the fitment of speed restriction devices and warning alarms.

Toyota MR2 Mk1
SPECIFICATIONS

Engine
1587cc in-line four, twin overhead camshafts, 16 valves. Alloy head, cast-iron block. Electronic fuel injection

Power
122bhp @ 6600rpm

Torque
105lb ft @ 5000rpm

Transmission
Five-speed manual, rear-wheel drive

Suspension
Front: Independent with MacPherson struts, triangulated lower links, anti-roll bar.
Rear: Independent with MacPherson struts, transverse and trailing links, anti-roll bar.

Brakes
Front: 259mm ventilated discs
Rear: 264mm solid discs
Servo-assisted

Weight
1066kg (2355lb)

Performance
0-60mph 7.7sec
Top speed 119mph

Value
Cost £11,808 new (1986)
Value now £1000-£4000

£112.80

FOOTMAN JAMES
Insurance specialists. At your service.

1986 Toyota MR2 T-bar
Value: £3000
Quote: **£112.80**
(£50x/s unlimited mpa)

»Info

TIMELINE
» 1983: MR2 Prototype is shown, badged SV-3, at the Tokyo motor show.
» 1984: Production MR2 is launched in Japan.
» 1985: First cars arrive in the UK in March. By October there's already a minor facelift, with colour-keyed bumpers, spoilers and skirts plus central locking.
» 1986: A T-bar roof is now offered, while all models get a deeper front spoiler, longer nose plus revised tail lights and air intake. There are also suspension tweaks while a 145bhp supercharged edition is introduced for markets outside Europe.
» 1988: Leather trim is now standard on the T-bar MR2.
» 1990: The Mk2 supersedes the first-generation car.

SPECIALISTS
» The MR2 Drivers' Club. 01487 710010, www.mr2dc.com
» Fensport, Cambs. 01354 696968, www.fensport.co.uk
» CASCU, Norfolk. 01493 748981, www.cascu.co.uk
» Nippon Automotive, Glos. 01242 584967, www.nipponautomotive.co.uk
» MR2 Breakers, Warks. 07950 300 235, www.justmr2breakers.co.uk

CLUBS
» MR2 Drivers' Club, www.mr2dc.com
» MR2 (Mk1) Club, www.mr2mk1club.com
» MR2 Owners' Club, www.mr2oc.co.uk

BOOKS
» Toyota MR2 Coupés and Spyders by Brian Long. Veloce, ISBN: 1-903706-16-5
» Toyota MR2 workshop manual, imported from US by Drivers' Club.

TRIUMPH SPITFIRE
(1962-1980)

Never dismiss the wonderful Spitifre – it's cheap but it's great fun
Words: Richard Dredge Photography: www.magiccarpics.co.uk

Thrills don't come much cheaper than with one of these; even less costly than an equivalent MG Midget or B, the Spitfire is perhaps the cheapest way of enjoying topless motoring. For £2000 you can buy a Spitfire that'll keep going; if you're handy with a socket set you could even pick up a project for just a few hundred.

The Spitfire was launched in 1962, aimed to compete with the Austin-Healey Sprite, but in the same year another rival also surfaced – the MGB. Thanks to its separate-chassis construction, Triumph's Herald provided the perfect platform from which to develop a new two-seater open-topped sportscar, even if the mechanicals were derived from the 1953 Standard Eight. There may not have been much power on offer, but with just 670kg to haul along, performance was better than you might think – especially as the 1147cc four-pot was fitted with twin carbs, a spicier camshaft

and a more free-breathing exhaust manifold.

During nearly two decades of production the engine grew, the bodywork was restyled and the suspension honed to make the car's handling more predictable. However, none of these cars is really fast and none will ever provide the élan of an Elan, but then you're not paying Lotus prices either.

There are plenty of project Spitfires about, but if you want to restore the car properly, even at home, you'll be doing well to break even if you buy something that needs a complete overhaul. However, you're better off buying one of these or a really good car rather than something in the middle, because there's a good chance that you'll pay over the odds for a car that needs plenty of work.

There's not much difference in values between the various Spitfire incarnations; the later cars are more usable but the earlier ones offer greater design purity. As a result,

they're all equally sought after – although the Mk3 is a particular favourite as it has nicer lines than the MkIV and 1500 yet it's relatively usable. If you're lucky you'll pick up a project car for £500 or so, but generally you should expect to pay more like £750 for anything worth putting back together.

If you want something roadworthy, expect to find £1500-£2500; once you've got more than £3500 available you can expect to get something really superb. The secret is to join the Triumph Sports Six Club; it's so large that there's a good chance you'll come across a Spitfire through its local branches.

Engine
There were three different engines fitted throughout the life of the Spitfire, with each one also fitted to other models in the Triumph range. Because the Spitfire was generally the most highly tuned of the lot, you need to

'For £2000 you can buy a good useable Spitfire or if you're handy with a socket set you could pick one up for a few hundred'

make sure the engine fitted is the one that belongs there, as less powerful units are often substituted from other Triumph models. All Spitfire engine numbers start with an F: FC in the case of the MkI/MkII, FD for the MkIII, FH for the MkIV (but FK for US cars) and FH for the 1500 (FM for US cars). However, there's a good chance that something else will be fitted, such as an engine starting G (Herald), D (Dolomite) or Y (1500 saloon).

MkI and MkII Spitfires were fitted with a 1147cc engine, but because these early cars are rare, you're unlikely to find a car with one of these rather gutless powerplants. Even if you do find a first or second-generation car, the chances are the engine will have been swapped for a later unit by now. The MkIII featured a 1296cc powerplant, which was carried over to the MkIV, but with less power because of emissions control equipment.

The 1147cc and 1296cc engines are very

durable, but all Spitfire engines must have the correct oil filter fitted if they're not to expire prematurely. This filter features a non-return valve to stop the oil draining back into the sump when the car is left; if there's much rattling when the car is started up, it's because the crankshaft's big-end bearings have had it, probably because the correct type of filter hasn't been fitted. Once this has happened, a bottom-end rebuild is necessary.

These two smaller engines will usually clock up 100,000 miles without problems, with the first sign of wear usually being a chattering top end because of erosion of the rocker shaft and rockers. Budget for a top end rebuild.

A problem that affects the 1296cc engine all too often is worn thrust washers, given away by excessive fore-aft movement of the crankshaft. The easiest way to check this is to push and pull on the front pulley; any detectable movement means possible disaster

as the crankshaft and block could ultimately be wrecked if the thrust washers fall out. MkIV Spitfires are especially prone to these problems; listen for rumbling from the bottom end as the engine ticks over.

The 1493cc engine fitted to the Spitfire 1500 has problems of its own, as the crankshaft can wear badly, along with the pistons and rings. That's why you need to listen out for rattling when starting up and look for blue smoke as you accelerate through the gears. If the engine has had it, your best bet is to fit an exchange rebuilt unit at around £1100.

Transmission

The first three generations of Spitfire featured the same four-speed manual gearbox, with synchromesh on all gears except first. The MkIV was fitted with the same transmission, but with synchromesh on all ratios, while the 1500 received a Marina-derived unit which is

the most durable of all the gearboxes. All of the gearboxes are reasonably long-lived, but big mileages will lead to rebuilds being necessary.

Synchromesh is usually the first thing to go, so check if there's any baulking as you go up and down the gears. Also listen for whining, indicating that the gears have worn, or rumbling, which signifies the bearings are on their way out. If there's any sign of trouble, your best bet is to budget for a rebuilt gearbox at £300 or so exchange. Replacing a gearbox is surprisingly easy as it pulls out from inside the car, once the seats and gearbox cover have been removed.

Many Spitfires have overdrive, which can also give problems. The first thing to check in the event of non-engagement is that the electrics are working okay; they're often the main cause of problems. If there's continuity in the circuit, the next most likely cause of trouble is an oil level that's fallen below the minimum required for the overdrive to operate. Fixing this is easy; you simply stick some EP90 in the gearbox and all should work once more. However, if the gearbox is leaking, there's clearly a problem to be addressed. If the oil is up to the level and the electrics are working fine, the overdrive unit probably needs cleaning out. If you budget for the worst – a rebuilt overdrive – you won't go far wrong. You can pick up an exchange unit for £250.

The rest of the transmission is simple, which means cheap and easy to repair – but there are various problems that can crop up. Most of these relate to wear of components such as universal joints or a propshaft that needs balancing, but these are nothing to worry about. If the propshaft needs balancing, there'll be a vibration at a certain road speed, which disappears once you accelerate. Worn universal joints are given away by clonks as the drive is taken up when moving off in forward or reverse.

Clutches don't give any particular problems, so just check for slipping as you accelerate, or juddering as you let the clutch out. The former is simply a worn clutch that needs renewing while the latter suggests there's oil on the pressure plate. This will also mean the clutch needs to be renewed, but there's also the issue of where the oil is coming from; Triumph engines aren't renowned for their ability to seal perfectly.

The final potential weak spot is the differential, which will whine when it's worn. Even when things sound really bad the rear axle will just keep going, but it's obviously not a good idea to just put up with the racket. A rebuilt unit is around £350, and while replacement is easy enough, it can get quite involved if you also find that the rear suspension needs work when you take everything apart.

Suspension, steering and brakes

Thanks to the flip-up bonnet, the Spitfire's front suspension is simplicity itself to work on. That's just as well because there are various bits that can give trouble – but it's all very cheap and beautifully simple to put right, especially if you can do the work yourself.

The nylon bushes in the brass trunnions can wear, so feel for play with a crowbar. Fresh bushes are just a fiver per side and even if the trunnion is past its best it's no disaster; a replacement is just £15. The main problem with the trunnions is wear of the threaded brass at the bottom, if EP90 oil hasn't been pumped in every six months or so. Without this, water gets in and corrodes the lower portion of the vertical link, weakening it and leading to the suspension collapsing when the wheels are turned at low speed. Replacement vertical links are available, at £100 each.

There are various other rubber bushes throughout the suspension, all of which will perish at some point – but they're cheap to buy if somewhat involved to replace if you want to fit a complete new set. Some repro stuff isn't especially durable and there are mixed views about the polyurethane items that are available. Some claim they make the ride too hard while others disagree; if yellow or blue bushes are in place, they're made of

TIMELINE
» 1962: Spitfire breaks cover, with 1147cc engine.
» 1965: MkII edition goes on sale, with more power and a stronger clutch.
» 1967: The MkIII arrives, with a 1296cc engine, a hood that's much easier to use and revised styling.
» 1970: The MkIV bring another facelift, plus an all-synchromesh gearbox and more predictable handling thanks to revised rear suspension.
» 1971: Seatbelts now fitted as standard.
» 1973: A 1500 edition makes its entrance, for the US market only. The bigger motor is needed because of all the emissions control equipment that has to be fitted. There's also a wider rare track, to overcome handling issues.
» 1974: Spitfire 1500 on sale in the UK.
» 1977: The interior receives minor fettling for greater comfort.
» 1980: The final Spitfire is made.

SPECIALISTS
» Anglian Triumph Services, Norfolk. 01986 895387, www.angserv.demon.co.uk
» Canley Classics, Coventry. 01676 541360, www.canleyclassics.com
» Chic Doig, Fife. 01592 722999, www.chicdoig.co.uk
» David Manners, W Midlands. 0121 544 4444, www.davidmanners.co.uk
» Jigsaw Racing, Kettering. 01536 763799, www.jigsawracingservices.co.uk
» Mick Dolphin, Leicester. 01530 271326, www.mickdolphin.co.uk
(continued overleaf)

polyurethane so you might want to pay particular attention to how hard the ride is when you take the car on a test drive.

The anti-roll bar links can also break, but at just £8 each that's nothing to worry about. The same goes for the rest of the front suspension; there are all sorts of potential weak spots but they're all quickly and cheaply fixed. The wheelbearings can wear, as can the track rods end, steering rack and upper ball joints that locate the top wishbone. The rubber steering rack mounts can also perish, usually after they've been marinaded in leaked engine oil. Your best bet is to feel for play by getting underneath.

The rear suspension can also give problems, but it's generally easy to overhaul, with one key exception; the wheel bearings. These wear out and are a pain to remove as a press is needed.

The only other likely problem, apart from worn or leaking shock absorbers, which are easy to replace, is a sagging leaf spring. If the top of the wheel has disappeared above the wheelarch, the spring needs to be renewed. A fresh one costs £100, but without the correct spring lifter, fitting it will be a pig of a job.

The rack-and-pinion steering is unlikely to have any problems, as it isn't under much strain, despite the Spitfire's fabulously tight turning circle. It's a similar story for the brakes; they're completely conventional so you just need to be on the lookout for leaking rear wheel cylinder, sticking caliper pistons and seized handbrakes. All parts are available.

Bodywork, electrics and trim

Corrosion is the Spitfire's main enemy; it can strike in the bodyshell as well as the chassis, and the sills are essential to the car's strength. Many owners restore their Spitfires at home and don't brace the bodyshell when the three-piece sills are replaced, twisting the bodyshell.

Start by looking at the integrity of the sills; the area where they meet the rear wings is where corrosion is the most likely, and once rot takes a hold, long-lasting repairs will require skill. Also take a look at the leading edge of each sill; there's a good chance of holes here. Water will get in, wreaking havoc throughout the sill.

There are plenty more rot spots to inspect too: the rear quarter panels, door bottoms, boot floor and the windscreen frame can all corrode badly. So too can the A-posts, wheelarches (inner and outer) plus the headlamp surrounds and front valance.

Spitfire 1500
SPECIFICATIONS

Engine
1493cc in-line four, 8 overhead valves. Cast-iron head and block. Twin SU carburettors

Power
71bhp @ 5500rpm

Torque
82lb ft @ 3000rpm

Transmission
Four-speed manual, overdrive optional Rear-wheel drive

Suspension
Front: independent with coil springs, double wishbones, telescopic dampers, anti-roll bar
Rear: independent with swing axles, transverse leaf spring, telescopic dampers

Brakes
Front: 229mm discs
Rear: 178mm drums
Servo-assisted

Weight
777kg (1710lb)

Performance
0-60mph 12.9sec
Top speed 101mph

Value
Cost £2383 new (1977)
Value now £1000-£5000

'The good news is that it's easy to spot a duffer from 100 paces, so buy with your eyes open and get set for some cheap fun'

The latter is double-skinned, so corrosion often spreads from the inside out; check for any bubbling, because what you see is likely to be just the tip of the iceberg.

Floorpans also corrode, sometimes because rot spreads from the sills and sometimes because the footwells have been allowed to fill up with water, which is then forced to eat its way out. The area behind the seats is likely to be particularly bad, as it's often not inspected very often; the front footwells also give problems so lift the carpets and see what state the metal is in underneath.

Next check the door shuts, which should be even all the way down. If a car has been badly restored, with the shell twisted in the process, the door won't be flush all the way down and neither will the shut lines be even. Putting this right is a huge job that if done professionally will cost more than the car is worth, because the whole structure needs to be realigned.

Accident damage is also a strong possibility, as these cars often appeal to inexperienced drivers after some cheap fun. If the car has been in a major shunt, the damage will be obvious; any prang big enough to distort the main chassis will have wrecked the car's delicate panels. It's the small knocks that are likely to cause you the most problems, as they may be harder to spot. However, if the panel fit is all over the place at the front, there's a good chance the front chassis rail, to which the valance attaches, has been knocked out of true.

With such a long list of potental problem areas with the bodywork, it's something of a relief to be able to report that the electrics and trim shouldn't pose any issues. Although there's a good chance that some sort of electrical problem will be present, it's usually only down to poor earths or the failure of some cheap-to-

replace component. Everything is available and there isn't anything that's a problem to fit.

Similarly, the trim shouldn't pose any problems as most of it is being remanufactured. Some bits for early cars are tricky to get hold of however, but if you're looking at a MkIV or 1500, you can retrim the car to original spec or upgrade it easily and relatively cheaply.

Conclusion

You're going to struggle to find anything that offers the same amount of fun as the Spitfire, if you're on a seriously tight budget, but such low values are a double-edged sword because there's a lot of rubbish available as a result. That's okay if you buy a project car knowing it needs a lot of work.

Most cars have been restored by now and originality is hard to find; suspension systems, exhausts, engines and wheels are often upgraded so don't expect to find a time-warp car. A lack of originality isn't generally an issue (although it may be to you), but poor restorations are a problem because many home restorers cut their teeth on cars like the Spitfire. The good news though is that it's easy to spot a duffer from 100 paces, so buy with your eyes open and get set for some cheap fun.

£91.80

FOOTMAN JAMES
Insurance specialists. At your service.

1975 Triumph Spitfire 1500
Value: £3000
Quote: **£91.80** (£50x/s unlimited mpa)

»Info

» Moss Europe, London. 0208 867 2020, www.moss-europe.co.uk
» Quiller Triumph, London. 0208 854 4777, www.triumphshop.co.uk
» Racetorations, Lincs. 01427 616565 www.racetorations.co.uk
» Rimmers, Lincoln. 01522 568000, www.rimmerbros.co.uk
» Southern Triumph Services, Dorset. 01202 423 687, www.southerntriumph.com
» Triumph Spares of Worcester, 01905 345222, www.users.globalnet.co.uk/~ngo/345222.htm

CLUBS
» Club Triumph, http://club.triumph.org.uk
» Triumph Sports Six Club, www.tssc.org.uk

BOOKS
» Triumph Spitfire & GT6, the complete story, by James Taylor. Crowood, ISBN: 1-86126-262-0
» Triumph Spitfire & GT6, a guide to originality, by John Thomason. Ebury, ISBN: 1-85223-893-3

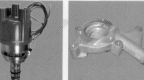

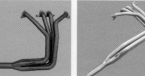

TRIUMPH GT6 (1966-1973)

Easy to work on and great to drive, the GT6 is still the 'poor man's E-type'   Words: Richard Dredge Photography: www.magiccarpics.co.uk

As soon as the GT6 hit the scene in 1966 it was christened the poor man's E-type, and for good reason. With a smooth straight-six nestling under a long bonnet (which like the Jag's was the whole front end of the car), there was no shortage of go or refinement. Nearly 40 years later not much has changed, although things like parts availability and ease of restoration are now more important, and once again, the Triumph scores highly.

Triumph's initial plan had been to use Spitfire mechanicals in a hatchback body and name it the Spitfire GT. But once the extra weight of an enclosed body had been taken into account, it soon became clear that the Spitfire's 1147cc four-cylinder unit would have struggled to offer a decent drive. So a bigger engine was called for, and after the 1596cc Vitesse powerplant was rejected, the later Vitesse's 1998cc straight-six was used instead. Because of this change of direction for the project, the planned 1964 launch turned into a 1966 debut, at the Earl's Court motor show. By then the Herald had spawned the Vitesse and Spitfire, making the GT6 the last of a quartet.

It's now 35 years since the last GT6 was built, and the cars are just as much fun now as

they were back then – but even more affordable. Any GT6 with an MoT is worth at least £1500 – even a restoration project is worth no less than half that. There's little difference in values between the different versions, although the Mk3 is slightly more desirable. The best show-winning cars will fetch £9000 while a really superb example is worth closer to £7000. A decent car that needs no work but won't win any prizes either costs around £3000 to buy.

Engine

The Triumph straight-six engine is renowned for its smoothness as well as its low-down torque. It's also famed for its oil leaks, and rattles at start up. But thankfully these 'characteristics' can be engineered out without too much difficulty or expense. If looked after with oil changes every 6000 miles it'll last 100,000 miles between rebuilds.

All parts are readily available, and it's an easy engine to cut your teeth on if you're buying a restoration project. Renew all oil seals while you have it apart, as it will save taking the engine out again later. If the engine has had it and you don't fancy rebuilding it

yourself, a running unit can be picked up for around £100 – although you'll need to pay twice that for a really good example.

If the original canister type of oil filter is still fitted it's worth investing £40 on a spin-on conversion. That will allow you to fit a modern filter with a non-return valve on it, meaning the bearings won't be starved of oil when you start it up, eliminating that start up rattle.

Transmission

The GT6's weakest link is its final drive, although if it's well looked after there's no reason for it to leave you stranded. The problem lies with the universal joints and diff, which can struggle to cope with the 2.0-litre engine's torque. They're an evolution of the Herald units – which in turn had evolved from Standard units of years before. The first Heralds had generated less than 40bhp and all GT6s put out more than double that, so if an owner has been over-enthusiastic with the thottle there may be rather more play in the system than there should be. Make sure the diff and gearbox aren't especially noisy – the gearbox is usually sturdy, but the diff will whine loudly if it's getting tired.

If there's clonking from the transmission as you manouevre backwards and forwards it's probably because some of the universal joints need replacing. New joints are only £10 apiece, and replacing them isn't tricky, but you might have to do all four if things are really bad.

The plastic bushes in the remote gearchange mechanism wear out eventually, but fitting a new set is cheap and easy – expect to pay around £20 for a pack. No GT6 had overdrive fitted as standard, but it was available as a factory-fitted option. Few Mk1 owners ticked the box but it became increasingly popular and most Mk3s owners specified it. A lot of cars have it nowadays because it's easy enough to retro-fit – and overdrive is worthwhile because it's more relaxed driving a car equipped with it if you raise the final drive ratio at the same time. Unusually, when new a GT6 with overdrive was no more relaxing to drive than one without. That's because the final drive ratio of cars not equipped with overdrive was lowered to 3.27:1 from the previous 3.89:1, to improve acceleration rather than make high-speed

cruising more relaxed. If overdrive is fitted but it's not working, the chances are that it's only an electrical connection somewhere that's playing up or a lack of oil pressure because the unit's internal filter needs a clean. If it's anything more serious, rebuilds are best left to a specialist, but if it has called it a day you can buy a rebuilt overdrive for £150 on an exchange basis.

If the car is fitted with a rubber doughnut Rotoflex coupling, make sure the coupling isn't about to disintegrate. Even the genuine Metalastik couplings last no more than 35,000 miles and cost at least £40 each side. If the car doesn't have Rotoflex couplings things are a lot simpler as you've then only got to be concerned with the rear bearings which last well and cost £18 per side.

Suspension, steering and brakes

The main thing to check with the rear suspension is the condition of the transverse leaf spring, which sags with age. Replacing it isn't especially pricey at around £100 (£80 for Rotoflex) but it can be a devil of a job unless you've got a spring

lifter to help you. If you have the swing spring (late Mk3) it will probably only need new rubber pads between the leaves. There's also a rubber bush at each end of the leaf spring along with bushes in the radius arms which locate the back axle and in each of the dampers. By the time the damper rubbers have gone the damper itself is likely to need replacing, which will set you back £32 for a pair.

Thankfully the front suspension doesn't give many problems. Sometimes the drop links that hold the anti-roll bar to the lower wishbone can break off, but these are available at £16 a pair. Tired springs or dampers might need to be replaced, but the job is easy and the costs are low at £47 and £32 respectively for a pair of each. The wishbones are fitted with rubber bushes, as are the anti-roll bar mounts and the steering rack mountings. These can all be replaced with polyurethane items and while you're checking to see if they've perished have a look at the ball joint at the top of the vertical link, to make sure it hasn't got a lot of play in it.

Although the Herald family of cars has a

'it's all put together like an overgrown Meccano kit – handy for taking apart and putting back together'

»

»Info

reputation for suffering from irritable trunnion syndrome, it's only if the car has been neglected that you're likely to have problems. If they've been lubricated as specified in the owner's manual, they'll be fine. But few owners know that every 6000 miles EP90 is supposed to be pumped in (not grease). The trunnions themselves are brass and don't give problems – it's the cast iron vertical link which threads into the trunnion which breaks. Replacement links cost £94 apiece and the easiest way of checking to see if they're about to give is by seeing how heavy the steering is. It shouldn't be especially heavy even with the weight of the straight-six sitting over the front wheels.

Pressed steel wheels were fitted to all GT6s as standard, but by now many have been swapped for alloys or wires. Because the GT6 has an unusual offset it's easy to buy wheels that suffer from clearance problems, so check that they're not rubbing if aftermarket wheels are fitted. If wire wheels have been put on, make sure that the spokes haven't broken and that the splines haven't worn. The widest tyres that will comfortably fit a GT6 are 175s.

Bodywork, electrics and trim

It's a full three decades since the last GT6 was built, so unless the example you're looking at has been really cherished, it will have had some remedial work performed on it at some point. That's no problem if it's been done properly, but if a full-scale restoration has been attempted, and the body and chassis haven't been separated, the work clearly hasn't been

done properly. It's not so much the bodyshell that's the problem as the chassis. The rear can be easily repaired, but ensure the front is aligned properly. The bonnet mountings (which are available new) are the most important here, because if they're not lined up correctly you'll never get the bonnet to line up properly.

The bodywork itself consists of two main sections: the front end (bonnet top, nose and front wings) and the main bodyshell (a tub made of the roof, floorpans and rear wings). The tailgate and doors attach to the tub and it's all put together like an overgrown Meccano kit – handy for taking apart and putting back together.

Although it's a good idea buying a bodyshell that's not full of holes, it's the chassis that gives the GT6 most of its strength. Thanks to the engine having a tendency to spray the underside of the car with oil, there's a good chance that the metal has been reasonably well preserved towards the front. It's worth buying replacement outriggers to patch up the chassis if the main rails are sound, but if the frame has rusted away comprehensively you'll be better off getting a replacement – you won't find a new one anywhere, but usable second hand ones can be picked up readily for £100 or so. But bear in mind that everything is based around the chassis, so if it needs replacing you're going to have to remove the brakes, steering, suspension and bodywork.

Even if the chassis doesn't need any work, there's a good chance the bodywork will. The first areas to check are the sills, floors and wheelarches. The GT6's sills are structural and if they along with the floorpans haven't been replaced yet, the chances are they will

»Info

- » Quiller Triumph, London. 0208 854 4777, www.triumphshop.co.uk
- » Racetorations, Lincs. 01427 616565 www.racetorations.co.uk
- » Rimmers, Lincoln. 01522 568000, www.rimmerbros.co.uk
- » Southern Triumph Services, Dorset. 01202 423 687, www.southerntriumph.com
- » Triumph Spares of Worcester, 01905 345 222, www.users.globalnet. co.uk/~ngo/345222.htm

CLUBS
- » Club Triumph, http://club.triumph.org.uk
- » Triumph Sports Six Club, www.tssc.org.uk

BOOKS
- » Triumph Spitfire & GT6, the complete story, by James Taylor. Crowood, ISBN: 1-86126-262-0
- » Triumph Spitfire & GT6, a guide to originality, by John Thomason. Ebury, ISBN: 1-85223-893-3

SPECIFICATION
Triumph GT6 Mk3

» **Engine**
1998cc in-line six, 12 overhead valves. Cast-iron head and block. Twin Stromberg 150CD carburettors

» **Power**
98bhp @ 5300rpm

» **Torque**
108lb ft @ 3000rpm

» **Transmission**
Four-speed manual, rear-wheel drive

» **Suspension**
Front: Independent with struts, coil springs, lower wishbones, telescopic dampers, anti-roll bar.
Rear: Independent with transverse leaf spring, lower links, semi-trailing arms, telescopic dampers.

» **Brakes**
Front: 246mm discs. Rear: 203mm drums

» **Weight**
918kg (2023lb)

» **Performance**
0-60mph 10.1sec. Top speed 112mph

» **Value**
Cost £1254 new
Value now £1500-£7000

need renewing before long. Nearly all panels are available new and are fairly easy to fit, but if somebody else has already done this, make sure the panels line up – putting else somebody else's bodge is far harder than starting from scratch.

Check under the false boot floor where the metal floor meets the arch – the passenger side is hidden under the petrol tank but the off-side will give a good idea of condition. All versions have a habit of corroding between the rear lights, and as new panels are not available you'll have to be handy with the MIG. Doors are rot-prone but thankfully the shells usually remain sound needing only a new skin.

Other rot spots include the bottom of the hatch aperture which fills with water then rots out and the double-skinned leading edge of the roof where it meets the windscreen surround – condensation collects in the seam and rots from the inside out. As if all this wasn't enough, it's quite common for the master cylinders on the bulkhead to leak brake fluid onto the metal panels below. Once this has stripped the paint, corrosion will follow, but the use of a silicone based brake fluid will avoid this.

Even if there's no discernible rust anywhere, the car may have been in an impact at some point. Poor shutlines are common on otherwise well-restored GT6s because aligning the panels can be very tricky. The easiest way of telling if the car has been shunted is to look at the chassis rails in front of the engine, which may be crumpled. Even if the car has been in a fairly big accident, if the chassis has been replaced properly along with the necessary panelwork, there's

no need to worry. That's the beauty of not using a monocoque – although if you do need to replace the bonnet, you'd better have at least £600 handy.

If the wiring has been hacked about you can buy a new loom for £170 and the few ancillaries that are fitted, such as wiper motor, dynamo/alternator and starter motor are cheap to buy.

If you find a GT6 with a completely trashed interior but it's on offer at a knock-down price, you're in luck as it's possible to buy new carpets (£130), door panels (£50/pr) and seat covers (£140) from Newton Commercial (01728 832 880). As far as exterior trim is concerned, Mick Dolphin is a good source.

Conclusion

With low parts prices, strong spares availability and the car's Meccano-like construction, even the tattiest GT6 can be revived – as long as you've got the patience. Even better is the fact that once built, the GT6 is great fun to drive – and it's even more fun if you mate a Spitfire with a GT6 to produce the drop-top that Triumph should have built.

TRIUMPH TR2 (1953-1955)

Triumph's tough little TR2 is a fun and surprisingly fast sports car that's as good in competition as it is on the road, yet doesn't cost a fortune to maintain Words: Malcolm McKay

The Triumph Sports Car

Above
Typical 1950s advertising for TR2 shows unfeasibly small occupants (or much larger TR...).

If you get your classic buzz from fresh air, lively performance, sporty looks and rugged rally potential, there's no better choice than a TR2. The Walter Belgrove styling is attractive and effective, with good interior and boot space, yet small frontal area which benefits the performance. And thanks to extensive pre-launch development by ex-BRM engineer Ken Richardson, it's compact, fast, strong, reliable and well protected underneath.

Competition success flooded in, with 1st/2nd on the 1954 RAC Rally and 15th overall at the 1954 Le Mans 24 Hours achieved by private entrants with near-standard cars. Richardson's works team went on to clock up many more successes with remarkably standard cars.

Though Standard-Triumph's plan was to win export dollars, overseas markets seemed wary of the unfamiliar marque and most TR2s were sold in Britain. Rapid improvements made them even more desirable with better

silencing, shorter doors with stiffer sills and an optional glassfibre hardtop, all by the end of 1954. During 1955, larger rear brakes, overdrive on second and third as well as top, and fresh air ventilation were added. However, it wasn't until the advent of the TR3 that autumn, with its egg-box grille, 100bhp and optional rear seat, that TR sales took off. When, in late 1956, the TR3 became the first British production car with front disc brakes, its success was assured.

Many TR2s have been updated over the years; try a few to decide if you prefer the genuine early-1950s feel or the extra grunt, tauter handling and sharper brakes and steering that can be achieved with more modern technology. Prices have risen in the last few years and really good TR2s now command over £15,000, but perfectly usable examples can still be found for under £10,000 and even expensively rally-prepared cars should be no more than £12,000

Engine

The wet-liner Standard Vanguard engine emulated the Citroën Traction unit and proved extremely versatile, detuned for Ferguson tractors and tuned up for TRs. In TR2 form it's still well below TR4 tune and is astonishingly economical, 30-35mpg being normal despite an ability to cruise all day at 80-85mph in overdrive top.

Over their 50-plus years, many TR2s have had component swaps, so check what you're getting. Original engine numbers closely (but not exactly) followed chassis numbers and TR2 engines run from TS 1E to TS 8996E. Anything that doesn't start TS is likely to be a Standard Vanguard engine: avoid. Cylinder heads were steadily uprated, TR3s being fitted with 1.75in H6 carburettors and opened-out inlet ports to extract an extra 5bhp, then from 9350E with the better-breathing 'Le Mans' head. All these were 'low port' with the inlet and exhaust ports almost

THE TRIUMPH SPORTS

FERGUS MOTORS, Inc. • NEW YORK CITY

SERVICE	SHOWROOM	SALON
444 W. 55th, West of 9th Ave.	1717 BROADWAY at 54th	290 PARK AVE. at 49th
JU 6-4045	CO 5-6494	MU 8-1841

Triumph TR2
SPECIFICATIONS

Engine
1991cc in-line four, pushrod ohv. Cast-iron head and block. Twin SU H4 carburettors

Power
90bhp @ 4800rpm

Torque
116lb ft @ 3000rpm

Transmission
Four-speed manual, optional overdrive, rear-wheel drive

Suspension
Front: independent via twin wishbones, coil springs, telescopic dampers. Rear: live axle with semi-elliptic leaf springs, lever-arm dampers

Brakes
Front: 10in drums. Rear: 9in drums (10in on later cars)

Weight
(940kg) 2072lb

Performance
0-60mph 11.6sec
Top speed 107mph

Value
Cost £844 new (1954)
Value now £2000-£17,000

---

in a line, but between 12606E and 13052E TR3s, the 'high port' head was phased in, with its inlet ports significantly above the exhaust ports. Of course, any head could be fitted to an earlier (or later) block so the engine number is no proof – but TR4s had a number stamped on the head adjacent to the front inlet port, so if you find 510084 there, it's TR4, while 511695 is TR4A and considered the best of the lot for power, if not for economy.

By the TR4A, Triumph had bored the engine out to 2138cc but, as all this is contained within the replaceable wet liners, what capacity is within the engine you're viewing is anybody's guess; relatively few engines are now 1991cc.

Well-maintained TR engines are extremely durable and can top 150,000 miles without major rebuild, but they do wear out eventually. Anything less than 50psi oil pressure at speed after a good run is likely to need new crankshaft bearings; listen for tell-tale rattles when loaded at low revs. Noisy tappets can usually be adjusted out, though some experts favour fitting an external oil feed to boost rocker lubrication; others condemn the external feed as more likely to fail itself and throw oil everywhere.

Performance should be lusty in any state of tune; anything else demands a compression check to ensure the head gasket, valves and rings are sound. If they are, suspect worn carburettors. Some TR2s have been fitted with twin Weber carburettors: these are of little benefit on the road unless very well set up with a mild camshaft. With a hot cam, they will flood the engine and stall it at the most awkward moments.

Transmission
Unlike most contemporaries, TR2s were high geared. Even without overdrive, cruising at the UK legal speed limit is relaxed. That

said, overdrive is a desirable bonus, adding £500-1000 to the value of a car, especially if it is the stronger unit operating on second and third as well as top.

Ratios are chosen to give the car an effective seven-speed gearbox, dramatically improving acceleration: though never tested in TR2 form, the use of overdrive second should cut the 0-60mph time to well under 11 seconds. These gearboxes were not originally optional until chassis TS6266, but many have been retro-fitted: you'll need to drive it (or lift the gearbox cover) to be sure what you have. A TR4 all-synchro gearbox also fits with minimal modification.

Gearbox wear starts with the layshaft and its bearings – listen for noise when in neutral at tickover, which disappears when you dip the clutch. A clattering in first gear or reverse means a chipped tooth and urgent attention needed. Few new gearbox internals are available, so a perfect gearbox

»

»Info

is a real bonus; specialists Revington TR offer conversion to a modern five-speed gearbox, retaining the original gearlever.

All TR2s were built with Lockheed brakes and the rear axle that used these is known as the 'Lockheed axle'. Many have been replaced with the later TR3/3A 'Girling axle' due to a reputation for the earlier axle breaking halfshafts. This is only likely on cars fitted with radial tyres and used very aggressively – or where halfshafts are swapped from side to side.

You're more likely to encounter problems with oil leaks from the axle ends, for which several modifications were made during the life of the TR2. The 'Girling axle' is unburstable, with stronger gears, halfshafts and bearings.

Suspension, steering and brakes
Though Triumph Mayflower derived, the front suspension is sturdy enough and with twin wishbones, coil springs and telescopic dampers was state-of-the-art in 1953. Lubrication every 1000 miles is essential to avoid rapid wear of the trunnions – check the vendor knows this. Rear suspension is simple and durable but check for broken springs and ineffective dampers.

No front anti-roll bar was fitted; with a low centre of gravity, body roll is not excessive and anti-roll bars for TRs were only available on the aftermarket until the introduction of the TR6. If you want modified suspension, go for a properly integrated package of springs, dampers, anti-roll bars and steering – half-measures just don't work.

The worm-and-peg steering box can be completely rebuilt with new parts: it wears fast if unlubricated or overloaded by wide tyres. If play is excessive (more than 1.5in at the rim) or the steering is stiff when on the move, budget to have it rebuilt. Converting to TR4 rack-and-pinion steering eradicates play and lightens feel, but loses the 1950s character as well as necessitating loss of the original steering wheel and Bakelite indicator/horn push set-up.

Stronger wheels were fitted retrospectively from May '54, widened from 4J to 4.5J, but narrow wheels are still around and even later ones can crack around the outside of the stud holes, so take the hubcaps off and check for cracks or welding. TR2s feel best and are wonderfully driftable on crossply tyres (Dunlop RS5 5.90x15 is the ultimate choice), though many choose radials for surer wet grip and longer life. Disadvantages are heavier steering at parking speeds and lower overall gearing, which increases fuel consumption and can cause clearance problems on rough rallies.

Drum brakes give effective retardation until over-used, but many owners prefer to fit late TR3/3A front disc brakes. The combined-reservoir Lockheed brake/clutch master cylinder is also sometimes changed for separate Girling units.

» Manvers Triumph, Elmswell, Suffolk.
01359 244417,
www.manvers-triumph.com
» Moss Europe, West London.
020 8867 2020,
www.moss-europe.co.uk
» Moss Bradford,
01274 735537
» Moss Bristol,
0117 923 2523
» Moss Manchester,
0161 480 6402
» North Devon Metalcraft, Barnstaple.
01271 322526, www.ndmetal.co.uk
» Parts4Triumph, Oldbury, West Mids.
0121 544 4444,
www.davidmanners.co.uk
» Picton Sportscars, Waltham Cross.
01992 634464,
www.picton-sportscars.co.uk
» Protek, Wallingford. 01491 832372
» Racetorations, Lincs. 01427 616565
www.racetorations.co.uk
» Revington TR, Somerset. 01823
698437, www.revingtontr.com
» Rimmer Bros, Lincoln. 01522 568000,
www.rimmerbros.co.uk
» TR Bitz, Warrington. 01925 861861,
www.trbitz.com
» TR Enterprises, Mansfield. 01623
793807, www.trenterprises.com
» TRGB, Huntingdon. 01487 842168,
www.trgb.co.uk
» TR Shop, London W4. 020 8995 6621,
www.trshop.co.uk
» Worcester Classic Cars, Worcester.
01905 345805,
www.worcesterclassic.co.uk

CLUBS
» TR Register, www.tr-register.co.uk
» TR Drivers Club, www.trdrivers.com
» Club Triumph, club.triumph.org.uk

BOOKS
» Original Triumph TR2/3/3A by Bill Piggott.
Bay View Books/MBI (out of print)
» Triumph TR by Bill Piggott. Haynes,
ISBN 1 85960 997 X
» Triumph by Name, Triumph by Nature
by Bill Piggott. Dalton Watson,
ISBN 1 85443 107 2
» TR for Triumph by Chris Harvey.
Haynes, ISBN 0 902280 94 5

Bodywork, electrics and trim

Though sparse and simple, the TR2's bodywork is the area needing closest scrutiny before purchase. Original British cars are likely to have rotted extensively at some point in their lives while US imports have often been heavily crashed and poorly repaired. Check the chassis carefully for signs of kinks, cracks or odd welding and for rust everywhere, but especially on body mounting outriggers and rear crossmembers. Fortunately all panels – even whole bodyshells or chassis – are available new, yet poor-quality repairs are not uncommon, so check panel gaps as well as rot.

Aluminium bonnets and spare wheel lids were used until February 1954 (TS550) and all panels can be bought in aluminium today. Small square rear lights were fitted until April 1954. Sliding sidescreens became available with the optional hardtop from October 1954 and on all cars from February 1955; hardtops are quite rare and add another £500-plus to value if in good order.

For pure TR2 looks, external hinges and wing beading should all be body colour, the latter originally self-coloured T-section plastic – one of the few parts unobtainable today (unless your TR2 is black or white).

Simple Lucas electrics are all available and generally reliable. Conversion of the heavy dynamo to an alternator is quite common, but usually entails a narrow fan belt designed to run at higher tension, which then knocks out water pump bearings.

Interior trim is simple and again all is available. Standard seats are remarkably comfortable and there's room to squeeze a friend behind the seats in an emergency.

Conclusion

Personal taste will dictate whether you go for a car in as original specification as you can find, to enjoy 1950s motoring in its purest form, or for a car with as many modifications from later TRs as can be squeezed into it, giving quite startling performance and more-modern feel.

Do make sure you know exactly what you're buying – Triumph TRs are such Meccano-cars that it's just as possible to buy a TR3A with a TR2 front as the reverse; a known history with a Production Trace certificate is a useful bonus.

£132.75

FOOTMAN JAMES
Insurance specialists. At your service.

1954 Triumph TR2
Value: £14,000
Quote: **£132.75** (£100x/s unlimited mpa)

TRIUMPH TR4, 4A, 5 AND 6 (1961-1976)

Fast and powerful, the TRs have a strong following   Words: Richard Dredge   Photography: www.magiccarpics.co.uk

Triumph TR6

SPECIFICATION

Engine
2498cc in-line six, 12
overhead valves. Cast-
iron block and head.
Lucas mechanical fuel
injection

Power
142bhp @ 5700rpm

Torque
149lb ft @ 3000rpm

Transmission
Four-speed manual,
optional overdrive
Rear-wheel drive

Suspension
Front: independent
with coil springs,
double wishbones,
telescopic dampers,
anti-roll bar.
Rear: independent with
semi-trailing arms,
coil springs, lever arm
dampers.

Brakes
Front: 276mm discs
Rear: 229mm drums
Servo-assisted

Weight
1122kg (2473lb)

Performance
0-60mph 8.2sec
Top speed 119mph

Value
Cost £1339 new
Value now
£5,000-£13,000

When Michelotti's sharp-suited TR4 was unveiled on the Triumph stand at the London motor show in 1961, the car looked thoroughly modern, especially when compared with the TR3A that it replaced. But the reality was that under the skin the car was still a TR3A – little more than the outer panels were new. Despite this the TR4, and TR4A which succeeded it, were among the fastest affordable sports cars on offer throughout the 1960s. Cheap to buy and run, the cars' road manners left room for improvement, but as stylish transport they were pretty much unbeatable.

Triumph repeated the trick in 1969 when it unveiled the TR6, which was little more than a reskinned TR5 (itself a rebodied TR4), but it had a lot of people fooled. Even with the mechanicals, main structure, doors, chassis and windscreen carried over, the car looked fresh enough to appear new. It was also the last of the true TRs in the eyes of many enthusiasts, yet it's still often overlooked by those wanting a proper British sports car.

If you fancy a post-sidescreen TR, bear in mind that TR5s are more sought after than TR4As, which in turn are more sought after than TR4s. The TR5 is by far the rarest and restoration projects are very hard to find. Even tatty runners aren't easy to source so expect to pay £6000 upwards for something that needs work. The best TR5 fetches around £20,000 while top TR4s command £13,000 – the nicest

TR4As are worth around £1000 more. TR4 and TR4A restoration projects typically command £4000, while you can expect to fork out £7500 for something decent.

TR6s are worth similar money to the TR4 and TR4A, with restoration projects starting at £3000, and something roadworthy costing around £7000. Good cars will fetch £10,000 while tip-top examples will command up to £13,000. However, these prices are all for genuine right-hand drive cars; knock 15 per-cent off if you're looking at an ex-US car that's been converted from left-hand drive.

Engine

The TR4/TR4A's 2138cc four-cylinder powerplant is simple, strong and reliable. Derived from the post-war Standard Vanguard unit, it'll cover 100,000 miles before needing significant attention, although oil leaks from the timing chain cover are an expected part of Triumph ownership. The scroll seal fitted at the rear of the crankshaft also lets oil out; this is only a problem when the engine is running but the vehicle itself isn't moving. Once the engine is up to running temperature you should be seeing 70psi on the gauge.

The TR5 and TR6's smooth 2.5-litre straight-six offers huge reserves of torque. With regular oil changes and proper servicing the units will take 120,000 miles quite happily – some owners have seen more than twice this before

major surgery is required.

Check for play in the crankshaft thrust washers by pushing and pulling on the bottom pulley. The job is made easier by depressing and releasing the clutch – there should be no more than 0.008in movement. It may also be possible to feel and hear a clonk as the crank moves. Any detectable movement means the thrust washers may have dropped out, which could be serious and may involve the sourcing of a replacement block or even engine. If the thrust washers are still in place it's possible to replace them with oversized ones, without having to remove the engine first.

See if the original canister type of oil filter has been replaced with a spin-on version – they cost less than £40 so if there isn't one there you'll get an idea of how well kept the car is. The original filters had no anti-drain valve, leading to the bearings being starved of oil on start up, whereas the spin-on type keeps the system primed allowing the oil to circulate much more quickly. Once up to temperature check the oil pressure; it should be showing 50-60psi on the dial at 2,500rpm.

The engine is also famed for oil leaks, and rattles at start up. Thankfully these characteristics can be engineered out without too much difficulty or expense. All parts are readily available, and it's an easy engine to cut your teeth on if you're buying a project.

It won't be hard to spot if the engine has

Clockwise from left
Very original TR4, twin SU lump, TR4A has independent rear suspension, tasteful TR4 cockpit

TIMELINE

» 1961: TR4 debuts; over the TR3A it gains rack and pinion steering, wider front and rear tracks and an all-syncro gearbox. The TR3's engine is bored out to 2138cc and there's a novel roof arrangement; a targa system. Because the panel was too bulky to fit into the car's boot, Triumph also offered a light framework and canvas assembly, the Surrey top

» 1965: The TR4A arrives; the chassis is tweaked comprehensively with a new design for the rear of the frame itself and independent rear suspension with coil springs with semi-trailing wishbones. However, for the North American market only, the original live-axled configuration is still offered.

» 1967: The TR5 goes on sale, with fuel-injected straight-six. Externally barely discernible from the TR4A, the new engine turns the TR into a genuine performance car. North American cars have twin carbs and are badged TR250.

» 1969: TR6 launched. UK cars and rest of World except US (CP series) get 150bhp fuel-injected 2.5-litre straight-six; US cars (CC series) get 104bhp carburetted version. Later that year, reclining seats and new wheels fitted.

» 1973: New models introduced; the CR series is for everywhere except the US; this has an injected engine detuned to 125bhp. The US gets the CF series; its carburetted powerplant now gives 106bhp. Wire wheels are no longer an option, and a new front spoiler is now fitted. There's also a tougher J-type overdrive to replace the A-type previously fitted.

» 1974: US cars get black bumpers.

» 1975: Last injected TR6 is built.

» 1976: Last carburetted TR6 produced.

worn out. Blue smoke when the car is accelerated points to bore and/or piston wear, while blue smoke when the engine is started indicates worn valve guides – and the requirement for a cylinder overhaul. Rebuilt unleaded heads are available for around £300 to fit yourself or from £500 to have someone do it for you. If you can see black smoke as the car is accelerated quickly, it's because the fuel-injection metering has been set up to run rich. Not only will this mean steep fuel bills but it will also make for premature bore wear if it's been that way for a while.

Other well known fuel injection problems revolve around difficult starting from hot, fuel vaporisation and misfiring on start up. These are well known problems and easily remedied by one of the many specialists, or the job can be done at home without any special tools. All parts for the injection system are readily available either on an exchange basis or even outright on a number of components. A common conversion on the fuel-injection system is the replacement of the Lucas pump with a Bosch item, which solves most of the problems of overheating for which the Lucas pump has achieved a reputation.

Replacement powerplants are readily available through the basic engine being common to the 2.5 saloons. Running second-hand engines can be bought from £50, although you'll have to spend at least £200 to get one that won't need rebuilding before long. However, for the purist who doesn't want a saloon engine with an MG prefix, genuine second-hand TR6 engines start at £250.

Transmission

The four-speed gearbox rarely gives problems, as it's just as tough as the engines. But once 100,000 miles have

been racked up the bearings will begin to grumble and it'll start to jump out of gear. Another common casualty is the layshaft bearings; when cruising you'll hear a rumbling in all of the intermediate gears, which disappears when top gear is engaged. It can also be identified when the car is stationary with the engine running, by a rumbling noise which disappears when the clutch pedal is pressed down. The only option is a rebuilt gearbox, for which you can expect to pay £350 plus your old one. Overdrive was fitted as an option to give a seven-speed 'box which gives few problems except for the classic electrical ones in which either the solenoid or the wiring loom play up.

If the clutch isn't set up properly on any of the cars there'll be problems. Make sure the clevis pin which connects the clutch pedal to the master cylinder isn't excessively worn and that the slave cylinder is mounted with the bleed nipple facing upwards – the cylinder can be fitted upside down very easily. This will allow the hydraulics to be bled properly, as if they're not, the baulk rings in the gearbox will take a battering through the clutch not giving the necessary clearance.

With around 145lb ft of torque available, the transmission will have taken quite a beating if the car has been driven hard. Accordingly, universal joints on the propshaft and half-shafts may be worn; listen for clonks as drive is taken up when the car is driven off. Also get underneath the car and look at the differential's mounting points, which can be distorted or even torn away by repeated fierce acceleration. Because of the torque levels, the clutch may have seen better days. Make sure it engages smoothly and disengages well before the pedal reaches the end of its travel.

»Info

Overdrive wasn't fitted as standard until 1974, and it's worth buying a car with it. If fitted but faulty, it's probably wiring problems, which are easily fixed. Look out for things like broken wires, dodgy relays or loose Lucar connections. It could be because the overdrive unit has clogged up inside or because the solenoid has packed up. CP, CC and CR series TR6 up to commission number CR641 had an A-type overdrive unit fitted. The CF and CR series cars (from CR567) were fitted with a J-type unit. Overdrive solenoids are available from £80, but if the unit just needs cleaning out it will take only a morning of your time.

Check for wear in the propshaft and driveshaft universal joints by using a wrench to turn the shafts while the brakes are on. Any play will be instantly noticeable and if the propshaft is worn out you'll have to pay around £150 to replace it. Also check for wear in the driveshaft splines which cost around £165 each side to fix – if you're having to replace these it's worth investing in a fresh, stronger set from Neil Revington, which are better made and longer lasting. Propshafts need to be greased every 3000 miles if they're not to seize and they can also go out of balance when the universal joints are replaced, so make sure they're reassembled in the correct way.

Suspension, steering and brakes

Neither the front nor the rear suspension have any inherent problems, although the rear of the TR4A can be improved by fitting telescopic shock absorbers. Uprated springs are available for the TR4, and these should be fitted without the aluminium spacer that normally lives between the top of the spring and the top spring mounting. But many DIY owners don't read the

instructions and end up fitting the whole lot, which raises the ride height and upsets the handling. You should be able to get just two fingers between the top of the tyre and the rear wheelarch – any more and it's sitting too high, probably because it's riding on the wrong springs.

The front trunnions have a habit of seizing because they haven't been lubricated properly when fitted. This strains other parts of the suspension – especially the drop link on the wishbone – so check their condition by jacking up the car from underneath the wishbone and making sure the trunnions are swivelling properly. Wheelbearings aren't renowned for their strength; play can be adjusted out, but count on having to replace them if you notice any play.

If wire wheels have been fitted, you need to check for loose or rusty spokes as well as rim corrosion. The splines that hold the wire wheel hubs in place can also wear, so jack up each corner and check for play by trying to rock then spin the wheel while the footbrake is applied. Any obvious movement between the wheel and the hub means the splines have worn. A replacement set costs around £250 including the spinners. Conversion between wires and steel wheels is easy on these cars because the same hubs are used for either model and conversion requires only shortened wheel studs to go along with the set of wire wheel spline adaptors.

Brakes have no inherent problems, but if there is a fault of any sort it'll be easy and cheap to fix. The brakes have an in-line servo as standard and unless the car has been uprated the stoppers are more than adequate for the purpose. However, the handbrake is poor even with everything in good condition.

Servo assistance was an option on the TR4 and TR4A,

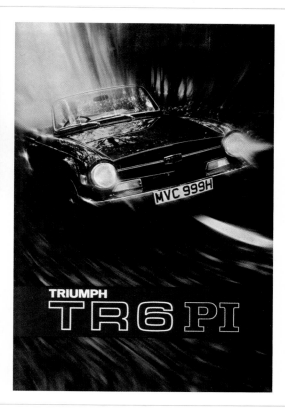

Clockwise from left
TR5 looks great with with
Surrey top; six-pot engine; front
and interior similar to TR4's.

TRIUMPH TR6 PI

but standard on the TR5 and TR6, so don't always expect to see one fitted to earlier cars. Whether or not there's one fitted, the brakes should be up to the job, but the handbrake is notoriously poor at holding the car on a hill.

Bodywork, electrics and trim

These cars have a separate chassis, which can rot in all sorts of places and can only really be repaired properly if the bodyshell is removed first. But the construction of the TR4A, TR5 and TR6 mean many chassis repairs can be undertaken with the body in situ. The worst-affected areas are usually the diff mounting brackets (which can snap off), so pay close attention to what state the offside front and nearside rear units are in, as these are most affected by the torque going through the diff.

The centre section of the chassis also needs careful analysis because it bulges as it gets weaker. TR4s survive the best because the chassis is less complex – the TR4A-TR6 have internal strengthening where the rear suspension is bolted to the chassis, and this is an area that corrodes quite readily. Also, because of the very different shape that the later cars have from the TR4, these suffer from flexing that can crack the chassis. These later cars also have differential mounting brackets that are more prone to problem than those on the earlier TR4. The TR5 and TR6 is the worst

affected of them all, because the amount of torque put through the diff can cause the mountings to break off altogether.

Poorly repaired accident damage is another probability. The chassis isn't especially hardy, so even small parking nudges can end up causing distortion. The areas most commonly afflicted are the front suspension turrets, the mounting brackets (the points from which the wishbones pivot), outriggers, steering rack mountings and the suspension itself. Look for distorted metal (particularly kinks where the chassis gets wider on either side of the sump), cracks, naff plating and uneven tyre wear which all give the game away.

Despite the use of a separate chassis, the bodyshell does give some structural strength, especially on the TR4A-TR6 which have a more flexible chassis. Because of this it's especially important to make sure the main shell is sound and that the doors, wings, sills and floorpans are in reasonable condition. Make sure the drain holes, which should be obvious on the underside of the sill, are all present and correct – if they're blocked up then the sills will probably be rotting through from the inside. The tops and bottoms of both the doors and wings can rot away, and where the front wings are concerned you have to inspect the inner as well as the outer wing very carefully. The battery sits behind the engine and the metal beneath it rots readily, so if it doesn't look too

great remove the battery and inspect more closely – you'll probably be glad you did.

Also check the door gaps as they can open up at the top if the chassis has been weakened by corrosion, or if the car hasn't been properly braced when the sills have been replaced. B-posts and door tops can also succumb to the dreaded tin worm as can the lip of the boot lid so ignore these and you might just regret it. But if the panel gaps are excessive or hideously uneven it could be because the car has been restored very badly. They weren't put together especially well on the production line, but most will have been restored by now. If a car has been badly rebuilt it'll be a lot more hassle putting that right than starting with an unrestored example.

Another sign of a bodged rebuild is missing beading along the seam between the top of the rear wings and the deck. The rear wings bolt on and filler is often used along the tops of them while the beading is left out. Speaking of bodges, make sure the footwells are in good shape, as a common bit of sharp practice is to weld replacement panels over already rusty ones – it might look OK but the corrosion will still be there and the car may well be weakened structurally as a result.

Incidentally, because TR5s are worth more than TR4As, it's not unknown for a six-pot engine to be dropped into a TR4A and passed off as a TR5 – it has to be a TR4A (and not a »

Above
TR6 brochure showed
off new frontal styling
and made much of new
fuel injection.

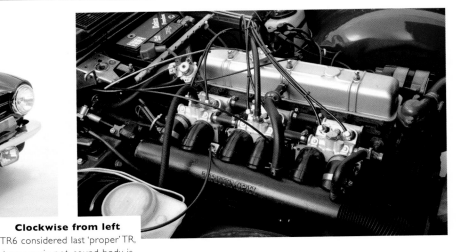

Clockwise from left
TR6 considered last 'proper' TR, torquey six pot, sound body is a must, attractive wood dash.

TR4) because of the independent rear suspension. A TR5 chassis number will start CP, while CT means it's a TR4, CTC is a TR4A and if it's a TR250 it'll start with CD. All these cars have a commission plate, which is located on the nearside front inner wheelarch – always worth a look.

Unless the interior resembles a scene from *The Young Ones*, a bit of scruffiness inside the car isn't anything to worry about because everything is available. The Surrey hard tops were always an option, and are now sought after – if the car you're looking at doesn't have one but you'd like one, expect to pay at least £400 for a decent example.

The electrics are straightforward; if there are any problems, everything can be fixed easily and cheaply. Replacement parts are cheap and apart from connections not connecting properly there's little to worry about. A new wiring loom is available for about £200 and it's not that tricky to fit – a specialist will charge £400-£500 to replace it for you. The only exception to this is if the windscreen wipers are playing up. If it's the motor that needs TLC there's very little to worry about, but if it's the

rack that's unhappy you'll have to remove the dash to get to it.

If the heater unit seems to be completely ineffective it's probably because the air vent at the base of the windscreen isn't open. Just raising the flap by a few degrees makes all the difference between a misted up windscreen and a clear one.

Conclusion

The Americans knew they were onto a good thing, which is why most of these were exported to the US. Now they're coming back here, and being converted to right-hand drive in the process. Such a job is quite involved but no problem if the car is being properly restored. Also, don't assume that if you're buying a car from the US that it'll be rust-free; they're often very corroded.

There's plenty of scope to buy something that will swallow all the money you throw at it, but if you take your time and look at plenty of cars, you'll see there are some superb examples to choose from.

Buy a good example of any TR, look after it and drive it sympathetically, and you'll be able

to sell it on without losing your shirt on it. If on the other hand you're looking at buying a car to treat as a project there are plenty of earlier cars on offer (TR5 projects are rarer) along with a decent supply of parts that means you won't grind to a halt because you're missing a crucial component.

Whichever route you choose, get ready to listen to everybody you ever meet while out in your TR, because they'll all want to relate at least one anecdote to you about their friends, relatives or neighbours who 'used to have one of those'.

» Thanks to Carl Kiddell of Revington TR, www.revingtontr.com.

£130.65 **FOOTMAN JAMES** Insurance specialists. At your service.

1974 Triumph TR6
Value: £9000
Quote: **£130.65** (£50x/s unlimited mpa)

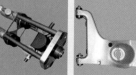 

TRIUMPH TR7 & TR8

At last the final incarnation of the TR line is now appreciated as a classic, but prices are still extremely favourable

Words: Richard Dredge Photography: www.magiccarpics.co.uk

Above
Mint condition, closed-roof TR7s command around £2500. Not much for a fun little coupé.

If ever there was a missed opportunity, the TR7 was it. Maligned since soon after its introduction, the last of the TR line (more or less) has been derided for years, thanks to so-so dynamics, appalling build quality in the early days and a controversial design that never offered any of the charm of its predecessors. Thanks to its poor reputation, the TR7 has always been something of a bargain, and while there are lots of ropey examples about, there are plenty of crackers too.

When the TR7 was unveiled in 1975, it seemed that the sports car's days were numbered. Triumph had penned its final TR design as a tin top only; convertibles were expected to be banned in the US, on safety grounds, and the oil crisis meant the motive power couldn't be anything too powerful, as it would then be too thirsty. The first cars were made in BL's Speke factory, complete with abysmal quality control and even worse employee relations; strikes were rife and the cars were incredibly poorly put together.

When production moved to Canley in 1978, things improved greatly. The standard of quality control improved massively and around 200 details were improved upon – but it was all too late.

Although press reports had generally been reasonably favourable, potential buyers stayed away, uninspired by the constant tales of woe coming from BL. Production moved once more in 1980, this time to BL's Solihull factory, with more improvements made to the 7, but the writing was on the wall and production ended altogether in October 1981.

More than a quarter of a century after the last TR7 was built, values have started to creep up after years in the doldrums. However, even with recent price rises you're not going to have to find much money to snap up a mint coupé – everyone is too busy focusing on the dropheads to worry about the closed cars. As a result, you'll pay around twice as much for a convertible as you will for an equivalent coupé.

Projects start at around £100 for a coupé or £500 for an equivalent convertible. If you can find a really good fixed head you'll have to find around £2500 to secure it, but if it's roofless that figure jumps to more like £4500. In between are the cars that are perfectly usable but a little tatty; £1500 will net you such a coupé while an equivalent convertible is £2000-£3000.

Engine

Apart from a handful of Sprint editions, all TR7s were fitted with an eight-valve 2-litre four-cylinder engine. It's a pretty lacklustre unit that's unique to the 7, but basically Dolomite 1850-sourced, and unless it's relatively pampered the engine will be fit for replacement by the time 70,000 miles have been racked up. However, as long as the timing chain has been replaced every 40,000 miles, and if the oil has been renewed regularly, it shouldn't be too difficult to notch up at least half as many miles again before major work is needed.

One of the keys to a long engine life is to ensure the cooling system is in tip-top condition, but it often isn't. Unless decent anti-freeze levels are maintained, the cylinder will corrode internally, leading to silting up of the waterways making things even worse. If the cylinder head does have to be replaced (or even just removed), brace yourself for a whole heap of grief. The retaining studs are at an angle, and this can cause all sorts of problems.

The viscous fan can also fail, which is why some owners fit an electric thermostatically controlled one instead. As if that isn't enough, the water pump has a habit of failing, so look for signs of it

TR7...6...5...4...3...2...1...

leaking coolant. It's located under the front carburettor and replacing it is a pain because of accessibility issues, so listen out for it making untoward noises as the engine is revved with the car at a standstill.

With just 105bhp on tap, the 2-litre engine hardly turned the TR7 into a serious sports car, which is why many owners have subsequently fitted a Rover V8 instead. It's a conversion that's well supported by various specialists and if done properly it can transform the car into a serious road burner. However, not all conversions are well engineered, with many cars upgraded on the cheap. Check the security of engine mountings, the strength of the transmission and also whether or not the brakes and suspension have been modified, if a V8 transplant has taken place.

If you're looking at a V8-engined TR, whether it's a genuine TR8 (which is unlikely) or an aftermarket conversion (much more likely), there are a few powerplant vices to be aware of. This V8 is durable as long as it's properly serviced, which means oil changes every 3000 miles. If this hasn't been done there's a good chance that the hydraulic tappets will have clogged up and the camshaft, followers and rocker shaft may have worn prematurely too. The giveaway is an especially noisy top end; these units should run very quietly even as the revs rise. Don't be too concerned by an oil pressure gauge that seems to read lower than you'd expect, as these engines run quite happily with just 15-20psi showing. Of more concern is knocking from the bottom end; this signals that a rebuild is due,

for which you can expect to pay £500 for the parts.

Oil leaks from pre-1973 V8s are par for the course, as they used rope-type seals for the front and rear bearings. These are ineffective, and replacing them means stripping down the engine. New neoprene front seals are £12 each but upgrading the rear one means machining the block.

As well as renewing the oil regularly, it's essential that the coolant is replaced every couple of years. Being an all-alloy unit, the V8 is prone to internal corrosion if anti-freeze levels are allowed to drop off, so check the temperature gauge once the car has been allowed to idle for a few minutes. If it gets ever hotter, it's probably because the radiator and block are full of deposits that need to be flushed out.

Transmission

Early cars were fitted with a four-speed manual gearbox, as seen in the Marina and Dolomite. It's not a very strong unit, so listen for bearing wear (there'll be rumbling when the car is under power), and also check that it doesn't jump out of gear when on the move. Four-speed cars can be converted to five-speed; you can buy a kit of used parts for around £350 to do the work yourself. Take your car to a company such as S+S and you'll pay around £800 for the work – or an extra £400 if you want reconditioned parts throughout.

From late 1976 there was an SD1-sourced five-speed box available as an optional extra on exported cars only, but from early 1978 it was also offered to UK

»Info

TIMELINE
» 1975: The TR7 coupé is launched, but it's for US buyers only. There are twin Stromberg carburettors fitted and a five-speed manual transmission.
» 1976: The car is launched in the UK, again as a closed car only, with twin SU carburettors and a four-speed manual gearbox. Overseas buyers can pay extra for a five-speed manual or three-speed auto.
» 1977: The Sprint edition is introduced, with a 16-valve engine, but just 60 are made. It doesn't help that the Speke factory, where the cars are made, goes on strike, stopping production altogether from October of this year until February 1978.
» 1978: The Speke factory closes with production transferred to Canley; there's also a five-speed gearbox now fitted as standard (continued overleaf).

Triumph TR7

SPECIFICATION

Engine
1998cc in-line four, eight
overhead valves. Alloy
head, cast-iron block.
Two SU carburettors

Power
105bhp @ 5500rpm

Torque
119lb ft @ 3500rpm

Transmission
Four/five-speed manual
or three-speed auto
Rear-wheel drive

Suspension
Front: Independent, with
MacPherson struts with
coil springs and anti-
roll bar
Rear: Live axle with
coil springs, radius arms,
telescopic dampers,
anti-roll bar

Brakes
Front: 241mm discs
Rear: 229mm drums
Servo-assisted

Weight
1070kg (2358lb)

Performance
0-60mph 10.7sec
Top speed 114mph

Value
Cost £5959 New (1980)
Value now £1500-£5500

buyers. It was also possible to specify a
three-speed automatic from 1976, but very
few UK buyers opted for this, and it's
unlikely that you'll find any such cars for
sale now.

All convertibles and some coupés left the
factory with an SD1 five-speed 'box; it's
plenty strong enough to cope with the
2-litre engine's torque, but it will wear out
eventually. The first sign of impending
expenditure will be from duff synchro on
second and third ratios, so feel for poor
selection as you change down.

The rest of the transmission causes few
problems. Hard-driven cars may be suffering
from a clutch that's past its best, but rear
axles are pretty much bulletproof. The
standard five-speed TR7 differential is
plenty strong enough to cope with the
torque of a Rover V8 – the four-speeder's
axle isn't tough enough however.

Suspension, steering and brakes

While the TR7 was never noted for its
performance, its ride was always a strong
point. The car was set up for US buyers,
who demanded soft suspension for their
long, straight, well-surfaced roads. As a
result the handling was never great, and

once the suspension bushes have started to
age the car will probably be all over the
place. If the car feels really unhappy
through the bends, and especially if there's
any sign of rear-wheel steering, budget on
spending £90 for a fresh set of rubber
bushes or £150 for polyurethane items.

The key is to rebuild the suspension,
upgrading it in the process, to give the TR7
the chassis that it should have had all
along. A fresh set of bushes, along with
upgraded springs and dampers, will work
wonders with the dynamics – with the right
attention to detail the car can be turned into
a truly sharp handler.

Although power steering was never
available from the factory, you can now buy
an electric system engineered by S+S
Preparations. This attaches to the steering
column underneath the dash, and it's yours,
fully fitted, for £1760.

The standard brakes were also marginal,
with thin discs at the front that wear all too
readily; they score and warp, leading to
squealing and judder.

The drums at the rear are fine, but it's
worth upgrading the front anchors with
harder pads, ventilated discs and twin-pot
callipers; if the car is still wearing a
completely standard braking system, expect

to pay £375 to fit a ventilated disc system
from a specialist.

Bodywork, electrics and trim

Corrosion has killed most TR7s; it takes a
hold all too readily and few owners are
prepared to spend the money needed to get
the car back to tip-top condition. Most of
the problems stem from the fact that there
are so many box sections; water gets in
then eats its way out, and by the time any
corrosion is evident it's all too late.

The sills give particular problems,
because they consist of four panels, and
tend to rot from the inside out. Repairs are
complex and bodges are rife, so take your
magnet with you and check they're not full
of filler. If structural repairs have already
been undertaken – and chances are they
have been – ask for photographic evidence
of the work, and who did it.

Other rot spots include all the classics;
inner and outer wheelarches, valances, door
bottoms and the boot floor. To these you
can add the footwells, spare wheel well,
windscreen frame, scuttle, and headlamp
panels. A-posts can also rust badly, along
with the inner wings, around the top mounts
for the MacPherson struts.

Although the floorpans usually survive

Clockwise from left
Dolomite-sourced lump, TR8 drop-top, cutaway with vinyl roof, standard TR7.

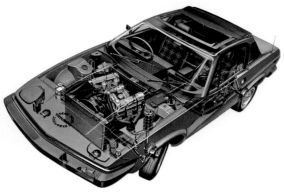

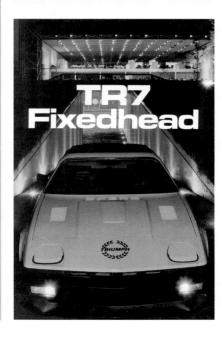
reasonably intact, you need to take a good look underneath the car to check what state the trailing arm mounting points are in. You'll also get a good idea of what's going on by lifting the carpet behind the seats and having a look at the condition of the bulkhead; any sign of cracks is bad news as the mountings are notorious for corroding, ultimately leading to some very interesting handling traits.

The TR7's electrical system is simple and reasonably reliable, but age will have taken its toll on some components. The headlamp pods frequently fail, and most people assume it's the motor. This isn't the case though – poor connections are usually to blame. The mechanism can also give trouble, as it seizes up if the car isn't used very much, and the headlamp motors often burn out as a result.

Interior trim isn't very durable as it's a mixture of cloth and vinyl, with poor quality stitching holding it together (or not as the case may be). The fabric wears through and the seams split, especially on the side bolsters where occupants get in and out of the car. It's not a disaster though, as replacement seats are available on either a new or used basis.

Most convertibles have had a replacement hood by now. As long as a decent quality roof has been fitted by somebody who knows what they're doing, all will be fine. But many owners skimp on the quality of the roof they buy and then get it fitted on the cheap – so it leaks and provides a deafening soundtrack when the car is driven at speed with the roof up.

Conclusion

Whether it's still got its original 2-litre four-pot or something with more cylinders (or a later four-cylinder, as fitted by S+S for example) and a lot more poke, the TR7 can make a great bargain sportster.

However, it can also be a whole lot of trouble, partly because of the original lousy build quality and partly because many owners have had mechanical alterations made that aren't always as well executed as they should be.

If you're hoping to buy a cheap standard car and just enjoy it then you'll probably end up with a dog. You're much better off spending extra cash on a car that's already had some upgrades, or buying a project that needs major mechanical work, so you can ensure that everything is done to a decent standard.

Take the latter route and the chances are you'll end up spending much more than the car will ever be worth – especially if major bodywork is needed – so you have to take the long-term view and do the car for keeps. ⚠

»Info

» 1979: The TR7 convertible is launched in America, along with open and closed editions of the TR8 – although the latter quickly dies.
» 1980: The TR7 convertible is now offered for sale worldwide.
» 1981: The final TR7 and TR8 are built; US cars fitted with Bosch L-Jetronic fuel injection for this year only.

SPECIALISTS
» Moss Europe, London. 0208 867 2020, www.moss-europe.co.uk
» Revington TR, Somerset. 01823 698437, www.revingtontr.com
» Rimmers, Lincoln. 01522 568000, www.rimmerbros.co.uk
» Robsport International, Herts. 01763 262263, www.robsport.co.uk
» S+S Preparations, Lancs. 01706 874874, www.ss-preparations.co.uk

CLUBS
» TR Register. 01235 818866, www.tr-register.co.uk
» TR Drivers' Club. 01562 825 000, www.trdrivers.com
» Club Triumph. 01425 274193, www.club.triumph.org.uk
» Triumph Sports Six Club. 01858 434424, www.tssc.org.uk

TVR VIXEN (1967-1973)

Often overlooked in favour of the V8s, a Vixen makes a great sports coupé

Words: Richard Dredge Photography: www.magiccarpics.co.uk

Above
It might not ooze power, but the Vixen is cheap and a hoot behind the wheel.

If you're one of those people who thinks that a TVR isn't a TVR unless it's got too much power and at least six cylinders – preferably a V8 – then the Vixen isn't for you. This is the TVR untouched by serious cubic inches, and it's none the worse for it thanks to a sharp chassis and low kerb weight.

Following on where the Grantura left off, the Vixen was the TVR for those who couldn't afford anything hairier; back in the 1960s, it was the four-cylinder cars that just about kept TVR in the black (well, most of the time anyway), with the V8 models for a minority only.

Although most TVR fanciers prefer something a lot more pokey, these small four-pot models have a loyal following. Values aren't especially high – the best cars will command little more than £8000; £6000 is more usual. However, if you want something that isn't all that pretty but is solid and will provide plenty of fun, £4000 will do the trick.

Engine

Most Vixens were fitted with a 1599cc Cortina GT engine; it's the Kent unit that's familiar to any Ford specialist so there's nothing to worry about in terms of parts availability. It'll be inexpensive and easy to overhaul, and at worst you'll need to buy a whole new unit,

but they're cheap and plentiful enough so it won't be a problem.

The first sign of trouble will be noisy valve gear, normally down to worn rockers, cam followers and the camshaft itself – by that stage the engine needs a top-end rebuild, although the camshaft is housed in the block.

Worn timing chains also cause problems – listen for rattles from the front of the engine – but compared with all these potential maladies, it's worn rings and bores that will blow the biggest hole in your wallet. Fumes from the oil filler cap and blue smoke from the exhaust will give the game away – spot these and a bottom end rebuild lies in store. The Kent engine is easy to work on and a rebuilt unit can be sourced for £750-£1000.

The various coolant hoses are unique to the Vixen, but they're all available through David Gerald. What can cause a bigger problem is the Cortina-sourced engine mountings; they're not that easy to find, so check the ones fitted are in good condition.

There were also 13 Vixens built with Triumph's 1300cc engine, but the chances of you finding one of those are virtually nil. However, you could well find a Vixen with Triumph's 2498cc straight-six, as fitted to the M-Series. For that engine's weak points, take a look at the M-Series guide on page 204.

Transmission

All Vixens featured a Ford four-speed manual 'box with no overdrive option. Synchromesh wearing out on second gear is the first sign of trouble, along with the transmission jumping out of top gear. If you're lucky it's because there's a broken spring in the gearchange fork rod, or the screw and lock nut which holds the selector fork rod together may be loose. But it could be more serious – the gearbox coupling dogs or selector fork rod could be suffering from serious wear. If this is the case, it's likely that there's major wear in the rest of the gearbox, in which case a reconditioned unit is the best solution. Expect to pick one up for around £350.

Universal joints have a habit of wearing quickly; TVR fitted its own driveshafts and they're designed in such a way that the joints wear out. But they're easy enough to find and fit; you'll pay £17 for each fresh one.

Suspension, steering and brakes

The front suspension is unique to the Vixen, while the rear set-up is a Triumph and TVR combo. It can all wear, but there's nothing to worry about because it's possible to source all the replacements you're likely to need.

In the front suspension it's the wheel

'Following on from where the Grantura left off, the Vixen was the car for those who couldn't afford anything hairier.'

bearings that are the most likely to give trouble as they're not really up to the job. Fitting fresh items regularly has been the only solution so far, but a conversion should be available soon, through Steve Reid.

The rear suspension is generally strong and easy to find fresh parts for, with the exception of the cast alloy upright which is at the heart of the whole set up. This has a habit of breaking, but it's either intact or it isn't. However, if the ones fitted look as though they might be the originals, budget to replace them soon as the metal will have aged by now. They're £312 a piece from David Gerald.

Something else that can give trouble is the quill shaft, which fails if the wheel bearings haven't been kept tight. Of course the obvious solution is to maintain the wheel bearings, but it's also possible to fit a much stronger quill shaft, made to aircraft standards – but they're £700 a pair, from Steve Reid.

The rack-and-pinion steering gives no trouble, so just feel for play as the rack will eventually wear to the point where it needs reconditioning. You can get an exchange rack for £40, but these tend to be little more than units that have been dismantled then reassembled with some shims; for £147 you can buy what's effectively a new rack from David Gerald. Alternatively, it's possible to fit

an Escort RS2000 rack, which is cheaper and stronger; it doesn't go straight on, but hardly any modifications are needed to make it fit.

Brakes are usually equally trouble-free; corroded pipes and warped discs are a possibility, but all parts are available to ensure the anchors are as good as new. Incidentally, the Series I featured a very simple braking system while later cars had a servo-assisted split-circuit system; it's possible to upgrade early cars to the later system.

Bodywork, electrics and trim

With its glassfibre panels, corrosion of the bodyshell isn't an issue at all – but poorly repaired crash damage is. Look for sunken paint, microblistering and fresh glassfibre matting that hasn't been let in properly, so the repairs are all too obvious. Also, abused cars may well be suffering from cracking and crazing of the panelwork, so inspect everything carefully; proper repairs are time-consuming and the skills aren't as common as those for fixing conventional steel panels. As a result, you could end up paying heavily even for what seem to be relatively minor repairs. There is some good news though; not only is the plastic very durable, but all replacement panels are available, right up to a replacement bodyshell.

Panel gaps should be reasonably tight and

even; if the bonnet clearly doesn't fit at all well, it's because the nose has been knocked out of shape. Once this has happened it's a major job to put everything right as the chassis will need to be fixed or nothing will ever line up properly again. Also have a close look at that large wraparound rear window; most were made of Perspex, but occasionally there was a glass item fitted. Glass replacements – heated or unheated – are available from Steve Reid, with prices starting at £1000. Polycarbonate rear windows are also available at £700 apiece. Incidentally, the windscreen is a Ford Consul/Zephyr MkII item, so finding a replacement shouldn't pose any problems.

Finally, check the state of the doors, which tend to drop when the hinges wear. Series I Vixens used TVR's own in-house hinges but later cars have Anglia 105E items; all are getting ever harder to recondition to a decent standard. Also look at the state of the alloy window frames, which fatigue then snap; repairs can get very involved.

The chassis is likely to have corroded at least a bit – and there's a good chance that it'll be really rotten in places. That's not necessarily a problem – and especially if you're buying a project car – because letting in fresh tubes isn't difficult. However, if the area around the differential has corroded badly, the chances

TVR Vixen S2
SPECIFICATIONS

Engine
1599cc in-line four, eight overhead valves. Cast-iron head and block. Weber 32DFM carb

Power
88bhp @ 5400rpm

Torque
96lb ft @ 3600rpm

Transmission
Four-speed manual

Suspension
Front: Independent with coil springs, double wishbones, telescopic dampers, anti-roll bar
Rear: Independent with coil springs, double wishbones, telescopic dampers, anti-roll bar

Brakes
Front: 231mm discs
Rear: 229mm drums
Servo-assisted

Weight
738kg (1624lb)

Performance
0-60mph 10.5sec
Top speed 109mph

Value
Cost £1493 new (1969)
Value now £3000-8000

are a new chassis will be needed because the frame has probably been weakened too much.

Although the diff area is the most important to check, the most likely corrosion hot spot is the side rails along the sills. Again, repairs are easy enough, although but the work is time consuming. Where it gets really involved is if you're looking at buying a Series I Vixen; these featured a bodyshell that was bonded to the chassis, whereas all later cars had a bolt-on shell.

Also take a look at the suspension mounting points; these corrode or can fracture if the metal has been weakened with time and hard use. Once the mountings have rusted, a new chassis (at £3000) is the best long-term solution; trying to weld everything up invariably leads to wheels pointing all over the place.

If there's a strong smell of fuel inside the car, it's because the steel fuel tank has corroded. It's out of sight underneath the rear window, so it's also out of mind. Aluminium tanks are available at £265, or you can spend about double this on a stainless steel item.

Electrics can suffer from poor earths or a brittle loom, but they're easily fixed. More problematic is missing or damaged instrumentation and switchgear on Series III and IV cars, as replacements are impossible to source. Series I and IIs used generic Lucas and Smiths parts, so finding new bits is much easier.

Any damaged or missing interior trim means you'll have to call on the services of a trimmer, as replacement bits aren't available. However, there's nothing in a Vixen's cabin that should tax any competent upholsterer – but if a fresh headlining is needed, along with new seats, carpets and trim panels,

the bill will add up very quickly. Exterior trim is also an issue, especially items such as door handles. Series I cars featured Standard Eight handles while later Vixens used Cortina MkII items; all are just about impossible to find. The alloy bumpers are also now extinct, but new glassfibre replacements are available at £20.

Conclusion
If we've convinced you that there's a Vixen-shaped hole in your life, you'd better start looking now because you might have to bide your time for the right car to come along. You'll find one through the TVR Car Club, and Steve Reid also often has early TVRs in stock. The Series II and III cars are generally the easiest to source, as well as being the most usable. They also feature a bodyshell that's bolted onto the chassis, so they're relatively easy to restore. However, whatever you buy you'll love driving; the Vixen is a hairy-chested sports car in the true sense; noisy, sometimes a bit of a handful and with a raw driving experience.

» **Thanks to Doug Elwood at David Gerald Sportscars, and Steve Reid.**

£119.10

1970 TVR Vixen
Value: £6000
Quote: **£119.10** (£50x/s unlimited mpa)

»Info

TIMELINE
» 1958: Grantura goes on sale.
» 1962: Grantura gets a new chassis; it's the same as the first Vixen's.
» 1964: V8-engined Griffith 400 is launched in the US.
» 1965: Griffith arrives in UK, but Grantura Engineering goes bust and all production stops, before Martin Lilley buys the company.
» 1967: V8 car now known as the Tuscan V8; new four-cylinder edition is the Vixen. This has a 1599cc Cortina GT engine and gearbox, installed in a Grantura bodyshell with a wheelbase of 85.5 inches.
» 1968: Series 2 Vixen has a 90-inch wheelbase, Cortina MkII tail lights and a larger rear window. The bodyshell is also now bolted to the chassis.
» 1970: Vixen SIII gets an 86bhp Ford powerplant and alloy wheels.
» 1972: Vixen SIV arrives, with an M-series chassis but an SIII bodyshell.
» 1973: The final Vixen SIV is built.

SPECIALISTS
» David Gerald TVR, Worcs. 01386 793237, www.davidgeraldtvr.com
» Steve Reid Classics, Cheshire. 01928 719267, www.classictvr.co.uk

CLUBS
» TVR Car Club, UK. www.tvr-car-club.co.uk

BOOKS
» TVR, an illustrated history by John Tipler. Haynes, ISBN 1-84425-235-3
» TVR, the complete story by John Tipler. Crowood, ISBN 1-85223-796-1
» TVR, all the cars by Ian Ayre. ISBN 978-1-84425-100-1

BOOKAZINES

(1972-1979)
TVR M-SERIES

It makes a superb daily or occasional driver – but what else
do you need to know about TVR's 1970s sportster?
Words: Richard Dredge Photography: www.magiccarpics.co.uk

**3000M
(1972-1979)**
SPECIFICATIONS

Engine
2994cc V6, 12 OHV. Cast
iron. Weber 40DFA carb

Power
142bhp @ 5,000rpm

Torque
174lb ft @ 3,000rpm

Transmission
Four-speed manual
Rear-wheel drive

Suspension
Front: Independent,
coil springs, double
wishbones, telescopic
dampers, anti-roll bar
Rear: Independent with
coil springs, double
wishbones, telescopic
dampers, anti-roll bar

Brakes
Front: 276mm discs
Rear: 229mm drums
Servo-assisted

Weight
998kg (2200lb)

Performance
0-60mph: 7.5sec
Top speed: 130mph

Value
Cost new: £4399 (1977)
Value now: £3000-£8000

It's hard to avoid talking in clichés where TVR's M-Series is concerned. Here's a genuinely hairy-chested British sportscar that has it all; performance, affordability, great looks and even a healthy dose of practicality and reliability – so where's the catch? Buy well and there isn't one; thanks to rugged components, great parts availability and excellent specialist support, the M-Series makes a superb classic used buy, whether it's for regular use or something more occasional.

Over an eight-year production span there were three engines offered in the M-Series; a Ford Kent 1.6-litre four-cylinder unit, a Triumph-sourced 2.5 straight-six and the well-known Ford Essex V6 in 3-litre form. Although the six-pot cars are much more sought after, they're not worth significantly more than a 1600M, whatever the condition. The typical premium is around £1000, with the best 2500Ms and 3000Ms usually fetching £8000 or so and an equivalent 1600M worth around £7000. More usable examples of the six-pot cars

change hands for £4000-£6000, while a 1600M in the same condition is around £3000-£5000. Taimars are worth the same as six-cylinder cars, while Convertibles fetch up to £10,000 in superb condition. However, the premium isn't so great if the car is in average condition; at the bottom end of the market you can pick up a usable machine for just £4000-£5000.

Engine
Aside from the Turbo, all M-Series engines are durable and cheap either to source second-hand or to rebuild. They're also easy to tune, so use a tired powerplant as a bargaining point.

It's the Essex unit that's the most common, as it was fitted to the 3000M, Taimar and Convertible. If serviced properly and not thrashed too much, this engine will clock up 200,000 miles before a rebuild is needed. Once the Essex motor has worn out, expect the classic symptoms; burning oil will be given away by blue exhaust smoke as the car is accelerated through the gears. The top end will also be noisy, while the

oil pressure will also be rather low; you should expect at least 50psi at 2000rpm once the engine has warmed up.

Few 2500Ms were sold outside the US, but there are examples in the UK, each fitted with Triumph's smooth and torquey TR6-derived 2.5-litre straight-six. Regular oil changes and proper servicing will ensure 120,000 miles are despatched with ease – some cars will see much more than this before major surgery is required. Whereas the TR6 featured Lucas fuel injection, the 2500M was fitted with twin Strombergs, dropping power to just 106bhp.

Check for play in the crankshaft thrust washers by pushing and pulling on the bottom pulley. The job is made easier by pushing and releasing the clutch – there should be no more than 0.015in movement. It may also be possible to feel and hear a clonk as the crank shifts. Any detectable movement means the thrust washers may have dropped out, which could be serious and may involve the sourcing of a replacement block or even engine. If the thrust

'Rugged build and great parts availability make M-Series a superb classic used buy'

washers are still in place it is possible to replace them with oversized ones, without having to remove the engine first.

If the motor has worn out, it won't be hard to spot. Blue smoke under acceleration points to bore and/or piston wear, while blue smoke when the car is first started up indicates worn valve guides – and the need for a cylinder overhaul. Rebuilt unleaded heads are available for around £300 to fit yourself or from £500 to have someone do it for you.

Replacement powerplants are easily sourced because the basic engine was also fitted to Triumph's big saloons as well as the TR6. Running second-hand motors can be bought for £50 upwards, although you'll have to spend at least £200 to get one that won't need rebuilding before long. However, for the purist who doesn't want a saloon engine with an MG prefix, genuine second-hand TR6 engines start at £200.

Not all M-Series buyers opted for six cylinders; a relatively small number chose the Ford Kent-sourced four-pot

1600M instead. This Capri GT powerplant offers performance that's far from thrilling, but it's an engine that's easy to tune so don't dismiss a 1600M too readily if the price is right. The first sign of trouble with the Kent unit is noisy valve gear, normally down to worn rockers, cam followers and the camshaft itself. If the engine has reached this stage, it needs a top-end rebuild.

Worn timing chains can also cause problems – listen for rattling from the front of the motor – but compared with all these potential issues it's worn rings and bores that will prove the most costly. Fumes from the oil-filler cap and blue smoke from the exhaust will give the game away. However, the Kent engine is very easy to work on and you should be able to track down a rebuilt unit for between £750 and £1000.

Because the M sits so low, the exhaust system can take a beating. Look at the system from underneath; check for dents, scrapes and pipes twisted out of true through coming into contact with speed bumps.

Transmission

All these cars were fitted with a four-speed manual gearbox, sourced from either Ford or Triumph depending on which engine was installed. They're all strong transmissions, with the 1600M unit being especially pleasant to use.

The first sign of trouble on a 3000M gearbox will be worn synchromesh, so check for baulking as you go up and down through the ratios. A noisy first gear indicates that the bearings are on their way out, and if the unit jumps out of gear it means that the mainshaft bearings have worn. If you find a car suffering from these symptoms, factor it into the buying price: you can expect to pay £475 for the exchange gearbox which will be needed before long.

From 1976, TVR offered overdrive on the 3000M, to allow more relaxed cruising. However, while this is usually a desirable option, when specified on the 3000M it makes the gearchange much less pleasant, so don't assume it's necessarily a good thing.

The Triumph gearbox was always ❯❯

offered with overdrive, and it's a transmission that generally lasts longer than the Ford-sourced one. However, it does wear out once 100,000 miles or so have been racked up, so watch out for a worn synchromesh – second gear is normally the first to go. If you do have to fit an overhauled gearbox, expect to pay £420 for an exchange unit, plus the same again if you want a reworked overdrive too.

Until 1977, all Ms featured a Triumph-sourced differential; after this date, a Salisbury 4HU unit was fitted. While it's the Salisbury axle that's the stronger and quieter of the two, it's the Triumph one that's the cheaper to rebuild. However, the Salisbury diff was also available with a limited-slip facility, which can come in useful if you're aiming to drive the car hard on a regular basis.

Suspension, steering and brakes

Although much of the suspension is TR6-derived, the wishbones, springs and dampers were all made specially by TVR. That doesn't pose any problems, though, as everything is available – and it's not especially costly either. The most likely problem is with the Triumph-sourced front trunnions, which should be injected with EP90 oil every few thousand miles but often are not. However, once again the parts are all readily available, the costs aren't exorbitant and the work is easy to do.

The only other likely suspension problem concerns rubber bushes that are past their best. Replacements can be picked up cheaply, or polyurethane items can be fitted for a bit more money; they're more durable but tend to make the ride a little firmer.

All Ms were fitted with disc brakes at the front and drums at the rear. However, because these machines are often driven hard, some owners prefer to upgrade the set-up by fitting four-pot calipers, vented discs and Aeroquip hoses.

Most Ms are still equipped with their original factory-fitted alloy wheels, but this isn't always the case. If you don't particularly care about keeping the car as it left the factory, fitting aftermarket alloys won't worry you. But if originality is a factor bear in mind that sourcing fresh wheels will be very tricky; they were made specially for TVR and they've been unavailable for many years.

Bodywork, electrics and trim

It's the usual story where the glassfibre bodyshell is concerned; although you don't have to worry about corrosion, there are all sorts of other things that can go wrong. While the shell is well made and the strong chassis ensures little in the way of flexing, there can be problems with cracking and crazing – but only if the car has been knocked or poorly repaired.

Although the bodyshell itself is extremely tough, there are other problems which can arise. The Convertible's windscreen frame is a stretched and lowered Jensen Healey item, consisting of a steel unit with some chrome trim on top. It rots but replacements aren't available; even decent used Jensen items are virtually impossible to find.

Another potential trouble spot is the underside of the car's nose. The whole front end tips forward, E-type style, for engine-bay access, and when all is well the ground clearance is marginal. However, when the car gets a punctured front tyre there isn't the space to open the bonnet fully – and the spare wheel is usefully stored above the front-mounted radiator... Some owners have fitted quick-release conversion kits to overcome the problem, but they're not that common.

Elsewhere, the doors can drop because the hinges are weak. These are Ford Anglia 105E units that can be rebuilt if necessary, as long as they're not too worn. At least one Vixen owner has had stainless steel replacements made.

The window frames can also give problems, because the extruded alloy channel that the glass sits in is attached to the door base by a steel channel. Electrolytic corrosion leads to weakening of the frame, causing it to break away – and once that happens, putting everything right again is a laborious process.

Paintwork can also give problems; the coat that TVR applied should have lasted well, but any remedial work needed since may have led to the colour losing its sheen. Microblistering is

Clockwise from far left
With sporty cabin and a choice of three engines, TVR is good to drive both on track and road.

also common, along with sunken paint, so check all the surfaces closely and pay particularly close attention to the corners.

The chassis is very robust but not completely immune from corrosion. Localised repairs aren't advised, so if one or two areas are badly affected by rust, you're better off replacing the whole frame – which isn't as onerous a job as you might think. The bodyshell is attached to the chassis at 10 points, and lifting it clear to fit a fresh unit is straightforward.

On the frame, the most likely place for corrosion to strike is the 'cage' area around the differential. In an attempt to reduce road noise, TVR fitted some felt soundproofing here, which soaks up the water then eats through the steel. Make sure the suspension mountings are intact, along with the chassis itself.

The electrical system is usually reliable enough, as long as the earths haven't been allowed to deteriorate. The wiring can also get brittle, and while fitting fresh wires can get involved (and pretty costly as a result), there's nothing that's insurmountable. Cars that have been modified are the most likely to give trouble, so look out for looms that have been hacked about with Scotchloks being spliced in all over the place.

A lot of these cars have been retrimmed, and not always to original specification. If done tastefully that's probably okay, but most buyers prefer factory spec for the seats and carpets. So bear in mind that even if you don't mind something a little different, you might not find selling the car later on too easy if it has a pink leather interior with mauve piping!

Make sure that the carpets haven't rotted, as they are prone to doing so if the windscreen seals are leaking. The door seals can also let in water and, of course, if the Convertible roof has seen better days it may be fighting a losing battle against keeping out the elements.

When it comes to exterior trim there isn't much to worry about. The badges are all available new, while most of the other components are borrowed from other mass-produced cars. Pre-1975 wing vents are taken from the Ford Zephyr/Zodiac MkIV, while the tail-lamps are from the Triumph TR6.

Conclusion

While the later V8 TVRs have massive appeal, as you can read from p206, the M-Series makes sense for much the same reasons; strength, performance, affordability and that delicious driving experience. Because the Griffith and Chimaera are now so affordable, the M-Series offers better value than ever; it's starting to get overlooked as the focus falls on TVRs from two decades later.

£103.35

FOOTMAN JAMES
Insurance specialists. At your service.

1972 TVR 1600M
Value: £4000
Quote: **£103.35** (£50x/s unlimited mpa)

»Info

TIMELINE
» 1972: The 1600M debuts, with a 1599cc Ford Kent engine; 149 are made. The 2500M also arrives, with Triumph TR6 power; 947 are built. In addition, there's the 3000M, with a Ford Essex V6 unit (2994cc); 634 are produced.
» 1975: The 1600M is re-introduced, having been killed off in 1973.
» 1976: The Taimar goes on sale; it's a hatchback edition of the 3000M. The name is derived from Tailgate and Martin (Lilley); 365 are built. The Turbo also debuts; developed by Broadspeed, its blown Essex V6 gives a 139mph top speed. Just 20 3000M-based editions are made, along with 30 Taimars and 13 Convertibles.
» 1977: The last 1600M and 2500M are manufactured.
» 1978: The Convertible joins the range; it's more than simply an open 3000M, as there are lots of new panels.
» 1979: The final cars are built.

SPECIALISTS
» Steve Reid Classics, Cheshire. +44 (0)1928 719 267, www.classictvr.co.uk
» David Gerald TVR, Worcs. +44 (0)1386 793 237, www.davidgeraldtvr.com

CLUBS
» TVR Car Club, UK. www.tvr-car-club.co.uk

BOOKS
» TVR, An Illustrated History by John Tipler. Haynes, ISBN 1-84425-235-3
» TVR, The Complete Story by John Tipler. Crowood, ISBN 1-85223-796-1
» TVR, All The Cars by Ian Ayre. ISBN 978-1-84425-100-1

TVR WEDGE (1980-1991)

You won't blend into the background in this sharp-nosed 1980s classic. Go on, be bold!

Words: Richard Dredge   Photography: www.magiccarpics.co.uk

Above
Open or closed, fast or plain outrageous, there is a Wedge for everyone.

If you're a shrinking violet, looking for a performance classic with which you can blend into the scenery, you might as well turn the page now. Few cars are as obvious as TVR's Wedge series, in terms of looks as well as noise, so consider one of these only if you're intent on making an entrance every time you take it out of the garage.

When the Tasmin was launched in 1980 it was a major departure for TVR, which until now had produced rounded cars that looked rather more subtle but were still decently quick. Over time the shape got more familiar – but performance levels also rose to the point where these models were snapping at the heels of far more costly machinery, even if reliability wasn't always too hot.

There's now a Wedge for everyone; the range spans open or closed bodies, from decently quick to indecently fast. However, the real beauty of these cars is how affordable they are – especially when you take the available performance into account. Falling values of Griffiths and Chimaeras have had a consequent effect on Wedge prices, to the point where you can now pick up a decent 2.8i model for under £2000.

The newer or more powerful a car is, the more it's worth, while convertibles typically command twice as much as equivalent coupés. The last models are still changing hands at up to £10,000 – but it needs to have been rebuilt for that money, or else be in truly superb original condition. For just half this amount, though, you can snap up a decent, usable 350i; look after it and it can only go up in value, while every journey in it will be a hoot.

Engine

There were three types of engine fitted to the Wedge. Rarest of the lot is Ford's Pinto unit in 2-litre form, with the 2.8-litre Cologne powerplant also relatively rare. By far the most commonly used motor though is the Rover V8, in various displacements ranging from 3.5 to 4.5 litres.

The Pinto engine will last forever as long as it gets regular oil changes and the timing belt is renewed every 60,000 miles or three years. The spray bar that keeps the top end lubricated should also be replaced regularly; it's a quick job and the parts needed cost just a fiver or so.

The Cologne unit should also be durable if looked after, although there are glitches to watch out for. For instance, the fuel injection can play up and the fibre timing gears can disintegrate, although it's possible to replace these with indestructible steel items. The main issue, though, is with blown head gaskets, so get a compression test done and take a look for oil and water having mixed by checking for white emulsion on the underside of the oil-filler cap.

Again, the Rover V8 is brilliantly long-lived as long as it's looked after, which means the oil should have been changed every 3000 miles. If previous owners have failed to do this there's a good chance the hydraulic tappets will have got clogged up, while the camshaft, followers and rocker shaft may have worn prematurely, too. The giveaway is an especially noisy top end; these units should run very quietly even as the revs rise.

Don't be too concerned by an oil-pressure gauge that reads low, as these engines run quite happily with just 15-20psi showing. Of more concern is knocking from the bottom end; this signals that a rebuild is due, for which you can expect to pay £500 for the

'Few cars are as obvious as TVR's Wedge series, in terms of looks as well as noise'

parts. As well as renewing the oil regularly, it's essential that the coolant is replaced every couple of years. Being an all-alloy unit, the V8 is prone to internal corrosion if anti-freeze levels are allowed to drop off, so check the temperature gauge once the car has been allowed to idle for a few minutes. If it gets ever hotter, it's probably because the radiator and block are full of deposits that need to be flushed out.

Transmission

Considering the torque some of the gearboxes have to endure, problems are surprisingly unlikely – unless the car has been truly neglected. Ford-engined cars were fitted with four- or five-speed boxes, while all V8 editions featured a five-speed SD1-sourced unit. You're unlikely to find an auto (only 16 were made), but if you do, check for slipping or jerkiness, signifying that a rebuilt unit will need to be fitted.

The SD1-sourced gearbox is a familiar unit that is easy to get rebuilt if necessary. However, it's also very tough,

so unless it's been abused or the car has covered a high mileage, it should be in fine fettle. After around 120,000 miles the bearings will probably need to be replaced, so listen for chattering from the transmission when the car is idling in neutral; the noise will disappear when the clutch is dipped. Also make sure you reverse the TVR, looking for the transmission jumping out of gear – once this happens, you'll need to budget for a rebuilt box at around £450.

The differential is a Salisbury-made unit, and despite the prodigious torque available in some of these cars, it's still well within its limits. However, you still need to be on the lookout for oil leaks, and listen for whining, which indicates that a rebuild is on the cards.

Clutches are also reasonably long-lived, with even hard-driven cars often giving few problems. They do wear out, though, and when they do it's a big job to fit a new one. That's because the engine has to come out to perform the operation, so budget at least £600 to get the work done.

The clutch hydraulics can also prove rather weak, so you should be suspicious of a baulky gearchange because of the clutch not fully releasing. The problem is down to the master cylinder wearing out, which it usually does after 60,000 miles or so. A £60 replacement is the only solution, but it's an easy task to perform.

Suspension, steering and brakes

There can be all sorts of problems with the rear suspension, which has several weak points. The key one is the hub nut, which can work loose causing complete havoc. Not only can the hub casting be wrecked if the nut loosens, but if it comes off altogether the wheel will eventually fall off. It's easy to see whether or not the nut has come off or is loose; just remove the wheel and see whether there's any play in the nut.

Before you take the wheel off, though, try rocking it with the back of the car lifted off the ground; if there's any detectable play, the wheelbearings need

TVR 350i
SPECIFICATIONS

Engine
3528cc V8, 16 overhead valves. Alloy head and block. Lucas L electronic fuel injection

Power
197bhp @ 5280rpm

Torque
220lb ft @ 4000rpm

Transmission
Five-speed manual
Rear-wheel drive

Suspension
Front: Independent with upper wishbone and lower stabilising lever, coil springs, telescopic dampers, anti-roll bar
Rear: Independent with lateral links, trailing arms, coil springs, telescopic dampers, anti-roll bar

Brakes
Front: 269mm discs
Rear: 277mm discs. Servo

Weight
1142kg (2520lb)

Performance
0-60mph: 6.6sec
Top speed: 136mph

Value
Cost new: £15,760 (1985)
Value now: £2000-£10,000

»Info

replacing. This isn't a big deal however; fresh bearings aren't costly, and replacing them isn't a difficult job.

Corrosion of the suspension can also be a problem, especially in the bracing tubes of the trailing rear arms. Even though the design was modified several times during production all are susceptible to rust, so make sure the metal hasn't been weakened by corrosion.

The brakes are up to the job unless they're given a regular hammering, such as on frequent track days. Despite the effectiveness of the stoppers, many owners like to fit stronger discs and calipers. Tower View Racing offers various levels of upgrade.

Original-spec alloy wheels are no longer available, and haven't been for years, so if you're keen on originality you'll need to make sure that what's fitted is in good condition. However, original tatty wheels are better than mint aftermarket ones because refurbishing the original rims is normally easy enough; sourcing a decent used set could prove tricky, depending on which model you're thinking of buying.

Bodywork, electrics and trim

It will come as no surprise that poorly-repaired accident damage is the number-one bodywork issue; lots of power, rear-wheel drive and a lack of electronic aids means many of these cars have left the road backwards, and rectification isn't always properly carried out. If the example you're looking at has been looked after it'll last indefinitely, because the glassfibre is of very good quality.

Early cars may be suffering from stress cracks and crazing around stress points, while paint can bubble and blister all too readily. As the Wedge evolved,

though, the quality got better and better; late models should be in superb condition. However, all cars can suffer from chipping of the nose, wheelarches and door mirrors, while the air dams may have made contact with the ground. Although everything is still available, the costs will add up when it comes to fitting and painting.

The steel chassis was plastic-coated when new, and as long as this coating is intact the metal should be fine. However, there's a good chance that the plastic will have got damaged from the car bottoming out, and once the steel is exposed it'll quickly rust. This rot will spread rapidly, with damp getting underneath the rest of the plastic and leading to more widespread corrosion. There's also the spectre of water then getting into the chassis tubes and rotting the chassis from the inside out, which is why lots of Waxoyl should be applied to the inside of these occasionally.

The most likely areas for corrosion are the outriggers, particularly behind the front wheels, along with the side rails that run from behind the front wheels to ahead of the rears. There's also a crossmember that sits in the nose of the car, which tends to rust; this corrodes after being battered by road debris. There are a few other areas which can corrode, including the rear body mounting and the underside of the main bottom chassis rails, as well as the tops of each main top rail.

If you're looking at a V6 car, make sure you inspect the tube just ahead of the diff, which sometimes cracks; when it does, it has to be replaced rather than welded up. Whatever the engine, you'll need to look at the fuel tanks as well as the pipes that connect them, plus the swirl pots and pump, all of which sit just ahead

Clockwise from left
Sharp-featured Tasmin snapped at heels of more costly exotica, even if reliability wasn't great.

»Info

SPECIALISTS
» Tower View Race Services, London.
+44 (0)208 452 6922,
www.t-v-r-services.co.uk
» Webbs, Bristol. +44 (0)1275 858461,
www.tvrspecialist.co.uk

CLUBS
» TVR Car Club, UK.
www.tvr-car-club.co.uk

BOOKS
» TVR, An Illustrated History by John
Tipler. Haynes, ISBN 1-84425-235-3
» TVR, The Complete Story by John
Tipler. Crowood, ISBN 1-85223-796-1
» TVR, All The Cars by Ian Ayre.
ISBN 978-1-84425-100-1

of the rear axle. Perished rubber and rusty steel are common, and there's a good chance that lots of new bits will be needed; a replacement fuel tank in aluminium is £235.

If the chassis needs lots of repairs it may be better to replace the whole thing; a new frame costs upwards of £3000. However, a fresh one is rarely needed, as a specialist such as RT Racing can normally rebuild the existing component. For a fixed price of £4100 it will lift off the bodyshell, repair and repaint the chassis, then put it all back together again. If things haven't got that bad the company also offers a preventative maintenance package for £350-£470, with the chassis cleaned, painted where necessary then undersealed.

Of course it isn't only corrosion that you need to look out for; accident damage is also common. If the chassis has been bodged the body will usually also be looking the worse for wear, but it's not unknown for the glassfibre to be repaired very well but for the chassis to be left untouched. Incidentally, up to the 350i the Wedge featured sill and air dams that were simply pop-riveted into place; on later cars the body were bonded to the chassis. As a result, there's a lot more work involved in separating shell and frame where these models are concerned.

Although early examples didn't feature much in the way of electrical equipment, later editions became increasingly gadget-laden. With the cars prone to leaks, and with earthing problems likely, that can be bad news – and can prove very frustrating when it comes to trying to trace faults.

The first thing to check is the headlamp motors; these TR7-sourced units can prove troublesome. They're prone to failure and hard to source, but they can be rebuilt – it's often only the diodes that need replacing. Electric-window motors can also give problems, just like the instrumentation. In the case of the latter, new parts aren't available so rebuilding is the only option, but that shouldn't pose any issues. ECUs can also play up; original ones are now unobtainable, so you'll have to have a custom unit installed and then set up on a rolling road to ensure it works properly.

Interiors often look tatty, but there's nothing that should faze a competent trimmer because it's all conventionally put together. However, if the upholstery has rotted because of water getting into the cabin you'll need to establish where it's coming from. It may be that the car has simply been left outside in the rain with the roof down, but more likely is water getting past the various weather seals. If the cabin has got damp the wood inserts will most likely have delaminated. That's why some owners take it all out and fit brushed aluminium or carbon fibre panels instead.

There isn't much in the way of exterior trim to worry about, but you do need to check that the hood frame hasn't rusted or twisted through ham-fisted use – and take a look at the roof itself, which may be tatty around the seams. Also check that the rubber seals for the doors and boot are intact.

Your final check is to the windscreen, which was made specially. It can delaminate, and once it does there's no alternative to fitting a new one. Replacements aren't always available, but when they are expect to pay upwards of £300 for the glass only. If you're looking at a coupé and its rear screen is damaged, be warned that you'll struggle to find a new one. When they do crop up, they usually have a four-figure price tag attached...

Conclusion
The biggest problem with the TVR Wedge is that some have been snapped up by inexperienced drivers who can't handle the power. As a result, you have to be really vigilant if you're not to buy a car that's been crashed. While everything is available to patch up even the worst damage, this model doesn't have to be in that poor a shape before it's not economically viable to revive.

Also make sure you get an insurance quote before buying; some early cars are surprisingly cheap to cover, while the much more powerful later editions can be horrifically expensive. However, stick it on a classic limited-mileage policy and suddenly the cost of cover will pale into insignificance. △

£99.15

1981 TVR Tasmin 2-Litre
Value: £1800
Quote: **£99.15** (£50x/s unlimited mpa)

TVR GRIFFITH & CHIMAERA

TVR may be consigned to the history books, but its cars still make a splash. Words: Richard Dredge Photography: www.magiccarpics.co.uk

If you listened to those who prop up the bar at the Red Lion, the chances are that you'd never even consider buying a TVR. After all, they apparently leak like sieves, are guaranteed to break down at least weekly and are driven only by those who are built like Viz magazine's Buster Gonad. But the reality is rather different; not only are these cars more usable than you'd think, but they're not inherently unreliable – as long as they are properly looked after.

Steve Reid of Classic TVR sums it up perfectly: 'TVRs are too often bought by people who are used to the reliability of a modern mass-market car. They think they can get it serviced every 10,000 miles and thrash it mercilessly without it breaking. These motors will take very hard use – but you have to service them much more often than a high-volume sportscar because they are highly specialist machines.'

The unveiling of the Griffith prototype at the 1990 British Motor Show meant TVR could leave the Tasmin and S-Series cars behind, and move into a new era of much more powerful, aggressively styled models. This first offering was essentially a rebodied V8-S, with a chassis that could cope with little more than 240bhp. TVR boss Peter Wheeler knew the Griffith would ultimately offer much more than this, so a fresh platform had to be devised. The solution was to base the new car on the Tuscan racer's frame, and at the 1991 motor show a completely rejigged Griffith was unveiled. The first cars were delivered in 1992, with either 3948cc or 4280cc

Rover V8s, but within a year a 5.0-litre unit was the sole choice.

While the Griffith looks fabulous, it doesn't offer much in the way of practicality – and even enthusiastic drivers sometimes need a healthy dose of usability. That's why the Chimaera was devised; it's a Griffith with a bigger boot and softer suspension, so it's just as fast but easier to live with – and some would also say more discreetly designed, too.

With the apparent demise of TVR and the fact that it's already six years since the final Chimaera was built (and seven since the last Griffith was produced), values for these cars are lower than ever. Indeed they're still a bit unstable, with good 5-litre examples sometimes advertised for the same money as ropey

Griffith 500

'They'll take very hard use – but you have to service them much more often than a high-volume sportscar because they're highly specialist'

4-litre ones, so shop around to get the best model for your money. An early (4-litre) Griffith is now down to around £10,000, but for little more you can have a 4.3-litre example, while £13,000 buys you a good 5-litre edition. Some optimistic dealers are still asking the thick end of £20,000 for a really good, low-mileage Griffith, but you don't need to pay that sort of money; £16,000 will net you something that's really superb.

If you'd prefer a Chimaera you're in luck because values are down a bit on the Griffith. These cars are more common and seen as less of a driver's machine, and as a result they're not so sought after – especially as these recent TVRs are now occasional playthings for most owners. A decent 4-litre Chimaera

can be yours for just £8-9000, while 4.5-litre editions are typically £11,000 for something nice. Pick of the bunch is definitely the 5-litre model, but just 10 per cent of the 6000 Chimaeras built were fitted with this engine; if you want one you'll need to find £15,000 if you're not to acquire a liability. After all, you wouldn't want to be joining the pundits at the Red Lion's bar, nodding in agreement at everything they say.

Engine
The Rover V8 may be from the old school, but it's reliable, easy to tune and dishes up plenty of horses. It is simply engineered and happy to keep going, too. The first thing to wear is the camshaft: whichever engine is fitted,

this usually needs replacing after 50,000 miles, costing £1500.

Another common weakness is oil leaks – so don't expect to see an exceptionally clean engine bay that looks as though it's just been steam cleaned. It's the rocker cover gasket that leaks, because the retaining bolts for the cover need to be tightened at every service – and they're usually not.

Listen for blowing from the exhaust; not only do the gaskets fail, but the manifolds are prone to cracking and new stainless items are over £600 per pair. Things aren't helped by the engine potentially getting rather hot, due to the failure of the relay that controls the radiator's thermostatic fan. Even if all is well here, check that the coolant

Above
The 340bhp Griffith 500 is the most common derivative, with 1640 examples manufactured before production finished.

»

'Make sure that nothing is damaged in the cabin, as the cost will be high if you have to rectify it'

hoses haven't perished; they'll probably need renewing by now. The radiator also has to be treated as a consumable; they rarely last much more than 25,000 miles before the sides split and coolant ends up all over the place. A new one is around £270 and fitting it means a fair amount of dismantling, but the job is easy enough to do at home.

Although exhausts are durable, those on earlier cars have generally had to be replaced in recent years. You'll pay around £500 for a new stainless system, and although this should be a fit-and-forget item, damage often occurs through grounding. As a result, it's a good idea to get underneath and check that the exhaust hasn't been bashed to within an inch of its life.

Transmission
The transmission is amazingly durable; it's conventional and over-engineered, so unless the car has been absolutely thrashed or driven to the moon and back, it shouldn't need anything major doing. The GKN limited-slip diff fitted until 1994 will whine when it wants attention, but it'll keep going for ages before giving in. Later cars featured a Salisbury unit; whichever back axle is fitted you'll need to ensure there are no oil leaks as they're common and fixing them is pricey.

Clutches are durable enough, even on

hard-driven cars, but the hydraulics can leak. It's the master cylinder that's usually the culprit, so check there's no brake fluid dripping down the clutch pedal; new master cylinders are £55 apiece.

Suspension, steering and brakes
The biggest problem with the suspension is that of worn bushes, although renewing them is cheap and easy. The best solution is to fit new bushes with the nylon washers as used on the later 500. Corrosion of the front wishbones is another problem, as the powder coating was of a poor quality. Replacement upper units complete with bushes cost £65 apiece, while the lower ones are double this.

Although power-assisted steering wasn't actually available until 1995, many earlier cars have had it retro-fitted. The surgery is complex but worthwhile, even though it costs around £2000. If the system is already in place and makes odd whirring noises on full lock, just make sure the reservoir hasn't been over-filled: it often is.

Even if the car is being hammered, the brakes are up to the job of stopping it squarely and without fade. That's why there's no need to upgrade the system, although it's obviously essential that everything is maintained in tip-top condition. Some

uprated set-ups produce a car that's less balanced to drive, so know what you're buying before parting with your readies.

It'll be no revelation that the tyres have a lot to contend with, so make sure they've still got some tread left. New ones are typically £175 apiece, but if you replace the tyres on a car whose alignment is out, they'll wear extremely quickly and you'll be back to square one. In the same way, be wary of a motor that's just had a new set of boots; it may be that the suspension is out and the tyres are wearing unevenly.

Bodywork, electrics and trim

You shouldn't be surprised to learn that the bodywork and chassis can throw up some pretty major problems, not least of all from accident damage. With no gadgetry to keep unskilled drivers out of trouble, there are plenty of Griffiths and Chimaeras that have made intimate contact with the scenery. Once the GRP has got damaged, it's usually a case of replacing panels wholesale.

It's not just about poor crash repairs, though; rust and age also take their toll on the glassfibre bodywork and the steel chassis. The nose is susceptible to stone

chips, so it's quite normal to have to fork out for a front-end respray – at £1000 a time. You also need to examine the corners very closely for evidence of scrapes, which occur all too easily because there are no bumpers.

While the glassfibre shrugs off minor knocks quite happily, it will only take so much before the bodywork erupts in a series of cracks and crazing. The Griffith 500 featured a different nose from the earlier cars, and for several years only the later panels were available. Therefore, if an early car has a later nose, you know it's been pranged; the earlier front is available once more now, though. The 500 features a grille that stretches from one driving light to the other, whereas the earlier one has separate nacelles for these.

You'll need to get underneath and check the state of the chassis; its powder coating gets chipped and cracks, leading to corrosion. Annual Waxoyling will keep rot at bay, but it's accident damage you also need to be wary of.

A major knock will push everything out of true, meaning that new panels and a fresh frame will be required – although it's surprising just how big a shunt it takes to cause distortion of the chassis. Everything is available to effect proper »»

1993 TVR Griffith 500
SPECIFICATIONS

Engine
4997cc V8, overhead valves, 16 valves. Alloy block and heads. Multi-point fuel injection, normally aspirated

Power
340bhp @ 5500rpm

Torque
350lb ft @ 4000rpm

Transmission
Five-speed manual

Suspension
Front: Independent with coil springs, double wishbones, telescopic dampers, anti-roll bar
Rear: Independent with coil springs, double wishbones, telescopic dampers, anti-roll bar

Brakes
Front: 259mm ventilated discs
Rear: 271mm solid discs
Servo-assisted

Weight
1075kg (2365lb)

Performance
0-60mph: 4.2sec
Top speed: 161mph

Value
Cost new: £32,995
Value now:
£12,000-£18,000

»Info

TIMELINE
» 1990: Griffith 4.0 prototype shown at British Motor Show, based on S-Series chassis.
» 1991: Reworked Griffith makes its debut at British Motor Show, this time based on the Tuscan racer chassis.
» 1992: Griffith 4.0 goes into production, with 3948cc Rover V8 giving 240bhp and 270lb ft; 308 are built. At same time, a 4280cc version is offered, with 280bhp and 305lb ft; 303 are sold. A few dozen big-valve 4.3-litre cars are also made, along with one or two 4.5-litres. The Chimaera also makes its debut, at the Earls Court Motor Show.
» 1993: Production of UK Griffiths is halted (export models are still built), as TVR gears up for Chimaera. This goes on sale early in the year in 3948cc and 4280cc forms, then the 340bhp Griffith 500 is unleashed; it's the most common derivative, with 1640 examples produced.
» 1994: There's now a Borg Warner T5 box, and the Chimaera 500 makes its debut, with a 5.0-litre Rover V8.
» 1995: Power-assisted steering becomes an option on the Griffith – but is quickly made standard.
» 1996: Facelifted Chimaera gets fresh nose based on Cerbera's. Horizontal bar replaces mesh grille.
» 1997: A 4.5-litre Chimaera is here; the original plan had been to fit TVR's own AJP engine but it wasn't ready in time.
» 2001: Final cars made, badged 500SE, with 100 run-out models offered. Chimaera now has enclosed headlights.
» 2002: Final Chimaera is built.

SPECIALISTS
» David Gerald TVR, Worcs. +44 (0)1386 793237, www.davidgeraldtvr.com
» Racing Green TVR, Hants. +44 (0)1252 894840, www.racinggreentvr.com
» RT Racing, Sheffield. +44 (0)114 281 7507, www.rtracing.co.uk
» Steve Reid Classics, Cheshire. +44 (0)1928 719267, www.classictvr.co.uk
» TET Mouldings, Lancs. +44 (0)1253 892342, www.b-link.co.uk/tet
» The TVR Shop, Oxon. +44 (0)1491 629219, www.racetechdirect.co.uk

Above
Poor crash repairs, rust and age can all take their toll on that distinctive glassfibre bodywork and steel chassis.

repairs, but the costs will soon mount if everything needs doing.

The TVR's electrical system is pretty robust where most of the major components are concerned, but it's usually the smaller stuff that packs up. That's why you need to make sure that the switchgear all works okay, along with things like the electric mirrors and powered side windows.

Starter motors aren't especially long-lived, so if the car still sports its original unit there's a good chance that a new one will be required before very long. They get cooked by the exhaust system; a reconditioned motor is £100, while a new one costs three times that. Also check that the speedometer works as it should. Because they're cheaply made, they frequently pack in – and that then throws into doubt the mileage displayed.

Interiors are generally hard-wearing, but if they have regularly got wet because of the roof having been left down in the rain, rotten carpets could be the result. A cabin retrim is unlikely to be needed, but you should make sure nothing is damaged anyway as the cost will be high if you have to rectify it. Pay particular attention to the state of the roof, which should be fine but which can suffer from perished seals. That's why you need to make sure there's no water in the footwells.

Conclusion

You needn't be put off by a relatively high-mileage TVR, but it has to have a fully stamped service book, with the work carried out by a specialist who knows what they're doing.

It doesn't matter which Griffith or Chimaera variant you buy, because they are all mind-bendingly quick. Condition is more important than model, age or – to a degree – mileage.

We'll leave the final word to Classic TVR's Steve Reid: 'The Griffith offers amazing value, but I reckon that prices could drop even further before they start climbing again. If you can find a really good one for the right money, dive in. It's the same for the Chimaera, which is even better value, more practical and largely the same as the Griffith underneath the skin. You will not get more performance for your money – anywhere.'

£302.85  **FOOTMAN JAMES**
Insurance specialists. At your service.

1994 TVR Chimaera 4.0ltr
Value: £11,000
Quote: **£302.85**
(£150x/s unlimited mpa)

»Info

SPECIALISTS CONT.

» Tower View Race Services, London. +44 (0)208 452 6922, www.t-v-r-services.co.uk
» Webbs, Bristol. +44 (0)1275 858461, www.tvrspecialist.co.uk

CLUBS

» TVR Car Club, UK. www.tvr-car-club.co.uk
» TVR Car Club of North America. www.tvrccna.org
» TVR Car Club, Holland. www.tvrcarclub.nl
» TVR Car Club, Belgium. www.tvrcc.be
» TVR Car Club, Sweden. www.tvrcc.org

BOOKS

» The TVR Griffith Story by Roger A Shackleton. Rufus, ISBN 0-9538244-1-1
» TVR, An Illustrated History by John Tipler. Haynes, ISBN 1-84425-235-3
» TVR, The Complete Story by John Tipler. Crowood, ISBN 1-85223-796-1

It's one of the most hardcore driver's cars from a mainstream marque in recent years, but is it a future classic?

Words: Richard Dredge Photography: www.magiccarpics.co.uk

VAUXHALL VX220

Manufactured on the same production line as its Elise cousin, Vauxhall's roadster never enjoyed the same cachet as the Lotus. Yet not only is the VX220 more usable, but it is also just as great to drive. It is more affordable, too.

The VX220 first went on sale in the UK in 2000 and was introduced at around the same time as the Elise S1 was being replaced by the S2. Fitted with a 145bhp version of Vauxhall's 2198cc Ecotec four-cylinder engine, its characteristics are quite different to those of the 1.8-litre K-Series fitted to the Elise. Its extra torque makes the car more relaxing to drive, but it's slower and less economical.

The VX220 shared just 10 per cent of its components with the Lotus, which is why it's subtly different in many ways. Although the Elise's basic tub was used, it featured a wheelbase that was 30mm longer and a rear track that was 20mm wider. As such, the car was heavier at 875kg, but it was still ferociously quick – and even more so when a turbocharger was bolted on (and the displacement reduced) in December 2002, to give 197bhp. Things got even hairier with

the VXR220 of 2004; with a stonking 220bhp on tap this is the ultimate VX, but you'll be lucky to find one as only 65 were built.

It's already three years since the VX220 went out of production, and you can now pick up a decent low-mileage example for just £10,000 or so; add an extra couple of grand to that and you can have a superb motor. You'll need to spend a third as much again for an equivalent Turbo, which must rank as one of the all-time great performance bargains. It's unlikely that you'll be lucky enough to find a VXR220; if you do, count on spending at least £20,000.

What to look for

The VX220 is ferociously quick, and many owners have come unstuck revelling in the performance on offer. That's why crash damage is at the top of your list of priorities; relatively few VXs have never had a skirmish of any kind. Get underneath and check the floorpans as well as the chassis and suspension components; look for rippling, cracks and dents.

Because that bluff nose sits so close to the ground, stone chips in the paintwork are par for

the course. A really caring owner will have had Armourfend fitted; that's the clear plastic film which protects a car's vulnerable bits from stray road debris. However, at £400 to get it applied, few cars boast such protection.

Not many VX220s have covered very high mileages; after all, they're not comfortable or practical enough for everyday use. As a result, few problem patterns have cropped up so far. Engines are proving tough and so are the transmissions. The suspension is also surprisingly durable; the only likely issue is with the bushes wearing out after 35,000 miles or so. By this point the outer wishbone ball joints may also have gone; if so, it'll be given away by the wheels vibrating on the test drive.

Interiors get scuffed all too easily, but as much of it is bare alloy that's not really a problem. The door trims are horribly flimsy and the roof can leak, so make sure it's been waterproofed recently; normally-aspirated cars can have their top upgraded to use the much-improved seals of the Turbo edition. Also, you should check that the doors don't shake; if they do, their retaining pins will need to be adjusted.

Vauxhall VX220
SPECIFICATIONS

Engine
2198cc in-line four, twin overhead camshafts, 16 valves. Alloy head and block. Bosch sequential fuel injection

Power
145bhp @ 5800rpm

Torque
150lb ft @ 4000rpm

Transmission
Five-speed manual
Rear-wheel drive

Suspension
Front: Independent coil springs, double wishbones, telescopic dampers, anti-roll bar
Rear: Independent coil springs, double wishbones, telescopic dampers

Brakes
Front: 288mm ventilated discs
Rear: 288mm ventilated discs
Servo-assisted

Weight
875kg (1925lb)

Performance
0-60mph: 5.6sec
Top speed: 136mph

Value
Cost new: £22,995 (2000)
Value now: £10,000-£14,000

'The VX220 shared just 10 per cent of its components with the Lotus Elise, which is why it's subtly different in many ways'

Check a VXR220 is the real thing by looking for its black Speedline alloys, VXR branding for the interior plus an all-black grille and windscreen surround.

Conclusion
Before you dismiss the VX220 because of its badge, think very carefully. Values are significantly lower than for an equivalent Elise, while the cars themselves are easier to live with – if still somewhat raw. Servo-assistance and anti-lock for the braking system were not offered by the Lotus (which to many is a good thing) but were standard on the Vauxhall. The interior was more lavishly trimmed, although there was still plenty of exposed alloy. However, because the VX is really for focused drivers only, many cars change hands quickly because they're snapped up by people who think the Vauxhall is more like a Mazda MX-5 than an Elise. Several owners on the V5 isn't necessarily an issue, but a lack of service history is; make sure the car has been maintained properly – and by somebody who knows what they're doing.

Even the normally-aspirated car is a hoot to drive, but the Turbo is something else. It came with tweaked suspension to help it stay the right

side up, and the ability to sprint from 0-62mph in just 4.9 seconds. For some, though, even this isn't enough; if you want to experience one of the most hardcore driver's cars on the planet, buy a VX220 Turbo and take along it to Thorney Motorsport (www.thorneymotorsport.co.uk) for some fettling; they can realise over 250bhp from the blown 2-litre four-pot for you, for truly insane performance.

However, you needn't go that far to appreciate the Vauxhall's qualities; you can have plenty of fun with the entry-level model's 145bhp. To get the most out of your VX, though, make sure you join the club (www.vx220.org.uk) – you'll find it invaluable whether you're aiming to keep the car standard, tune it or thrash it regularly around the track. ⚠

£273.45

FOOTMAN JAMES
Insurance specialists. At your service.

2001 Vauxhall VX220
Value: £10,000
Quote: **£273.45** (£250x/s unlimited mpa)
Max NCD - VX220 Club member

»Info

TIMELINE
» 2000: The Vauxhall VX220 goes on sale, with a normally-aspirated 2.2-litre four-pot engine.
» 2001: A special edition is unleashed on the roads, called the Lightning Yellow. A mere 100 are produced, and it boasts yellow paint and anthracite alloy wheels along with a colour-coded hardtop.
» 2002: VX220 Turbo arrives, equipped with a blown 2-litre powerplant giving 197bhp.
» 2004: The ultimate VX goes on sale, the VXR220. It packs a 2-litre turbocharged engine offering 220bhp.

VW KARMANN GHIA (1955-1974)

German cruiser combined cutting-edge styling with tried-and-tested mechanicals – but rot is the buyer's biggest enemy

Words: Richard Dredge Photography: www.magiccarpics.co.uk

Below
Sleek 'designer' looks belied Karmann Ghia's sturdy Beetle running gear and platform.

It doesn't matter that the VW Karmann Ghia is slow and has indifferent handling: for those million-dollar looks you'd just forgive it anything. This rebodied Beetle – or, to give it its official title, the Type 14 – was first seen in coupé form in 1955, with just 30 rear-mounted horses from an 1192cc Beetle flat-four. The car was expensive and the convertible that followed in 1957 was pricier still – but hey, what price style?

In 1961 an alternative Karmann Ghia arrived, called the Type 34 or 'Razor Edge'. The new model was based on the recently-introduced Type 3 which marked the company's move away from the long-running Beetle, but unlike the earlier car the fresh offering didn't prove very popular. In seven years of production just 42,500 Ghias found buyers – although it wasn't sold in the US, which didn't help. Whereas the Type 14 was all curves, the Type 34 was very angular and relatively ungainly; nowadays they rarely come up for sale and only a small number in the UK are in roadworthy condition.

In 1974 the Karmann Ghia handed over the baton to the Golf-based Scirocco. This may have been a rather more modern machine, but it never matched the style of its predecessor. In total, 364,401 Karmann Ghia coupés were made and 80,899 convertibles. But most of them have since rotted away, and it's now getting very hard to find a decent example.

If you do track down a restoration project, it'll cost at least £2500 whether it's coupé or cabriolet – the latter carrying a premium above basket-case status. As usual, you're better off buying a decent car that doesn't need a complete rebuild; expect to pay around £6500 for a tin-top and £8000 for a drop-head. If you're feeling flush, the best coupés are worth £10,000 while an equivalent cabriolet is £12,750, but such cars rarely come onto the market. As the lion's share were exported to the US, many cars have been imported back from Stateside, so left-hand-drivers are rather easier to source.

Engine

The engines used in the Karmann Ghia would all be familiar to any Beetle fan. The 1285cc boxer four entered the fray in 1964 and four years later the 1493cc powerplant arrived. The final incarnation of the car used the 1584cc motor with a heady 55bhp, but it could still manage only 86mph.

Sharing engines with the Beetle means good news and bad – indifferent performance is tempered with plentiful parts availability, as well as the chance to embark on some easy tuning. The motors are straightforward and don't

'The Karmann Ghia was expensive – but hey, what price style?'

need masses of attention to keep them running happily. Many VW enthusiasts will tell you that this reliability is the cause of the unit's reputation for noisiness, since they're so very often neglected and left unserviced for high mileages. Changing the oil and checking the valve clearances every 3000 miles is worthwhile. If looked after properly, a Karmann Ghia's engine will last 100,000 miles quite happily.

Check the level and condition of the oil – don't be surprised if there are minor leaks from the rocker covers or pushrod tubes, which are visible on the underside of the engine when you look beneath the rear of the car. But if there's oil leaking from the rear crankshaft seal it could be because it has failed due to crankshaft end float. Once this happens the only answer is to rebuild or replace the engine, but the parts are available from any Beetle specialist and you can pick up a complete replacement unit for just a few hundred pounds.

Exhaust systems are generally long-lived, but rotten heat exchangers will lead to fumes getting into the cabin via the heater. Also, if any of the cooling fins that stop the engine from cooking itself are missing, it could be bad news. Top-end problems are rare with normal use, but can include valves dropping (usually number three), while the twin-port cylinder head of the 1600 engine can suffer from cracking. Both will lead to uneven idling and misfiring, and the former will also manifest itself in clattery valvegear.

If the engine runs badly it could be because there's a blockage in the fuel system. Sediment has a habit of building up in the tank, which then blocks the outlet. Things are worse on pre-1961 cars which, instead of a fuel gauge, were fitted with a reserve petrol tank and tap. These incorporated a filter and small pipe – but over the years many will have become blocked up and even rusted away, causing petrol leakage and erratic 'dirt in the fuel line' problems.

Transmission
First gear had no synchromesh until 1961,

but the later gearbox was even more reliable than the earlier unit and it was also more refined. The transmission and differential share a common casing and both of them are pretty tough. The first sign of trouble is the transmission jumping out of first gear, although oil leaks are also pretty common.

If the box runs dry, things will get pretty noisy and it'll start jumping out of gear. Fitting a decent used unit is normally more cost-effective than having your duff one rebuilt – you should be able to get something for around £50. On pre-1968 cars the gearbox oil also has to lubricate the wheel bearings so it's especially important that the level isn't allowed to drop too far. Post-1968 cars featured semi-trailing arm rear suspension, and you need to check the driveshaft CV joints for split boots.

Suspension, steering and brakes
Until 1965 the front suspension used kingpins, on which the hubs swivelled. These can wear, so check for play in

'Convertibles have been known to corrode until they sag in the middle'

**Karmann
Ghia 1500
Coupé**
SPECIFICATIONS

Engine
1493cc flat-four,
eight overhead valves.
Alloy heads and block,
cast-iron barrels.
One Solex carburettor

Power
53bhp @ 4200rpm

Torque
78lb ft @ 2600rpm

Transmission
Four-speed manual

Suspension
Front: Independent
with twin trailing arms,
transverse torsion bars,
telescopic dampers,
anti-roll bar
Rear: Independent
with swinging semi-
axles, trailing arms,
transverse torsion bars,
telescopic dampers

Brakes
Front: 250mm drums
Rear: 250mm drums

Weight
1310kg (2889lb)

Performance
0-60mph: 21sec
Top speed: 82mph

Value
Cost new: £1282 (1969)
Value now: £5000-£10,000

the system; later cars were fitted with balljoints instead, which are less prone to wear and both easier and cheaper to fix. Dropping the suspension is popular, to make the car look sportier as well as to improve its handling. But this is not to everyone's taste, and if you want to return the set-up to standard it may mean a new beam at the front because the original one will have been cut down – unless you're lucky enough to acquire a car with an adjustable beam.

At the back it's just a case of turning the torsion bars on their splines – but this isn't a job for the faint-hearted as you have to de-tension the spring bar itself and a great deal of care is needed since the torsion bars have a 'vernier' arrangement and no reference marks. It has been known for the suspension to be reassembled with one spline different from side to side, with a correspondingly unequal ride height. The bushes that support the front axle beam wear out eventually, and although it's a bit fiddly to replace them, it's not too pricey or tricky to do it yourself.

Check the steering for play, as there's a good chance that the steering box will have some wear, as might any of the various linkages that make up the system. New, used or reconditioned boxes are all available – expect to pay upwards of £75

for something decent. All the balljoints and linkage arms are also available at low prices and they're easy to swap – so there's no excuse for having a Karmann Ghia that drives like a bag of bolts.

Pre-1967 cars were fitted with drum brakes at the front, then discs arrived. Either system is up to the job, but they don't take hard use – and if a caliper has seized, which happens, they'll be decidedly below par. Converting from drum to disc is easy enough, and it's also affordable as the whole thing costs under £200.

All models left the factory with pressed-steel wheels as standard. Five-stud fixings were used until the introduction of disc brakes, when they were superseded by four-stud hubs. The standard tyre size is 165x15, which isn't a common size any more, although you can still buy new rubber at reasonable prices. Many cars had the optional chrome trims fitted, and these are still a popular aftermarket accessory.

Bodywork, electrics and trim

When Karmann Ghias were new they had excellent panel fit because they were essentially hand-made. The only exception is the bonnet, which often isn't aligned very well. Unfortunately, rust-proofing wasn't too high on the list of priorities and

as a result cars can rot quickly. Most examples have now been restored. All models are vulnerable, but convertibles have been known to corrode to the point where they sag in the middle – look out for closing-up door gaps by checking shutlines very carefully. Jacking up the car and checking to see if the gaps change in the process will give the game away.

Original panels have all but disappeared, and with all those compound curves it's not easy trying to effect repairs unless you're pretty accomplished. But decent repair panels are available, as are good second-hand ones, usually imported from America. As well as rust, you need to check for bodged accident-rectification work because the slender bumpers don't offer much protection from impacts.

Consequently, it's worth going over the whole car with a magnet to check for filler – although many cars left the Karmann works with some plop, which was sometimes used instead of lead-loading. Don't despair, as good cars are out there; you have to be very careful and examine any prospective purchase very closely.

The nose cone and front panels in the luggage compartment are the first places to look, for rot as well as accident damage. Check around the air vents as well as the headlights, before analysing the leading

TIMELINE

» 1955: Type 14 Karmann Ghia launched at Frankfurt Motor Show, with four-speed gearbox and 30bhp.
» 1957: Type 14 convertible announced at Frankfurt Motor Show.
» 1959: New front wings. Rear lights also updated and right-hand-drive arrives.
» 1960: Power increases to 34bhp, and first gear gets synchromesh.
» 1961: Type 34 is launched, with 1493cc engine and 'Razor Edge' styling.
» 1965: Type 14 engine goes up to 1285cc, giving 40bhp. Type 34's engine enlarged to 1584cc and disc front brakes arrive.
» 1966: Type 14 gets 1493cc flat-four and disc brakes. 12-volt electrics supersede 6-volt on Type 34 and three-speed semi-auto becomes an optional extra.
» 1969: Final Type 34 is built and larger rear lights are fitted to Type 14.
» 1970: Type 14 gets larger, 1584cc engine.
» 1971: Bigger bumpers, front indicators and rear lights arrive, plus matt black fascia and padded steering wheel.
» 1974: Last Karmann Ghia Type 14 rolls off the production lines in June.

SPECIALISTS

» Big Boys Toys, Essex. +44 (0)845 2300101, www.bigboyztoys.co.uk
» Cool Air, Kent. +44 (0)1322 335 050, www.coolairvw.co.uk
» JAVA – John Abbott VW Accessories, Birmingham. +44 (0)121 558 9135, www.vwjava.com
» German, Swedish & French. +44 (0)870 60 60 153, www.gsfcarparts.com
» Karmann Ghia Centre, Herts. +44 (0)1442 236 333, www.kgcentre.co.uk
» Status VW, Lancs. +44 (0)1524 272 915, www.status-vw.co.uk
» VW Heritage, West Sussex. +44 (0)1273 495 800, www.vwheritage.com

CLUBS

» Karmann Ghia Owners' Club, www.kgoc-gb.org

BOOKS

» Karmann Ghia by Malcolm Bobbitt. Veloce, ISBN 1-903706-05-X
» Essential Karmann Ghia by Laurence Meredith. MBI, ISBN 1-870-979-524

edge of the bonnet, the wheelarches and the lower rear edges of the wings. Pay close attention to the door bottoms, rear quarter panels, wheelarches and valance, plus the trailing edge of the bootlid.

These areas are easy enough (if potentially rather pricey) to repair. But the sills are less straightforward, and they can corrode very badly. Their complexity is due to the heater channels which are incorporated within the panels to duct air warmed by the engine forward into the passenger compartment. The easiest way to tell if they're badly rotten is to look under the wheelarches to see if there's rust in the sill closing panels. At the rear of each outer sill there should also be a circular plate, which gives access to the torsion bars – this is often welded over by bodgers.

Regardless of the condition of the sills, make sure the floorpans are intact where the two meet. There should be a set of bolted fixings visible where the sills attach – it's common for these to be welded over. This helps the car get through an MoT, but long-term owners like to keep the model as original in this area and a serious restorer will want to retain the body's ability to be separated from its rolling chassis.

Also look at the footwells and under the rear seat – the latter area being especially rust-prone where convertibles are concerned. Next lift the lid of the front luggage bay and see if the inner wings and spare wheel well are all present and correct, before making sure the battery tray, which sits in the engine bay, hasn't dissolved in its own juices.

Quite a lot of exterior trim was fitted to the Karmann Ghia, and it's now hard to find original parts. Most items such as the chrome parts and badges are available through specialist suppliers, as it's remanufactured in the US. Easier to source is the multi-layer hood, but it's expensive to buy and not easy to fit. But it does do a good job of sealing the car and it's reasonably quiet, too.

Interior trim is easier, thanks to Newton Commercial (01728 832880) remanufacturing carpet sets for all variants. Dashboard pads split thanks to exposure to sunlight and carpets tend to rot as the cars often aren't very watertight. Neither are the seats particularly durable, eventually splitting and tearing through general use.

Conclusion

Although the Karmann Ghia is less practical and harder to restore than the equivalent Beetle, and tracking down parts that are unique to it is more difficult, people will happily pay a hefty premium over its stablemate. But those Bug mechanicals make it a practical proposition for the daily driver. ⚠

OTHERS TO CONSIDER...

We've covered most of the major models, but here are the specifications of a few more. Enjoy!

Words: Jack Carfrae Photography: Michael Bailie

Abarth Fiat Zagato 750
Engine
747cc in-line four, overhead valve
Power
44bhp @ 6000rpm
Torque
44lb ft @ 3000rpm
Transmission
Four-speed manual
Suspension
Front: Independent, trailing arms
Rear: Independent, coil springs
Brakes
Drum all round
Weight
559kg
Price at launch
£2248
Performance
0-60mph 15.8secs
Top speed 95mph

Alfa-Romeo SZ
Engine
2959cc V6, overhead camshaft
Power
210bhp @ 6200rpm
Torque
181lb ft @ 4500
Transmission
Five-speed manual
Suspension
Front: Independent, coil spring
Rear: de Dion axle, coil spring
Brakes
Disc all round
Weight
1260kg
Price at launch
£40,000
Performance
0-60mph 6.9secs
Top speed 153mph

Alfa GTV/Spider
Engine
1970cc in-line four, double ohc
Power
150bhp @ 6200rpm
Torque
137lb ft @ 4000rpm
Transmission
Five-speed manual
Suspension
Front: Independent, coil spring
Rear: independent, coil, spring
Brakes
Disc all round
Weight
1353kg
Performance
0-60mph 9.4secs
Top speed 122mph

Alfa Romeo GTV6
Engine
2492cc V6, overhead camshaft
Power
160bhp @ 6000rpm
Torque
157lb ft @ 4000rpm
Transmission
Five-speed manual
Suspension
Front: Independent, torsion bar
Rear: de Dion axle with coil springs
Brakes
Disc all round
Weight
1210kg
Price at launch
£9495
Performance
0-60mph 8.8secs
Top speed 130mph

Alfa Giulietta
Engine
1290cc in-line four, double ohc
Power
80bhp @ 6300rpm
Torque
72lb ft @ 3500rpm
Transmission
Four-speed manual
Suspension
Front: Independent, coil spring
Rear: Beam axle, coil spring
Brakes
drum all round
Weight
860kg
Price at launch
£2116
Performance
0-60mph 11.8secs
Top speed 113mph

Alfa 2600 Spider
Engine
2584cc in-line six, double ohc
Power
145bhp @ 5900rpm
Torque
156lb ft @ 4000rpm
Transmission
Five-speed manual
Suspension
Front: Independent, coil spring
Rear: Beam axle, coil spring
Brakes
disc all round
Weight
1257kg
Price at launch
£2979
Performance
0-60mph n/a
Top speed 124mph

Alfa Giulia 1600
Engine
1570cc in-line four, double ohc
Power
92bhp @ 6200rpm
Torque
108lb ft @ 3700rom
Transmission
Five-speed manual
Suspension
Front: Independent, coil spring
Rear: Beam axle, coil spring
Brakes
drum all round
Weight
905kg
Price at launch
£1729
Performance
0-60mph 12.9secs
Top speed 107mph

Alpine 1600S
Engine
1565cc in-line all-alloy four, two valves per cylinder, fed by twin 45DCOE Weber carburettors
Power
138bhp @ 6000rpm
Torque
117lb ft @ 5000rpm
Transmission
5-speed manual, rear-wheel-drive
Suspension
Front: Ind. wishbones, coil springs, telescopic dampers, anti-roll bar
Rear: Ind, swing axles with coil springs and telescopic dampers
Brakes
Disc all round
Performance
0-60mph 6.3sec
Top speed 132mph

Berkeley
Engine
322cc Anzai vertical-twin, 2-stroke
Power
15bhp @ 5000rpm
Torque
16lb ft @ 3500rpm
Transmission
Three-speed manual, non-synchro, chain-driven
Suspension
Front: Independent, coil springs,
Rear: Independent, swing axles, coil spring
Brakes
drum all round
Weight
Price at launch
Performance
0-60mph n/a
Top speed 60mph (est)

BMW 507
Engine
3168cc V8, overhead valve
Power
150bhp @ 5000rpm
Torque
174lb ft @ 4000rpm
Transmission
Four-speed manual
Suspension
Front: Independent, torsion bar
Rear: Beam axle, torsion bar
Brakes
Front: disc. Rear: drum
Weight
1330kgs
Price at launch
£4201
Performance
0-60mph 9.5secs
Top Speed: 124mph

Chevrolet Corvette Sting Ray
Engine
5360cc pushrod V8, overhead valve
Power
360bhp @ 6000rpm
Torque
352lb ft @ 4000rpm
Transmission
Four-speed manual
Suspension
Front: Independent, coil spring
Rear: Independent, transverse leaf-spring
Brakes
Drum all round
Weight
1461kg
Price at launch
£3323
Performance
0-60mph 6.2 sec
Top Speed 147mph

Datsun 240Z
Engine
2393 in-line six, overhead cam
Power
151bhp @ 5600rpm
Torque
146lb ft @ 4400rpm
Transmission
5-speed manual
Suspension
Independent, coil springs
Brakes
Front: disc. Rear: drum
Weight
1036kg
Price at launch
Performance
0-60mph 8.0secs
Top speed 125mph

Datsun 260Z
Engine
2565cc in-line six
Power
162bhp @ 5600rpm
Torque
152lb ft @4400rpm
Transmission
Five-speed manual
Suspension
Front: Independent, coil spring
Rear: Independent, coil spring
Brakes
Front: disc. Rear: drum
Weight
1164kg
Price at launch
£2896
Performance
0-60mph 10.1secs
Top speed 115mph

Dodge Viper
Engine
7997cc V10, overhead valve
Power
400bhp @ 4600rpm
Torque
450lb ft @ 3600rpm
Transmission
Six-speed manual
Suspension
Front: Independent, coil springs
Rear: Independent, coil springs
Brakes
Disc all round
Weight
n/a
Price at launch
£55,000
Performance
0-60mph 4.6secs
Top speed 146mph

Elva Courier
Engine
1489cc in-line four, overhead valve
Power
72bhp @ 5000rpm
Torque
77lb ft @ 3500rpm
Transmission
Four-speed manual
Suspension
Front: Independent, coil spring
Rear: Beam axle, coil spring
Brakes
Drum all round
Weight
705kg
Price at launch
n/a
Performance
0-60mph 12.7secs
Top speed 98mph

Fiat 124 Spider
Engine
1438cc in-line four, double ohc
Power
90bhp @ 6000rpm
Torque
80lb ft @ 3600rpm
Transmission
Five-speed manual
Suspension
Front: Independent, coil spring
Rear: Beam axle, coil spring
Brakes
Disc all round
Weight
945kg
Performance
0-60mph 12.6secs
Top speed 106mph

Fiat 850 Spider
Engine
843cc in-line four, overhead valve
Power
49bhp @ 6200rpm
Torque
43lb ft @ 4200rpm
Transmission
Four-speed manual
Suspension
Front: Independent, transverse leaf spring
Rear: Independent, coil spring
Brakes
Front: disc
Rear: drum
Weight
735
Price at launch
£1000
Performance
0-60mph n/a
Top speed 92mph

Fiat 1200 Cabrio
Engine
1221cc in-line four, overhead valve
Power
58bhp @ 5300rpm
Torque
61bhp @ 3000rpm
Transmission
Four-speed manual
Suspension
Front: Independent, coil spring
Rear: Beam axle, semi-elliptic
Brakes
Drum all round
Weight
905kg
Price at launch
£1460
Performance
0-60mph 19.1secs
Top speed 90mph

Fiat X1/9
Engine
1290cc in-line four, overhead cam
Power
75bhp @ 6000rpm
Torque
72lb ft @ 3400rpm
Transmission
Four-speed, manual
Suspension
Front: Independent, coil spring
Rear: Independent, coil spring
Brakes
Disc all round
Weight
912kg
Price at launch
£2997
Performance
0-60mph 12.7secs
Top speed 99mph

Fiat Barchetta
Engine
1747cc in-line four, double overhead camshaft
Power
130bhp @ 6300rpm
Torque
121lb ft @ 4300rpm
Transmission
Five-speed manual
Suspension
Front: Independent, coil spring
Rear: Independent, coil spring
Brakes
disc all round
Weight
1069kg
Price at launch
£13,995
Performance
0-60mph 8.7secs
Top speed 118mph

Fiat Coupé
Engine
1995cc in-line four, double overhead camshaft
Power
142bhp @ 6000rpm
Torque
135lb ft @ 4500rpm
Transmission
Five-speed manual
Suspension
Front: Independent, coil spring
Rear: Independent, coil spring
Brakes
disc all round
Weight
1244kg
Price at launch
£17,349
Performance
0-60mph 9.5secs
Top speed 124mph

Ginetta G4
Engine
997cc Ford in-line four, overhead valve
Power
40bhp @ 5000rpm
Torque
53lb ft @ 2700rpm
Transmission
Four-speed manual
Suspension
Front: Independent, coil springs
Rear: Independent, beam axle
Brakes
Front: disc
Rear: drum
Weight
490kg
Price at launch
£697
Performance
0-60mph n/a
Top speed 85mph (est)

Ginetta G15
Engine
875cc Rootes/Sunbeam in-line four, overhead camshaft
Power
50bhp @ 5800rpm
Torque
49lb ft @ 4500rpm
Transmission
Four-speed manual
Suspension
Front: Independent, coil springs
Rear: Independent, coil springs
Brakes
Front: disc
Rear: drum
Weight
501kg
Price at launch
£1024
Performance
0-60mph 12.9sec
Top speed 94mph

Ginetta G33 V8
Engine
3946cc Rover V8, overhead valve
Power
198bhp @ 5280
Torque
220lb ft @ 3500
Transmission
Five-speed manual
Suspension
Front: Independent, coil spring
Rear: Independent, coil spring
Brakes
Disc all round
Weight
874kg
Price at launch
£18,187
Performance
0-60mph 5.3
Top speed 137mph

Honda S800
Engine
791cc In-line four, double overhead camshaft
Power
70bhp @ 8000rpm
Torque
49lb ft @ 6000rpm
Transmission
Four-speed manual
Suspension
Front: Independent, torsion bar
Rear: Beam axle, coil springs
Brakes
Front: disc
Rear: drum
Weight
768kg
Price at launch
£779
Performance
0-60mph 13.4secs
Top speed 94mph

Jaguar XK120
Engine
3442cc in-line four, double overhead camshaft
Power
160bhp @ 5000rpm
Torque
195lb ft @ 2500rpm
Transmission
Four-speed manual, with overdrive
Suspension
Front: Independent, torsion bar
Rear: Beam axle, semi-elliptic springs
Brakes
Drum all round
Weight
1296kg
Price at launch
£1263
Performance
0-60mph 10secs
Top speed 125mph

Lotus Elite
Engine
1216cc in-line four, overhead camshaft
Power
71bhp @ 6100rpm
Torque
77lb ft @ 3750rpm
Transmission
Four-speed manual
Suspension
Front: Independent, coil springs
Rear: Independent, coil springs
Brakes
discs all round
Weight
660kg
Price at launch
£1951
Performance
0-60mph 11.4secs
Top speed 112mph

Lotus Europa
Engine
1470cc in-line four, overhead camshaft
Power
78bhp @ 6500
Torque
76lb ft @ 4000rpm
Transmission
Four-speed manual
Suspension
Front: Independent, coil spring
Rear: Independent, coil spring
Brakes
Front: disc
Rear: drum
Weight
706kg
Price at launch
£1996
Performance
0-60mph 7.0secs
Top speed 117mph

Lotus Esprit
Engine
1973cc in-line four, double overhead camshaft
Power
160bhp @ 6200rpm
Torque
140lb ft @ 4900rpm
Transmission
Five-speed manual
Suspension
Front: Independent, coil springs
Rear: Independent, coil springs
Brakes
Disc all round
Weight
1006kg
Price at launch
£7883
Performance
0-60mph 5.3
Top speed 135mph

Lotus Eclat
Engine
1973cc in-line, four, double overhead camshaft
Power
160bhp @ 6200rpm
Torque
140lb ft @ 4900rpm
Transmission
Four/five-speed manual or automatic
Suspension
Front: independent, coil springs
Rear: independent, coil springs
Brakes
Disc all round
Weight
1107kg
Price at launch
£5729
Performance
0-60mph 7.9secs
Top speed 129mph

Marcos 1800
Engine
1778cc Volvo in-line four, overhead valve
Power
114bhp @ 5800rpm
Torque
110 @ 4200rpm
Transmission
Four-speed manual with overdrive
Suspension
Front: Independent, coil spring
Rear: Independent, coil spring
Brakes
Front: disc
Rear: drum
Weight
767kg
Price at launch
£1645
Performance
0-60mph 91.secs
Top speed 115mph

Marcos 3.0-litre
Engine
2994cc Ford in-line six, overhead valve
Power
136bhp @ 4750rpm
Torque
193lb ft @ 3000rpm
Transmission
Four-speed manual with overdrive
Suspension
Front: Independent, coil spring
Rear: Beam axle, coil spring
Brakes
Front: disc
Rear: drum
Weight
884kg
Price at launch
£2350
Performance
0-60mph 7.8secs
Top speed 125mph (est)

Marcos Mantis
Engine
2498cc Triumph in-line six, overhead valve
Power
150bhp @ 5700rpm
Torque
158lb ft @ 3000rpm
Transmission
Four-speed manual with overdrive
Suspension
Front: Independent coil springs
Rear: beam axle, coil springs
Brakes
Front: disc
Rear: drum
Weight
1043kg
Price at launch
£3185
Performance
0-60mph n/a
Top speed 125mph

Marcus LM500
Engine
4998cc Rover V8, overhead valve
Power
320bhp @ 5250rpm
Torque
330 @ 3900rpm
Transmission
Five-speed manual/automatic
Suspension
Front: Independent, coil spring
Rear: Independent, coil spring
Brakes
Disc all round
Weight
1101kg
Price at launch
£44,650
Performance
0-60mph 4.6secs
Top speed 169mph

Mazda RX-7
Engine
2292cc twin rotor Wankel
Power
105bhp @ 6000rpm
Torque
106lb ft @ 4000rpm
Transmission
Four or five-speed manual, or automatic
Suspension
Front: Independent, coil spring
Rear: Beam axle, coil spring
Brakes
Front: disc
Rear: drum
Weight
1024kg
Price at launch
£8549
Performance
0-60mph 9.9secs
Top speed 117mph

Morgan 3-wheeler
Engine
933-1172cc in-line four cylinder, sidevalve
Power
25-42bhp
Torque
n/a
Transmission
Two-speed bevel 'box, non-synchro, chain drive, no reverse
Suspension
Front: Independent, coil spring
Rear: quarter-elliptic leaf-spring
Brakes
mechanical drum
Weight
n/a
Price at launch
n/a
Performance
0-60mph n/a
Top speed 73mph (Super Sports)

Opel GT 1900
Engine
1897cc in-line four, overhead camshaft
Power
90bhp @ 5100rpm
Torque
108lb ft @ 2800rpm
Transmission
Four-speed manual
Suspension
Front: Independent, transverse leaf-spring
Rear: Beam axle, coil-spring
Brakes
Front: disc
Rear: drum
Weight
956kg
Price at launch
£1882
Performance
0-60mph 12.0secs
Top speed 115mph

Toyota 2000GT
Engine
1988cc in-line six, double overhead camshaft
Power
150bhp @ 6600rpm
Torque
n/a
Transmission
Five-speed manual
Suspension
Front: Independent, coil spring
Rear: Independent, coil spring
Brakes
Disc all round
Weight
n/a
Price at launch
n/a
Performance
0-60mph n/a
Top speed 137mph

Toyota MR2
Engine
1588cc in-line four, double overhead camshaft
Power
122bhp @ 6600rpm
Torque
105lb ft @ 5000rpm
Transmission
Five-speed manual
Suspension
Front: Independent, coil spring
Rear: Independent, coil spring
Brakes
Disc all round
Weight
1052kg
Price at launch
£9295
Performance
0-60mph 7.7secs
Top speed 116mph

Triumph TR3
Engine
1991cc in-line four, overhead valve
Power
90bhp@4800rpm
Torque
117lb ft @ 3000rpm
Transmission
Four-speed manual with overdrive
Suspension
Front: Independent, coil springs
Rear: Beam axle, semi-elliptic
Brakes
Drum all round
Weight
838kg
Performance
0-60mph 11.9sec
Top speed 103
Price at launch
£787

Triumph TR3A
Engine
1991cc in-line four, overhead valve
Power
95bhp @4800
Torque
117lb ft @ 3000rpm
Transmission
Four-speed manual with overdrive
Suspension
Front: Independent, coil springs
Rear: Beam axle, semi-elliptic
Brakes
Drum all round
Weight
901kg
Performance
0-60mph 12.5sec
Top Speed 102mph
Price at launch
£976

Triumph Stag
Engine
2997cc V8, overhead camshaft
Power
145bhp @ 5500rpm
Torque
170lb ft @ 3500rpm
Transmission
Four-speed manual with overdrive or automatic
Suspension
Front: Independent, coil spring
Rear: Independent, coil spring
Brakes
Front: disc
Rear: drum
Weight
1273kg
Price at launch
£1996
Performance
0-60mph 9.7secs
Top speed 117mph

TVR Griffith 200
Engine
4727cc V8, overhead valve
Power
195bhp @ 4400rpm
Torque
282lb ft @ 2400rpm
Transmission
Four-speed manual
Suspension
Front: Independent, coil spring
Rear: Independent, coil spring
Brakes
Front: disc
Rear: drum
Weight
864kg
Price at launch
£1620
Performance
0-60mph n/a
Top speed 140mph (est)

TVR Tuscan V6
Engine
2994cc V6, overhead valve
Power
128bhp @ 4750rpm
Torque
173lb ft @ 3000rpm
Transmission
Four-speed manual with overdrive
Suspension
Front: Independent, coil spring
Rear: Independent, coil spring
Brakes
Front: disc
Rear: drum
Weight
907kg
Price at launch
£1930
Performance
0-60mph 8.3
Top speed 125 (est)

TVR Taimar
Engine
2994cc V6, overhead valve
Power
142bhp @ 5000rpm
Torque
174lb ft @ 3000rpm
Transmission
Four-speed manual
Suspension
Front: Independent, coil spring
Rear: Independent, coil spring
Brakes
Front: disc
Rear: drum
Weight
1025kg
Price at launch
£4260
Performance
0-60mph 7.7secs
Top speed 121mph

TVR S 2.9
Engine
2933cc V6, overhead valve
Power
170bhp @ 5700rpm
Torque
172lb ft @ 3000rpm
Transmission
Five-speed manual
Suspension
Front: Independent, coil spring
Rear: independent, coil spring
Brakes
Front: disc
Rear: drum
Weight
9897kg
Price at launch
£15,450
Performance
0-60mph 6.8secs
Top speed 136mph

TVR Cerbera 4.2
Engine
4185cc V8, overhead camshaft
Power
350bhp @ 6500rpm
Torque
320lb ft @ 4500rpm
Transmission
Five-speed manual
Suspension
Front: independent, coil spring
Rear: independent, coil spring
Brakes
Disc all round
Weight
1177kg
Price at launch
£37,000
Performance
0-60mph 4.0sec
Top speed 185mph

Westfield SE 1.6
Engine
1596cc in-line four, overhead camshaft
Power
108bhp @ 5600rpm
Torque
104 lb ft @ 4500
Transmission
Five-speed manual
Suspension
Front: Independent, coil spring
Rear: Independent, coil spring
Brakes
Disc all round
Weight
680kg
Price at launch
£11,750
Performance
0-60mph 7.3secs
Top speed 108mph

HOW TO BUY AT AUCTION

You coud pick up a bargain at a classic car auction. Or you could get carried away and bid away too much... Here's how to get it right

Words: David Lillywhite

Choose your sale
The big-name sales aren't generally the places to buy common-or-garden classics, they're all about big cars for big money. But if one does sneak in, you might find it tacked on the end, when the big guns have headed home. Time for a bargain? Generally, though, the provincial sales are bargain territory.

Decide what you're after
Don't be too random about your buying target because you must do your homework before a sale. You need to know the model's potential weak points – don't be embarrassed to take crib notes.

Get a catalogue
Order an auction catalogue as early as possible, to give yourself plenty of time for your research. Mark off a selection of cars that appeal, but don't set your heart on them.

Decide how much to pay
Set yourself a limit. And stick to it! Do not get carried away!

Give yourself plenty of time
Find out the viewing times and get there early to check out the cars in peace, before the hoards arrive.

Remember to register
Classic mistake. You spot the car you want, you try to bid, but you haven't regsitered with the auction house. You'll need to give bank details and show proof of identity (passport or driving licence).

Check the car's documents
The auction staff will hold all the documentation for the cars. If you're lucky there might be contact details for an old owner – ring them! You want lots of history, receipts, MoTs, etc.

Question the auction staff
The staff will know more about the history. Some might have driven the car you're interested in.

Be sneaky
Don't be polite – listen in on the conversations of other potential buyers

to see if they mention any faults or let drop how much they're willing to pay. When you're bidding, postion yourself where you can see the other bidders.

Don't bid first!
And if no-one bids, seek out the auctioneer after the sale.

Be ready to walk away
There will always be another one!

Don't leave early though
If you stay to the bitter end, the casual buyers will have left or tired of the action and you might just pick up a bargain.

Don't assume the sale is over
Sometimes it's not clear to a novice whether or not a car has sold. If the auctioneer hasn't declared a sale then it's not sold – find him afterwards for a deal.

Plan ahead
Think about how you'll get a car home if you are successful. You'll need insurance or transportation, for example. Good luck!